GRAHAM HOUGH GOULDEN, 1908-

The Last Romantics

UNIVERSITY PAPERBACKS

METHUEN : LONDON

BARNES & NOBLE : NEW YORK

First published 1947 by Gerald Duckworth & Co Ltd
First published in this series 1961
Reprinted lithographically in Great Britain
at the University Press, Oxford
by Vivian Ridler, Printer to the University
Catalogue No. (Methuen) 2/6768/27

University Paperbacks are published
by METHUEN & CO LTD
36 Essex Street, Strand, London WC2
and BARNES & NOBLE INC
105 Fifth Avenue, New York 8

En effet, lorsque l'époque où un homme de talent est obligé
de vivre, est plate et bête, l'artiste est, à son insu même, hanté
par la nostalgie d'un autre siècle.

Chez les uns, c'est un retour aux ages consommés, aux
civilisations disparues, aux temps morts; chez les autres, c'est
un élancement vers la fantastique et vers le rêve, c'est une
vision plus ou moins intense d'un temps à éclore dont l'image
reproduit, sans qu'il le sache, par un effet d'atavisme, celle des
époques révolues.

J. K. HUYSMANS

We were the last romantics—chose for theme
Traditional sanctity and loveliness;
Whatever's written in what poet's name
The book of the people; whatever most can bless
The mind of man or elevate a rhyme.

W. B. YEATS

PREFACE

THE best way to explain the purpose of this book is to trace it backwards. During the war, most of which I spent as a prisoner of the Japanese, I was fortunate enough to have with me a copy of Yeats's poems; and in the intervals of more pressing activities I read and thought about them a good deal. Continuing to ruminate on these matters, in pleasanter circumstances later on, I became interested in the genesis of Yeats's ideas from those of the small poetic circle with whom he associated in the nineties. They in turn seemed to owe almost everything to Pater and the pre-Raphaelites, and from them I was inevitably led back to Ruskin. At this point I came to a stop. The new ideas about the arts and their relations to religion and the social order all seemed to originate somewhere in the dense jungle of Ruskin's works. So I formed the intention, of which this book is the result, of tracing this movement of thought and feeling, and of trying to show its relevance to our own day. Occasional digressions occur into more general critical questions: for I believe it is time we thought again about a good deal of nineteenth-century writing, and that in doing so we shall have to modify some of the critical canons of the last thirty years.

I have necessarily involved myself in painting and the visual arts, which are not my proper business: if what I have to say about them is inadequate, it may serve a limited purpose—to indicate some of the connections that have been made in the last hundred years between different kinds of imaginative experience. To this end I have also had to say a little, again quite inadequate, about the influence of French literature: but to deal with this topic at all fully would require a separate book. In matters of art-history I am conscious of a great debt to Mr. R. H. Wilenski's *John Ruskin*, Sir Kenneth Clark's *Gothic*

vii

PREFACE

Revival, Mr. Michael Trappes-Lomax's *Pugin*, and Mr. James Laver's *Whistler*. Detailed obligations, to these and other writers, are recorded in the notes.

I am indebted to Mrs. Yeats and to Macmillan and Co. Ltd., the publishers of W. B. Yeats' *Collected Poems* and other works, for permitting me to quote freely from Yeats' work.

Part of Chapter I, part of Chapter IV, and the whole of Chapter VI have appeared in the *Cambridge Journal*, and my thanks are due to the editors for permission to reprint. I should also like to thank my wife for all her help in typing and preparing the book for the press.

G. H.

University of Malaya
   Singapore

viii

CONTENTS

CONTENTS

x

INTRODUCTION

In the troubled waters of nineteenth-century thought two main currents can be discerned, the one scientific, positivist and radical, the other antiquarian, traditional, conservative. In England, though opposed, they were not harshly antagonistic. On the whole they contrived to live pretty comfortably together, and there were many bridges between the two territories—participation in a common literary renaissance and a common code of practical ethics. Nineteenth-century England is notorious for having reform bills instead of revolutions, and there is little of the ferocious Continental antagonism between clericals and anti-clericals, liberals and reactionaries. Hazlitt the Radical abused Scott the Tory, but could still admire Scott the picaresque novelist. The agnostics gave up the traditional religious sanctions, but maintained on the whole the traditional moral scheme. Probably the central religious movement of the age is the broad-church syncretism of F. D. Maurice and Tennyson, in which so many incompatibles were reconciled. The only intransigents were the early Oxford reformers, for they were the only people who maintained absolute and immutable standards. But later they too settled down to something more like the English compromise. Often the two currents of thought met and mingled in the same person. Gladstone remained both a High Churchman and a liberal, and retained the friendship of both Manning and John Bright. More strikingly, and with greater difficulty, Lord Acton remained both a liberal and a Roman Catholic. And George Eliot passed her personal life among the philosophic radicals, yet became the great novelist of the traditional sanctities of pastoral England.

The rival mythologies of the romantic age, the myth of the past and the myth of the future, come to a similar accommodation. History is very generally used as a support for contem-

porary attitudes. Scott, rather curiously, had provided a
romantic stimulus for the Oxford Movement; and tears suffuse
the eyes of Charlotte M. Yonge's High Church heroines at the
mention of King Charles the martyr. Browning's travels in
Renaissance clerical and artistic circles were understood because
they were so clearly the medium of quite nineteenth-century
views of human character and conduct. And Tennyson's later
dealings with Arthurian legend seemed right and natural
because they were used as the vehicle of a clearly seen moral
and political purpose. His knights would have put the Grail to
some useful social purpose if they had found it, and the haunted
forests of Lyonnesse were thoroughly illuminated by advanced
scientific thought and the belief in progress.

Meanwhile the dual supremacy of the landed interest and the
Church declined: the county member and the high-and-dry
rector were no longer the twin pillars of society. And the
Manchester liberals who had been admitted to a share of power
were changing their own position in other ways as well. After
the mid-century they were no longer in the vanguard. Free
trade and *laisser-faire*, originally the battle-cries of reform,
had become the props of the new mammonism. Carlyle begins
to describe the old ruling class as a do-nothing aristocracy who
go gracefully idle in Mayfair, and Arnold to describe the new
one as Philistines who alternate between a dismal and illiberal
life in Birmingham and a dismal and illiberal life in Manchester.
But the great estates remained undivided, and Manchester and
Birmingham continued to grow.

The political minds, the organisers and administrators, were
not fundamentally distressed. Accustomed to the clash of
opposing principles, and trained in the belief that this was the
inevitable condition of progress, they could, without too much
strain on the imagination, look forward to a future in which
liberty and prosperity would go hand in hand. Both had
manifestly increased since the close of the eighteenth century.
The age was essentially one of practical achievement, and its
intellectual leaders are those who can comment on practical
achievement, or criticise it, or celebrate it imaginatively. We
value Tennyson to-day mainly as a pure lyrist, but his work as

a whole is meant to express in poetry the social and moral structure that his age had built up, even, occasionally, to celebrate its political and material triumphs. The mid-century novelists are primarily commentators on the social scheme: so is Carlyle, for all his German metaphysics. Arnold, in spite of his condemnation of the intellectual who rashly meddles with practice, is above all a writer with an immediately practical aim. Essentially the great Victorian writers write as parts of a system. The fact that they mostly criticised it does not matter —the necessity of free criticism was also part of the system. All write to maintain something or to change something, and only as an occasional indulgence to contemplate, to experience, to accept the immediate impact of the moment as it comes. They form a great school (the last of them, Mr. Bernard Shaw, is still with us) and on the whole they have had little reason to be dissatisfied with the world as they found it. There are always plenty of causes that need to be maintained and plenty of things that need to be altered. Those, however, who lived more by their immediate sensibilities than by the large apprehension of the practical intellect found in the later half of the nineteenth century less and less in which the life of the imagination could be satisfied. In spite of the real probity and sobriety of public life, national ideals were becoming more and more purely material: in spite of a prevailing and genuine devoutness, spontaneous and imaginative religious experience was harder than ever to come by: in spite of material progress, the world was getting steadily uglier.

It is perhaps not surprising that the dissatisfaction should be felt most clearly by those whose main concern was with the visual arts. Painting is less easy to harness to social and moral ends than letters, and painters are more clearly dependent on their direct sensuous apprehensions. It is Ruskin who first attributes the passion for nature and the romantic admiration for the past to the blank ugliness of nineteenth-century England.

> Though still forced, by rule and fashion, to the producing and wearing all that is ugly, men steal out, half-ashamed of themselves for doing so, to the fields and mountains; and, finding among these the colour, and liberty, and variety, and power,

which are for ever grateful to them, delight in these to an extent never before known; rejoice in all the wildest shattering of the mountain-side, as an opposition to Gower Street, gaze in a rapt manner at sunsets and sunrises, to see there the blue, and gold, and purple, which glow for them no longer on knight's armour or temple porch; and gather with care out of the fields, into their blotted herbaria, the flowers which the five orders of architecture have banished from their doors and casements.

The absence of care for personal beauty, which is another great characteristic of the age, adds to this feeling in a twofold way: first, by turning all reverent thoughts away from human nature; and making us think of men as ridiculous or ugly creatures, getting through the world as well as they can, and spoiling it in doing so; not ruling it in a kingly way and crowning all its loveliness. . . . It is not, however, only to existing inanimate nature that our want of beauty in person and dress has driven us. The imagination of it, as it was seen in our ancestors, haunts us continually; and while we yield to the present fashions, or act in accordance with the dullest modern principles of economy and utility, we look fondly back to the manners of the ages of chivalry, and delight in painting, to the fancy, the fashions we pretend to despise, and the splendours we think it wise to abandon.[1]

Since that time the habit has become endemic: we are so accustomed to compare the eagles and the trumpets with the buttered scones of a thousand A.B.C.'s that it no longer seems worthy of remark. Members of the cultivated classes are by now born with this kind of nostalgia, though directed perhaps to a different part of the historical past: and they are scarcely more aware of it than they are of their pituitary glands. There is a general melancholy agreement that art and the sense of beauty have a rougher time in the modern world than they ever had before; and this may well be true; but our acquiescence in the belief has become hereditary. We are universally convinced of it, not only by the evidence of our own senses, but also because Ruskin and Morris, Rossetti and Pater, the nineties, and, in our own century, Yeats, have directly or indirectly habituated us to this way of feeling.

> We were the last romantics, chose for theme
> Traditional sanctity and loveliness . . .

This homesickness for the merely human past is foreign to the earlier romantics, who had visited history as spectators, intelligent tourists, not as exiles from a lost paradise.

It is natural that the first signs of this recoil from the mere physical apparatus of the contemporary world should be seen in Ruskin. Typical representative of Victorian culture as he was, and profoundly immersed in its social and moral preoccupations, he was also, as Roger Fry has said, a man to whom the life of the imagination was a necessity. It is actually in his work that we can see the life of the imagination asserting its rights against the external social order, beginning even, though without Ruskin's consent, to make some sort of claim to autonomy. It is significant that about 1850 the word "artist", which had formerly meant either scientist, artisan, or specifically painter, acquires also a new meaning—that of imaginative creator in general.† This suggests that about the middle of the century something was happening to change the position of the imaginative artist, to make him more conscious of his status and of his community with his fellows. In fact several things were happening. In 1847 Ruskin published the first volume of *Modern Painters*, a work which at once gave an enormous stimulus to interest in the visual arts. It not only inspired painters; still more it touched the general cultured public, and gave the pleasures of the eye a metaphysical status they had never enjoyed in England before. In 1848 the pre-Raphaelite Brotherhood was formed, a society of painters with strong literary interests, whose protagonist, Rossetti, was as much poet as painter—a fusion of two kinds of imaginative experience that England had never yet seen except in the isolated case of Blake. In 1850 the P.R.B. brought out *The Germ*—the first, as it turned out, of a long array of magazines devoted exclusively to propagating a special artistic point of view.

Social and religious forces too were combining to bring about a scarcely conscious coalition of imaginative minds. Disappointment with the results of the industrial revolution, as we have said, was coming to a head in the forties. By the

† The first use of the word in the new sense recorded in the *O.E.D.* is by F. D. Maurice in 1853.

end of that decade the Oxford Movement had lost much of its original force; but it had left behind it a great deal of undirected devotional sentiment, some of which was ready enough to flow into aesthetic channels. By 1857 when Rossetti was painting his ill-fated decorations on the walls of Oxford Union it was evident that something like a movement was under way. The break it made with the older culture is neatly illustrated in one of Max Beerbohm's cartoons. Jowett is represented, stocky, shovel-hatted and inquiring, watching Rossetti at work on a large mural of some Arthurian theme. "What were they going to do with the Grail when they found it, Mr. Rossetti?" he inquires. To the elder Victorian moralists, an eminently reasonable question; but one which the aesthetic generation could hardly be expected to answer. The Grail stood for all those values which needed no utilitarian justification.

Victorian culture with its strong ethical and social bias was beginning to produce within itself its own antithesis, though this was hardly to become apparent till the sixties, with the appearance of Pater's *Renaissance*. The earlier manifestations of the change were naturally not fully understood, even by those who produced them. The pietistic jargon of *Modern Painters* found ready acceptance, but I doubt if the full implications of that rich, extensive and confusing work have been fully realised to this day. The pre-Raphaelites were never a united body, and their aims were never particularly clear-cut. They were first reproved for Romanist and Tractarian leanings, and then reviled for distortion and affectation. By the time Rossetti and Millais were making their fortunes in the sixties, they had lost most of the purity of intention with which they had begun their career. Morris's work as a designer and manufacturer is a fresh start in a new direction. It is not until after Pater that anything like a school doctrine begins to develop out of this variety of effort. We shall not find, then, among the writers discussed in this book any one clear direction of thought. What they share is a common passion for the life of the imagination, conceived as an all-embracing activity, apart from the expression of it in any one particular art. Hence a tendency to assimilate the different arts to each other, to allow their values

INTRODUCTION

to interpenetrate each other, forming together a realm of
transcendent importance, for which a status has somehow to
be found in an inhospitable world. This endeavour becomes
so absorbing that it leads to a gradual severance, increasingly
apparent from Ruskin onwards, of art from the interests of
common life, and a constant tendency to turn art itself into the
highest value, to assimilate aesthetic to religious experience.

Ruskin does for the painter's imagination what Coleridge
had done for the poet's—exalts it into one of the central and
dominating seats in the hierarchy of human faculties. Many
of the results of this teaching he could not foresee; the conse-
quence he himself drew from it was that all men should be
artists. But others built on Ruskin's foundations a doctrine
that he would certainly have regarded as heretical—a belief
in the special position of the arts, in their autonomy, and
their essential independence of social and ethical considerations.
Obviously ideas of this kind are ideas about conduct as well as
ideas about art. Both Ruskin's statement and the rival one
appear in several forms, some defensible, some merely silly.
The general upshot is a movement to extend the values of art
to the whole of life, to judge religion, morals and society by
aesthetic standards. In the field of criticism the new interpre-
tation of the word artist imports into literature values that had
formerly been thought more appropriate to other and "purer"
arts. Pater's "All art aspires to the condition of music" is an
example; and Verlaine's "De la musique avant toute chose".
And there is the denial of accepted literary standards implied
by the campaign against rhetoric in the nineties. Rossetti's
painting displays the opposite process—much of it is illustration
of his poetry, or of Dante's, or at least of ideas that have been
"poetically" rather than visually conceived. Interwoven with
all this, and often concealing a real scepticism, are threads of
strong quasi-religious sentiment. The doctrines of Ruskin and
Pater were each referred to in their day as a "religion of

INTRODUCTION

hieratic solemnity on purely artistic matters which had not formerly been thought to require it. By the seventies these several currents had coalesced sufficiently to form a definable stream, and it was already possible to refer to the aesthetic movement—with approval or disapproval, as the case might be, but never, perhaps, quite neutrally.

Even now the implications of the phrase are so ambiguous that it is almost necessary to use it in inverted commas. English "aestheticism" carried suggestions of triviality that the parallel Continental movement, French symbolism, did not. French symbolists traced their origins to Baudelaire—a major poet and a serious moralist: and they included Rimbaud, perhaps the greatest revolutionary influence on modern French verse, and, whatever standard of judgment one adopts, a formidable moral phenomenon. Swinburne, or our own *poètes maudits* are small beer by comparison; and much that went on in the nineties was merely affected or eccentric. But towards the *fin-de-siècle* the French influence began to be important in England. Swinburne was an admirer of Gautier and Baudelaire. Verlaine's *Art Poétique* and the poetical doctrine of Mallarmé, as far as that was understood, became exciting critical stimuli in the nineties. In life as well as in art the poets of the tragic generation, *laeti et errabundi*, made valiant efforts to follow the practice of their Parisian prototypes. Slowly it became apparent that the English aesthetic movement had been working, in isolation and in a provincial environment, in the same direction as a literary movement of European dimensions. In 1899 Arthur Symons wrote *The Symbolist Movement in Literature*, partly to explain what was going on in France and partly as propaganda for a similar movement in England. The early essays of Yeats, with their continual citation of Verlaine and Mallarmé, their discussions of the nature of symbolism, show that the stream which had flowed through the pre-Raphaelites and the nineties had now joined the larger Continental river. Yeats him be summed up in any schematic way, and the same is true of its English counterpart. The movement in England, as also probably in France, is a natural consequence of social and economic development. A spreading bourgeois and industrial society left less and less room for the arts; they no longer had any natural place in the social organism, and the cluster of ideas we are describing is a continual effort by the artists to carve out an enclave of their own, emancipated as far as possible from contemporary circumstance. In England, with its strongly established routine of social and moral effort, this first took the Ruskin-Morris form—the attempt to make the world fit for artists to live in; if society would not have art, society must be changed. In France it more typically took the form of a violent negation of the claims of society, as in the career of Rimbaud; or of aristocratic seclusion and self-assertion, as in Villiers de l'Isle Adam, of which we find the Irish echoes in Yeats. We are faced with the history of an immense number of explorations, many false starts and blind alleys, and not a few personal tragedies, all directed to finding some sort of accommodation between art and a bourgeois industrial society. This involved many experiments, in ethics, aesthetics, poetical and artistic technique. No English or French writer of this movement can be said to have solved his problem, or ended in an Olympian calm; and we shall hardly find it possible to record any final messages of ripe wisdom. It is probably because the problem was insoluble that so many of the personal stories of this period end unhappily. Many of the technical experiments have borne their fruit, and some of them seem already out of date: but society to-day is no more hospitable to the artist than it was in the late nineteenth century. So most of the difficulties of this epoch still remain, and a study of the earlier attempts to solve them is an indispensable preliminary to an understanding of the literary situation at the present day.

Chapter I

RUSKIN

I. THE EDUCATION OF THE SENSES

Ruskin is the earliest (perhaps the only) English writer of first-rate intellectual power to devote himself mainly to the visual arts. This is not altogether surprising; the English have commonly taken the view that they do not know anything about art, but know what they like: and they have commonly been content to like whatever the current fashion, often derived from abroad, happened to dictate. This critical apathy is in striking contrast with the continual discussion of literary principles and methods since Tudor times. Even in Europe as a whole it is perhaps true to say that, from the first, literary criticism was a public business, while the artistic tradition was handed down mainly as a set of studio secrets, and discussed in the esoteric dialect of connoisseurs. Education was so essentially literary that the discursive intellect was given an almost irrecoverable bias towards the study of some form of rhetoric or dialectic, and the cultivation of other modes of apprehension was either neglected or used as a mere auxiliary. In England, without a strong native artistic tradition, this was even more likely to be so; and it is not unnatural to find that the most powerful minds had hardly concerned themselves about the plastic arts at all. Reynolds, critic and theorist as well as painter, may seem to be an exception; but his classic *Discourses*, highly instructive essays in applied aesthetics though they are, are after all mainly the formulation of a school doctrine. Reynolds offers a far more consistent and more civilised point of view than Ruskin, but he does not convey any sense of personal authority or individual insight. It would be unfair to say that

1

he writes only as President of the Royal Academy, but is it true that he writes as a practical painter, concerned mainly to train students in conformity to the canons of the age: and beneath his air of lucidity and completeness lurks a fair amount of philosophical confusion. After him there is no one. Hazlitt's art criticisms are genial and sympathetic, but generate more warmth than light; painting to him was a region of happy day-dreams, and his writing about it is an attempt to re-create this "sober certainty of waking bliss". And when we come to the Victorian periodical critics, to Thackeray for instance, we find ourselves faced with the cheerful philistinism, tempered in his case by a little technical knowledge, that pervades the mid-nineteenth-century attitude to art. It is worth quoting him, for he is typical of the *ambiente* in which Ruskin's writings arose.

> I must tell you, however, that Mr. Turner's performances are for the most part quite incomprehensible to me. . . . On n'embellit pas la nature, my dear Bricabrac; one may make pert caricatures of it, or mad exaggerations, like Mr. Turner in his fancy pieces. O ye gods! why will he not stick to copying her majestical countenance, instead of daubing it with some absurd antics and fard of his own? Fancy pea-green skies, crimson-lake trees, and orange and purple grass—fancy cataracts, rainbows, suns, moons and thunderbolts—shake them well up, with a quantity of gamboge, and you will have an idea of a fancy picture by Turner.[1]

On Wilkie's *Grace before Meat*:†

> . . . which, a little misty and feeble, perhaps, in drawing and substance, in colour, feeling, composition and expression, is exquisite. The eye loves to repose upon this picture, and the heart to brood over it afterwards. When, as I said before, lines and colours come to be translated into sounds, this picture, I have no doubt, will turn out to be a sweet and touching hymn-tune, with rude notes of cheerful voices, and peal of soft melo-dious organ, such as one hears stealing over the meadows on sunshiny Sabbath-days, while waves under cloudless blue the peaceful golden corn.[2]

---

† Ruskin comments drily on the same painter: "Wilkie became popular, like Scott, because he touches passions which all feel, and expresses truths which all can recognise." It is true that Ruskin himself sometimes writes very like the passages above, but these are his lapses; Thackeray's criticism never seems to rise above this level.

For further evidence of the general level of art-criticism at the time it is only necessary to turn to the Academy notices in *The Times* or some of the early critiques of the pre-Raphaelites.

With Ruskin, it is evident at once that we are dealing with a mind of an entirely different order. Wherever we open his works we are liable to find prolixity, prejudice and a choice assortment of manias and phobias; but everywhere there is evidence of intellectual power and a delicate and practised sensibility. It is easiest to illustrate this by examples chosen from outside his own particular field. The critique of visual appearances to which Ruskin devoted so much of his time is, as he practised it, almost a new genre: there is nothing with which it can be compared. In other fields it is easier to estimate his status at once. His political writings, unprofessional and emotional as they are, probably did more than anyone's to awaken a new social conscience in the uncritical believers in *laisser-faire*. In the passages on literature that are scattered through his writing we are constantly compelled, in spite of frequent disagreement, to acknowledge the energy and acuteness of his judgments. The passage on the pathetic fallacy in the third volume of *Modern Painters* is a case in point. A more compact example is the admirable piece of criticism in *The Stones of Venice* in which he contrasts Milton's treatment of the powers of evil with Dante's.

> It is not possible to express intense wickedness without some condition of degradation. Malice, subtlety, and pride, in their extreme, cannot be written upon nobler forms; and I am aware of no effort to represent the Satanic mind in the angelic form, which has succeeded in painting. Milton succeeds only because he separately describes the movements of the mind, and therefore leaves himself at liberty to make the form heroic; but that form is never distinct enough to be painted. Dante, who will not leave even external forms obscure, degrades them before he can feel them to be demoniacal; so also John Bunyan: both of them, I think, having firmer faith in their own creations, and deeper insight into the nature of sin. Milton makes his fiends too noble, and misses the foulness, inconstancy, and fury of wickedness. His Satan possesses some virtues, not the less virtues for being applied to evil purpose. Courage, resolution, patience, deliberation in council, this latter being eminently a wise and

holy character, as opposed to the "Insania" of excessive sin: and all this, if not a shallow and false, is a smoothed and artistical, conception.[3]

Whatever our views of sin and its relation to noble external form, there can be little doubt that this does analyse, with the greatest penetration, the different treatments by Dante and Milton of the power of evil.

The amount of sheer patient recording and cataloguing that has gone into his works on architecture reveals an immense tenacity of purpose: a quality which is not particularly rare, but one which can easily become mechanical. What is extremely rare is to find it allied with perpetual vitality and sensitiveness. Many of the things that Ruskin writes about do not lend themselves naturally to discourse: no doubt one of the reasons that literary criticism has always been so much further advanced than art criticism is that it is relatively easy to discuss in words what has already been expressed in words, but far harder to discuss things seen. Here Ruskin has an immense source of strength in the vigour, range and flexibility of his prose. The prevalence in the early part of the century of *Gems from Ruskin* in limp purple suède has set up an unduly guarded attitude towards this side of his work. We should be wrong, however, to allow a contemporary dislike of the twopence coloured to blind us to the scale of his achievement as a prose writer. Leaving aside the passages of exhortation and denunciation, often extremely powerful, consider only the capacity for detailed physical description that enables him to handle masses of the most unpromising material without ever allowing his writing to go flat or dead. And his more emotional descriptions are not mere bottled moonshine. The account of the approach to Venice with which the first volume of *The Stones of Venice* concludes is an enchanting piece of writing, but it is also functional; it does all that it is meant to do in creating an anticipatory excitement about the detailed discussion of the city's architecture that is to follow. It is not made up out of a dreamlike succession of silver domes and purple mists: it is made up of such elements as blighted fragments of gnarled hedges, the smell of garlic and crabs, a straggling line of low and confused

4

brick buildings which might be the suburbs of an English manufacturing town. It is by complete fidelity to the thing actually seen and experienced that Ruskin achieves his best effects. Even more impressive is his power of blending his impressions into an imaginative synthesis; as in this passage where he develops the contrast in physical character between the northern and the southern countries.

> Let us for a moment try to raise ourselves even above the level of the birds' flight, and imagine the Mediterranean lying beneath us like an irregular lake, and all its ancient promontories sleeping in the sun: here and there an angry spot of thunder, a grey stain of storm, moving upon the burning field; and here and there a fixed wreath of white volcano smoke, surrounded by its circle of ashes; but for the most part a great peacefulness of light, Syria and Greece, Italy and Spain, laid like pieces of a golden pavement into the sea-blue, chased, as we stoop nearer to them, with bossy beaten work of mountain chains, and glowing softly with terraced gardens, and flowers heavy with frankincense, mixed among masses of laurel, and orange, and plumy palm, that abate with their grey-green shadows the burning of the marble rocks, and of the ledges of porphyry sloping under lucent sand. Then let us pass farther towards the north, until we see the orient colours change gradually into a vast belt of rainy green, where the pastures of Switzerland, and poplar valleys of France, and dark forests of the Danube and Carpathians stretch from the mouths of the Loire to those of the Volga, seen through clefts in grey swirls of rain-cloud and flaky veils of the mist of the brooks, spreading low along the pasture-lands.[4]

An astonishing piece of prevision: one would say that Ruskin himself had flown over Europe, with Turner beside him to paint what they had seen.

It is in employing these imaginative and descriptive powers on the visual appearance of things that Ruskin's originality lies. Minds of this degree of delicacy and range had applied themselves before to ideas and to literary form, but never before to the appearance of nature, and their representation in art. The individual criticisms in *Modern Painters* are nearly always from the representational point of view, and many people would doubt nowadays how far this kind of criticism is worth doing. (All painting, even the most abstract, is nevertheless some kind of commentary on visual appearances; and Ruskin is dealing mostly with descriptive artists.) What cannot, however, be doubted is that Ruskin is not repeating studio or academy commonplaces, that he has really looked both at pictures and at the natural world: and this is clear even in the most pedestrian pieces of criticism; for instance, his remarks on Copley Fielding:

> It is perhaps one of the most difficult lessons to learn in art, that the warm colours of distance, even the most glowing, are subdued by the air so as in nowise to resemble the same colour seen on a foreground object; so that the rose of sunset on clouds or mountains has a grey in it which distinguishes it from the rose colour of the leaf of a flower; and the mingling of this grey of distance without in the slightest degree taking away the expression of the intense and perfect purity of the colour in and by itself, is perhaps the last attainment of the great landscape colourist. In the same way the blue of distance, however intense, is not the blue of a bright blue flower; and it is not distinguished from it by different texture merely, but by a certain intermixture and undercurrent of warm colour, which are altogether wanting in many of the blues of Fielding's distances; and so of every bright distant colour; while in foreground, where colours may be, and ought to be, pure, they yet become expressive of light only where there is the accurate fitting of them to their relative shadows which we find in the works of Giorgione, Titian, Tintoret, Veronese, Turner, and all other great colourists. Of this fitting of light to shadow Fielding is altogether regardless, so that his foregrounds are constantly assuming the aspect of overcharged local colour instead of sunshine, and his figures and cattle look transparent.[5]

The particular purpose of *Modern Painters* is to show the superior truth to nature of the modern English school, Turner especially, to the landscape painters of the seventeenth century —Claude and Salvator on the one hand, and the Dutch school on the other. But this purpose springs from a more general opposition to the ethos of the High Renaissance, based on a daunting mixture of religious, moral, scientific and aesthetic reasons. Raphael especially is singled out for reprobation, because he first substituted an elegant convention for the sincere depiction of actualities. In the following passage on Renaissance painting, beneath the rant and the pietism, we can still discern the main lines of Ruskin's criticism—the insistence on personal vision of fact as far above any science of picture-making.

> Now, the evil consequences of the acceptance of this kind of religious idealism for true, were instant and manifold. . . . Whatever they could have fancied for themselves about the wild, strange, infinitely stern, infinitely tender, infinitely varied veracities of the life of Christ, was blotted out by the vapid fineries of Raphael: the rough Galilean pilot, the orderly custom receiver, and all the questioning wonder and fire of uneducated apostleship, were obscured under an antique mask of philosophical faces and long robes. . . . Raphael ministered with applause to the impious luxury of the Vatican, but was trampled under foot at once by every believing and advancing Christian of his own and subsequent times; and thenceforward pure Christianity and "high art" took separate roads, and fared on, as best they might, independently of each other.
>
> But . . . certain conditions of weaker Christianity suffered the false system to retain influence over them; and to this day, the clear and tasteless poison of the art of Raphael infects with sleep of infidelity the hearts of millions of Christians. . . . A dim sense of impossibility attaches itself always to the graceful emptiness of the representation; we feel instinctively that the painted Christ and painted apostle are not beings that ever did or could exist; and this fatal sense of fair fabulousness and well-composed impossibility, steals gradually from the picture into the history, until we find ourselves reading St. Mark or St. Luke with the same admiring, but uninterested, incredulity with which we contemplate Raphael.[6]

What chiefly makes *Modern Painters* confusing is that Ruskin is fighting on two fronts. On the one hand he is attacking the doctrine of the Grand Style—the doctrine represented in England by Reynolds; on the other hand, a pedestrian realism. Against Reynolds, he attacks the classical doctrine of generalisation. Painting for Reynolds, like poetry for Johnson, was not to "number the streaks of the tulip, or distinguish the several shades in the verdure of the forest". Ruskin had little difficulty in showing that this precept had led to a serious neglect of the study of natural form; and he illustrates his point effectively enough by reproducing some of Claude's drawings of trees and stones. On the other hand, the work of the "various Van-somethings and Back-somethings", by reason of an unpoetical dullness of perception, is dead to all the subtlety and beauty of natural effect. That both these classes of painters may have had other admirable qualities does not seriously occur to Ruskin; there is prejudice and crankiness enough in his judgments, and they are quite without any impartial view of the historic development of painting. But his independence is not that of mere caprice, it is the independence of a man who has looked at pictures direct with his own eyes, not in the mirror of a convention.

Ruskin's own drawings are evidence enough of his minute delicacy of perception. They often make one wish that he had drawn more and written less. Whether they are mere diagrams, slight pen-sketches to give a summary notion of some particular form that he is discussing, or detailed studies of plants, clouds or mountains, they show an astonishing refinement of the visual sense. Ruskin neither possessed nor desired the post-Cézannesque faculty of reducing organic form to a few simple and fundamental geometrical ones: but he has what is perhaps even rarer, the power of seeing the essential lines of life, growth and structure beneath all the diversities of natural appearance, and without sacrificing any of these delightful accidents on the way.

Most of *Modern Painters*, indeed, is not about painters at all, but about what the natural world really looks like. It is here that Ruskin's observation rises to a level that can reasonably be called creative. It is a commonplace of Ruskin's aesthetic theory that the truth of nature is not to be perceived by the uneducated senses, and that men usually see little of what is before their eyes. He sets out therefore to provide an intensive education of the visual sensibilities which will open men's eyes to the richness and delicacy of all that is to be seen around them. Up to now, Ruskin implies, only a few great painters have been capable of this kind of perception, and many reputedly great painters have been without it. Connoisseurs of art have pretty uniformly failed both to perceive the world as it really appears, and to judge rightly the perceptions of the artists. The predominance of the representational point of view makes Ruskin's judgments seem to us violently eccentric. The average

RUSKIN

modern reader would be more at home with those of Sir
Joshua Reynolds, in spite of his preoccupation with relatively
neglected painters of the *seicento*. But the importance of what
Ruskin was doing does not lie in his individual judgments. Its
importance is that he is opening the eyes of an age by whom
the sense of sight was left uncultivated as it had probably never
been before. The point about mid-Victorian domestic interiors
is not just that they were ugly, but that they were filled with
decorations that were hardly meant to be looked at; they were
there because they called to mind pleasant holidays or absent
relatives or great thoughts. The visual sense was so thickly
overlaid with association and reflection that it hardly contrived
to function in its own right at all. To Ruskin, too, visual
sensations are heavily charged with moral and reflective over-
tones; but he does believe that without the accurate and lively
(Ruskin would say loving) use of the visual sense, the attendant
reflections would be inevitably false and distorted.

It is to the re-creation of the sense of sight as applied to
nature that most of *Modern Painters* is devoted: hence the long
sections on truth of clouds, on truth of rocks, on truth of trees,
which to many readers both of his own and of a later generation
have seemed to have nothing to do with art at all. The con-
temporary gibe was that Ruskin wanted painters to be botanists
and geologists as well; and he himself did not deny this; but
actually his interests were not primarily scientific. He some-
times uses botany, geology and so forth as descriptive tools,
but in fact he is inventing a new line of research of his own,
different in aim from scientific study of natural forms, and
different too from the eighteenth-century study of the pic-
turesque with which it seems at first to have some kinship.
His description of the cirrus clouds, for instance, tells us nothing
about the weather or the way such clouds are formed, nor is it
concerned with any particular conventions of picture-making:
but it reveals a beauty and complexity in their organisation
that nine out of ten ordinary observers would never have been
able to see for themselves.

They are nearly always arranged in some definite and evident
order, commonly in long ranks reaching sometimes from the

zenith to the horizon, each rank composed of an infinite number of transverse bars of about the same length, each bar thickest in the middle, and terminating in a traceless vaporous point at each side; the ranks are in the direction of the wind, and the bars of course at right angles to it; these latter are slightly bent in the middle. Frequently two systems of this kind, indicative of two currents of wind, at different altitudes, intersect each other, forming a network. Another frequent arrrangement is in groups of excessively fine, silky, parallel fibres, common radiating, or having a tendency to radiate, from one of their extremities, and terminating in a plumy sweep at the other; these are vulgarly known as "mare's tails". The plumy and expanded extremity of these is often bent upwards, sometimes back and up again, giving an appearance of great flexibility and unity at the same time; as if the clouds were tough, and would hold together, however bent. The narrow extremity is invariably turned to the wind, and the fibres are parallel with its direction. The upper clouds always fall into some modification or other of these arrangements. They thus differ from all other clouds in having a plan and system; whereas other clouds, though there are certain laws which they cannot break, have yet perfect freedom from anything like a relative and general system of government. The upper clouds are to the lower, what soldiers on parade are to a mixed multitude: no men walk on their heads or their hands, and so there are certain laws that no clouds violate; but there is nothing, except in the upper clouds, resembling symmetrical discipline.[7]

Equally the following passage about the fir tree tells us. nothing about its growth or formation in the botanical sense: but it reveals to us something we have probably never realised about its effect upon the visual perceptions.

There is perhaps no tree which has baffled the landscape painter more than the common black spruce fir. It is rare that we see any representation of it other than caricature. It is conceived as if it grew in one plane, or as a section of a tree, with a set of boughs symmetrically dependent on opposite sides. It is thought formal, unmanageable and ugly. It would be so, if it grew as it is drawn. But the Power of the tree is not in that chandelier-like section. It is in the dark, flat, solid tables of leafage, which it holds out on its strong arms, curved slightly over them like shields, and spreading towards the extremity like a hand. It is vain to endeavour to paint the sharp, grassy, intricate leafage until this ruling form has been secured; and in the boughs that approach the spectator, the foreshortening of it is just like that of a wide hill-country, ridge just rising over ridge in successive distances.[8]

It seemed to Ruskin that only by patient and minute study of this kind could the sense of form be quickened and fertilised: without this, it becomes conventional and dead: hence his objection to much Renaissance ornament, and his own endless analyses of the curves of leaves, rocks and the wings of birds. "All beautiful works of art must either intentionally imitate, or accidentally resemble natural forms."[9] This belief leads Ruskin into his fantastic habit of talking of Nature as an artist, entirely concerned with formal effects. He explains, for instance, that the curves of a mountain crest are radially related to each other in the same way as those of a bird's wing:

> All groups of curves set beside each other depend for their beauty on the observance of this law; and if therefore the mountain crests are to be perfectly beautiful, Nature must contrive to get this element of radiant curvature into them in one way or another. Nor does it at first sight appear easy for her to get, I do not say radiant curves, but curves at all: for in the aiguilles she actually bent their beds; but in these slaty crystallines it seems not always convenient to her to bend the beds; and when they are to remain straight, she must obtain the curvature in some other way.[10]

Some of this anthropomorphism is so preposterous, yet so solemn, that one hardly knows whether to take it at its face value, or to regard it as an example of that sort of avuncular playfulness which is the besetting vice of Ruskin's writing. But it is probably quite seriously intended: to Ruskin, especially at the stage when he was writing *Modern Painters*, Nature was only a convenient term for the physical operations of God; and in regarding them as he does he is only extending the eighteenth-century physico-theology of the school of Paley, showing how the wisdom of God is manifested in the works of creation. But for him the exquisite contrivance of Nature is shown not so much in practical adaptation as in beauty of form.

God is thus revealed in beauty as well as in utility; and this is not merely an emotional phrase, but can be illustrated in a precise, detailed, almost scientific way. It is notable that Professor J. E. Marr's *The Scientific Study of Scenery*, an introductory treatise on geomorphology, quotes several considerable passages from *Modern Painters*; refers to Ruskin as one of the acknowledged masters of the study of scenery; and reproduces a very Ruskinesque illustration by W. G. Collingwood, who was one of Ruskin's Oxford pupils. But to appreciate this it is first necessary to learn to see. Thus the disciplined exercise of the visual sensibilities which Ruskin is trying to teach becomes a morally and metaphysically important occupation. "The greatest thing a human soul ever does in this world is to see something, and tell what it saw in a plain way. Hundreds of people can talk for one who can think, but thousands can think for one who can see. To see clearly is poetry, prophecy and religion all in one."[11] Of course anything that Ruskin likes doing is apt to become poetry, prophecy and religion all in one: in this case it is not hard to explain the large claim he is making for his revelation. Ruskin is trying to bring about a psychological revolution, one of those revolutions which, according to the psychology of Jung, must periodically occur in individuals and in cultures if the flow of psychic life is to continue without being blocked and frustrated. The neglected faculties must be released from their archaic existence in the unconscious and set free to function in the daylight. This is what Ruskin is trying to do for the sense of sight—to release it from the bondage to utility and convention and to set it free to operate in its own way; he is vindicating the rights of the senses. This emergence of a buried faculty always comes with something of the force of a revelation; and it was as such that Ruskin's younger disciples accepted his gospel. He himself begins to feel this as the wide tracts of *Modern Painters* open out before him. Early in the second volume he realises that his business "is not now to distinguish between disputed degrees of ability in individuals, or agreeableness in canvases; it is not now to expose the ignorance or defend the principles of party or person; it is to summon the moral energies of the nation to a forgotten duty, to display the use, force and function of a great body of neglected sympathies and desires".[12]

II. ART AND THE MORAL LIFE

We have remarked already that Ruskin's views on perception start from the belief that the uneducated senses are not capable of perceiving what is around them. He connects this belief with Locke, and quotes from the Essay: "This is certain, that whatever alterations are made in the body, if they reach not the mind; whatever impressions are made on the outward parts, if they are not taken notice of within; there is no perception."[13] Locke does not really suit Ruskin's purpose at all well; the doctrine that has more usually and more legitimately been derived from Locke is Wordsworth's

> The eye, it cannot choose but see,
> We cannot bid the ear be still,
> Our bodies feel, where'er we be
> Against or with our will.

In fact Ruskin states this doctrine immediately below. "The eye, during our waking hours, exercises constantly its function of seeing; we always, as far as the bodily organ is concerned, see something, and we always see in the same degree. . . ." But he goes on to deduce from this that we become so used to this merely habitual sense of sight that without particular attention to it, we do not really see at all. And numbers of men being too preoccupied with cares or business to pay this particular attention to impressions of sight, they receive from nature "only the inevitable sensations of blueness, redness, darkness, light, etc., and except at particular and rare moments, no more whatsoever".[14] Which may be true enough, but it is not what Locke was talking about. Locke is distinguishing between sensation and perception (the physical fact and its psychic result); Ruskin between inattentive and attentive perception. Ruskin would really have been happier with the German idealists, but had apparently read little of them. His main concern is to connect the senses with the moral life, and to do this he uses such philosophy as he knows. His beliefs are not dependent on any attempt to link them with formal philosophy, and the connection he wishes to establish between sense perception and morals is eventually made by a little simple sleight-of-hand.

He proceeds to argue that men's ignorance of external nature depends partly on the number of their alien preoccupations, mentioned above, and partly on "a natural want of sensibility to the power of beauty of form, and the other attributes of external objects". Needless to say, this natural want of sensibility is a completely new factor, and has nothing to do with the pseudo-Lockian argument from which we started: nor is it clear whether it is want of sensibility to beauty or a physical defectiveness of sense-perception which is in question. However, it does not greatly matter, for this is only a preamble, and what Ruskin really wants to say appears clearly enough a few lines lower down—that physical acuteness of perception is intimately connected with the higher kind of perception that we call moral:

> With this kind of bodily sensibility to colour and form is intimately connected that higher sensibility which we revere as one of the chief attributes of all noble minds, and as the chief spring of real poetry. I believe this kind of sensibility may be entirely resolved into the acuteness of bodily sense of which I have been speaking, associated with love, love I mean in its infinite and holy functions, as it embraces divine and human and brutal intelligences, and hallows the physical perception of external objects by association, gratitude, veneration, and other pure feelings of our moral nature.[15]

This is a mild attempt to assimilate to an associationist psychology a belief which in Ruskin is independent of any acquired psychological theory. Collingwood has argued cogently that the underlying principle from which nearly all Ruskin's practical thinking springs is the unity and indivisibility of the human spirit, that this betrays the presence of a comprehensive belief about the human mind, "the belief, namely, that each form of human activity springs not from a special faculty —an organ of the mind, so to speak—but from the whole nature of the person concerned: so that art is not the product of a special part of the mind called the 'aesthetic faculty', nor morality the product of a special 'moral faculty', but each alike is an expression of the whole self".[16] It is often felt that

Ruskin's belief on this matter can be summed up in the statement that good art is produced only by good men, and that this is an almost desperate attempt to accommodate an interest in art to the evangelical pietism of his parents. Most men's beliefs are affected in one way or another by those of their parents, but their value is not to be judged on that ground. Whatever its origin Ruskin made use of his conviction of the unity of the human spirit to develop a more comprehensive and humane view of human activities than most of his contemporaries. It is the whole from which many late nineteenth-century ideals— tempering Hebraism with Hellenism, burning with a hard gem-like flame, treating life as a ritual—are broken fragments.

This underlying conviction of unity can find expression in a number of different forms: when it is only half-consciously realised it is apt to be expressed in a series of vaguely para-doxical identifications—statements that art is morality, that life is art, that religion is poetry. The particular content of the statement will depend on the particular interests of its author. Ruskin's particular interests are in art: his aim is to show that it is the expression of man's totality and that it must therefore be justified in terms of his whole nature, not by any partial appeal such as that to utility or a special aesthetic sense. And as the art with which he is concerned is one which depends primarily on visual sensibility, it is his business first to show the connection of visual sensibility with the rest of the psychic life.

Large areas of his work are essentially concerned with this question, but the place where he attempted to expound it philosophically is that part of the second volume of *Modern Painters*, on the theoretic faculty. By this time he has forgotten about Locke and taken up with Aristotle. He is no longer concerned with sense-perception as such, but with the faculty by which beauty is apprehended; and he has decided that the operation of it can be identified with the Greek Theoria. His first concern is to distinguish the Theoretic faculty from the Aesthetic; "aesthesis" properly signifying, he says, "mere sensual perception of the outward qualities and necessary effects of bodies". If Ruskin were merely drawing a distinction between the perception of objects and the perception of beauty it would hardly be necessary to underline it so heavily; his expression is obscure, but he is making, I believe, the same distinction as Roger Fry makes between the apprehension of beauty as sensuous charm and the apprehension of beauty as a satisfying emotional order. "Beauty in the former sense belongs to works of art where only the perceptual aspect of the imaginative life is exercised, beauty in the second sense becomes as it were supersensual, and is concerned with the appropriateness and intensity of the emotions aroused."[17] The first Ruskin dismisses as mere "Aesthesis" (the accident that he happened to use this term in 1846 gives him a handy stick to beat the later aesthetic movement in 1883): the second, or Theoria, is the only means by which beauty is truly apprehended at all.

> The Theoretic faculty is concerned with the moral perception and appreciation of ideas of beauty. And the error respecting it is, the considering and calling it Aesthetic, degrading it to a mere operation of sense, or perhaps worse, of custom; so that the arts which appeal to it sink into a mere amusement, ministers to morbid sensibilities, ticklers and fanners of the soul's sleep.[18]

The key word here is "moral", which we will discuss later: but the above outlines sufficiently clearly the field which he intends Theoria to cover.

He next proceeds to argue that Theoria is produced by the systematic training of the senses, and to illustrate the power we have over the impressions of sense, he takes an example from the sense of taste. When the palate first experiences two different things, it is not in our power to control the immediate preference. But if the same two things be submitted to judgment frequently and attentively, it will often be found that their relations change. The palate will come to perceive in both, qualities at first unnoticed, which on continued experience become more influential than the first impressions; and it will finally reach a settled preference which will be regarded by the person who feels it, and will be received by others, as more correct than the first. As an account of the way in which most people who have the opportunity ultimately come to prefer Stilton to Australian Cheddar, this seems adequate. But from the nutritive point of view, as a cabinet minister has pointed out, there is nothing to choose between them; the faculty which discriminates between these two cheeses performs no biological function. Ruskin proceeds, then, to distinguish between the purely instrumental uses of the senses and those which are ends in themselves. The lower senses of touch and taste are mainly instrumental, mainly subservient to the purposes of life; though even they can to a limited degree become ends in themselves without detriment to the total organisation of our nature. But sight and hearing are manifestly more than instrumental.

> They answer not any purposes of mere existence; for the distinction of all that is useful or dangerous to us might be made, and often is made, by the eye, without its receiving the slightest pleasure of sight. We might have learned to distinguish fruits and grains from flowers, without having any superior pleasure in the aspect of the latter; and the ear might have learned to distinguish the sounds that communicate ideas, or to recognise intimations of elemental danger, without perceiving either melody in the voice, or majesty in the thunder. And as these pleasures have no function to perform, so there is no limit to their continuance in the accomplishment of their end, for they are an end in themselves, and so may be perpetual with all of us; being in no way destructive, but rather increasing in exquisiteness by repetition.[19]

There is a duty attached to every power we possess: in this case the duty " to bring every sense into that state of cultivation in which it shall form the truest conclusions respecting all that is submitted to it, and procure us the greatest amount of pleasure consistent with its due relations to other senses and functions ".[20] And when we practise the cultivation of the senses in this way we are led to realise, not only their self-sufficiency, but also a sense of purpose and adaptation to our desires; out of which perception arise joy, admiration and gratitude. For the pleasures of the senses are not scattered and chance distributed, but form part of a scheme which training and practice enable us to perceive. Thus we cannot go far in the cultivation of the senses without going beyond the purely sensual. Aesthesis, or "the mere animal consciousness of the pleasantness", passes into Theoria, or "the exulting, reverent and grateful perception of it". And this perception Ruskin calls moral.

Ruskin is such an inveterate preacher, and uses so often the language of evangelical exhortation, that this is often taken to mean that he would include the perception of beauty in the perception of right and wrong. Although a number of isolated passages of *The Seven Lamps* or *The Stones of Venice* may seem to support this view, a reading of these two books as a whole, and of volume two of *Modern Painters,* should be sufficient to dispel it. By saying that the perception of beauty is moral, Ruskin does not mean that it is a perception of right and wrong; nor is he using "moral" in any special sense of his own: he is simply using it in the quite common sense of "pertaining to character and conduct". He means in the first place that the perception of beauty is not isolated from the rest of human life, secondly that it is not an affair of the intellect or purely of the senses, but of the emotions. The extent to which we are capable of receiving impressions of beauty depends on the quality of our emotional life in general; and the quality of the emotional life is to Ruskin, as indeed I do not see how it can help being to anyone, a moral concern. There is, in fact, a relation between the kind and amount of beauty that we can perceive, and the moral quality of our lives. This relation can be expressed in two ways; Ruskin's tastes and education being as they were, he constantly expresses it by treating art from the moral point of view. But Pater and the later aesthetes who insisted on treating morals from the point of view of art were only expressing the same relation from the other end. Perhaps one of the reasons that Ruskin was so bitter against them was that he had provided most of the training which made it possible for them to do so. But they are essentially of the same party as Ruskin, and the real opposition is between them and those who regard beauty as the province of a special aesthetic sense, unrelated to the rest of human experience.

Moralist as he is, Ruskin is nevertheless perfectly clear that the requirements of art cannot be merely short-circuited by ethical and emotional considerations. His individual judgments are so capricious that to establish his real and substantial view

18

is always a matter of sifting and collating: to quote any one passage as final lays one open to the charge of being as arbitrary as Ruskin himself. But there is a passage in *The Stones of Venice* which seems to sum up this aspect of the matter as well as any, and which I do not know to be contradicted by any other of similar weight. It suggests that whoever in his age may have attempted to impose a moral Puritanism on art, Ruskin did not do so.

> I perceive a tendency among some of the more thoughtful critics of the day to forget that the business of a painter is to *paint*, and so altogether to despise those men, Veronese and Rubens for instance, who were painters *par excellence*, and in whom the expressional qualities are subordinate. Now it is well when we have strong moral or poetical feeling manifested in painting, to mark this as the best part of the work; but it is not well to consider as a thing of small account, the painter's language in which that feeling is conveyed; for if that language be good and lovely, the man may indeed be a just moralist or a great poet, but he is not a painter, and it was wrong of him to paint. He had much better have put his morality into sermons, and his poetry into verse than into a language of which he was not master. . . . On the other hand, if the man be a painter indeed, and have the gift of colours and lines, what is in him will come from his hand freely and faithfully; and the language itself is so difficult and so vast, that the mere possession of it argues that the man is great, and that his works are worth reading. So that I have never yet seen the case in which this true artistical excellence, visible by the eye-glance, was not the index of some true expressional worth in the work. Neither have I ever seen a good expressional work without high artistical merit: and that this is ever denied is only owing to the narrow view which men are apt to take both of expression and of art; a narrowness consequent on their own especial practice and habits of thought.[21]

He goes on to reprove the modern purist, who out of affection for Angelico would despise Rubens: each is the expression of his own time and country: the moral climate which produced the monk's visions of Italy was different from "the fleshy, substantial, iron-shod humanities" of Flanders: but Rubens's "masculine and universal sympathy" is as much an expression of man's moral experience as the delicate devotion of Angelico.

Ruskin is arguing in effect that the connection of art with

morality is not that it expresses any particular kind of morality, but that it does inevitably express, not merely the technical skill but the whole ethos of the artist himself and of the civilisation that produced him. *The Seven Lamps* and *The Stones of Venice* are continuous illustrations of this. Their importance to their age was that they appeared to translate aesthetic matters which most people felt they did not understand into terms of a morality which they felt quite sure about. This point of view is felt to be so repugnant or so incomprehensible at the present day that it is worth examining Ruskin's practice in the matter a little further. Let us begin by recognising some of the absurdities. The chapter on the Cornice and the Capital in *The Stones of Venice*[22] will provide examples. In Plate XVI Ruskin gives illustrations of a number of cornices, all Byzantine or Italian Gothic, ranging from extreme formalism to extreme naturalism of design. Ruskin has decided, in response to one of his manias, that Catholicism is Heathenism in disguise, that Protestantism is the only true Christianity. He then decides to regard the formal designs as the expression of Catholic Heathenism, and the naturalistic ones as the expression of Protestant Christianity.

But in both these cornices the reader will notice that while the naturalism of the sculpture is steadily on the increase, the classical formalism is still retained. The leaves are accurately numbered, and sternly set in their places; they are leaves in office, and dare not stir nor wave. . . . What is the meaning of this? . . .

These cornices are the Venetian Ecclesiastical Gothic; the Christian element struggling with the Formalism of the Papacy, —the Papacy being entirely heathen in all its principles. That officialism of the leaves and their ribs means Apostolic succession, and I don't know how much more, and is already preparing for the transition to old Heathenism again, and the Renaissance.

Now look to the last cornice. That is Protestantism,—a slight touch of Dissent, hardly amounting to schism, in those falling leaves, but true life in the whole of it. The forms all broken through, and sent heaven knows where, but the root held fast; and the strong sap in the branches; and best of all, good fruit ripening and opening straight towards heaven, and in the face of it, even though some of the leaves lie in the dust.[23]

This is the sort of thing that makes the modern reader despair of Ruskin: it would be hard to imagine anything more capriciously absurd. If formalism were constantly found in the ornament of Catholic churches and naturalism in that of Protestant ones, it would indeed not be unreasonable to trace some connection between the type of religious thought and the type of decorative art it produces: it would be to trace a connection between two more or less demonstrable and objective sets of facts. But here, Protestantism is not actually in question at all; it has come out of Ruskin's private stock of obsessions. He does not produce or attempt to produce the slightest evidence that the growth of naturalism in design runs parallel with a growth of Protestant religious sentiment. As all the examples are pre-Reformation Italian it is difficult to see how he could. He is quite arbitrarily ascribing a religious character that he likes to a style of decoration that he likes. And this is the sort of corruption to which Ruskin's habit of discussing formal characteristics in moral terms is always liable.

What is important, however, to realise is that absurdities of this kind do not invalidate Ruskin's whole attitude and method. Indeed I believe that Ruskin is only doing continuously and on principle what almost all critics of art do more or less. You cannot say very much about the formal qualities of a design without going beyond purely formal terms: if criticism is to be more than pure technical analysis it can hardly avoid doing so. Roger Fry, who more than most critics is credited with insistence on the purely formal qualities of art, continually makes this transition.

> In all that concerns the building up of a composition by the adjustment and balance of lighted and shaded planes Guercino must be accounted a scientific, if not an inspired master. . . . Guercino was in a double sense an eclectic, since he learned his design from Lodovico Caracci, and combined with that the strong light and shade of the Naturalistic school. In his choice of types, and in his conception of the subject also, he stands between the two schools, but inclines much more nearly to the Bolognese. For all that, there is a virility and force about this St. Bruno which the Caracci would perhaps have considered vulgar and wanting in ideality.[24]

There are three kinds of estimate at work here, the formal, the historical, and lastly the emotional. But the terms in which this last is discussed, virility, force, vulgarity, ideality, are in Ruskin's sense moral terms, terms descriptive of the ethos, the moral nature of the artist, as when he says that "the characteristic or moral elements of Gothic" are savageness, changefulness, naturalism, grotesqueness, rigidity, redundance. It is hard to see how the critic of art could get on without using such terms: but there is a limitation to their use. They should not be employed as a short cut, to avoid really looking at the work under discussion; their use should arise naturally out of a consideration of its visual and formal qualities. Thackeray's remarks about Wilkie's Grace before Meat, quoted above, tell us that it is sweet and touching and arouses the feelings associated with Sunday in the country; but give no evidence that he has ever really looked at the picture at all. For all his moralising Ruskin rarely falls into this kind of nebulous catalogue: however eccentric his judgments, he nearly always succeeds in connecting them with the thing seen. This, in fact, is the aim of Ruskin's writings on art—to show how certain formal characteristics are significant in terms of man's life as a whole.

The Seven Lamps of Architecture and *The Stones of Venice* must in this respect be regarded as complementary to each other, parts of a continuous whole: *The Seven Lamps* concerned with the moral qualities which we can expect to find expressed in all great architecture, and *The Stones of Venice* concerned with the detailed illustration of this in practice. It is very unlikely that they have any influence on the way people look at buildings now: most people who are interested in architecture would revolt at the suggestion that a building expresses obedience, or sacrifice; though curiously enough they would not mind saying that it expresses power. And this leads one to the suspicion that the objection to Ruskin's aesthetics is not so much to his moral preoccupations as to his particular scheme of moral values, and to the order in which he arranges his ideas. If he always did his formal analysis first, and if he deduced from them only those moral qualities which the twentieth century can talk about without embarrassment, his point of view would no longer seem particularly strange. Indeed, the thesis of these two books—that plastic art is an expression of the ethos of the men and of the culture that produced it—if expressed in uncoloured unruskinian prose becomes almost a truism: when Roger Fry, in his essay *Art and Life*, attempts to deny this thesis, it is he who has the air of maintaining a paradox. The Marxists, conscious Hegelians as Ruskin was perhaps an unconscious one, would be on Ruskin's side. So, if he analysed his ideas on the matter, would the plain man: the people who hated the late Picasso pictures in 1946 did so partly, it is true, from ignorance of the conventions employed: but still more because they hated a moral atmosphere that they only half-consciously divined. All of which means that a great deal of Ruskin's aesthetic doctrine has found its way into the general current of ideas. The mention of Marxists and plain men suggests too that Ruskin's art-criticism is constantly on the verge of passing over into something else; for neither of these classes of persons commonly fix their attention on aesthetic matters for very long. But the tendency to pass over into something else is common to all imaginative criticism of the arts, to all criticism that is not either history or technical analysis. If you talk long enough about poetry you find yourself talking about religion, ethics or politics, and it is the same with the visual arts. The most illuminating criticism is done in moments of transition between technicalities and philosophy of one kind or another. Ruskin, as we have seen, spends most of his time in this borderland; but it is not only with ethics and politics that he links up his aesthetic criticism; it is also with religion, and it is the connection he makes between art and religion that we must now attempt to trace.

III. ART AND RELIGION

The religious tone of Ruskin's writings on art has perhaps been the greatest stumbling-block to his later readers. In the first place, he often appears to make his artistic doctrines dependent on his religious beliefs; they are thus apt to appear in something the same light as, say, medieval physics; interesting in themselves, but dependent for their validity on the assumed truth of a quite different set of ideas, which the later reader frequently does not share. Secondly, his religious beliefs changed in the course of his development: he does not, in his published works, make this change at all clear, and the result is a good deal of confusion, often reflected in footnotes to later editions of his books, denying or amending positions previously upheld. Many readers no doubt regard Ruskin's religious tone as a sort of stucco front of Biblical phraseology imposed upon beliefs held on other than religious grounds. But the connection is actually far more organic; nor is it a matter of trying to accommodate aesthetic doctrine to an inherited evangelical piety. The attempt to find a connection between art and religious experience is a major preoccupation of the later nineteenth century, though some of the attempts were trivial and incomplete. Rossetti's poetry is filled with Christian imagery; Pater is obsessed by the conflict between pagan and Christian religious ideals, and many of the aesthetes of the nineties found that the worship of beauty could be satisfactorily consummated only within the Catholic Church. A French critic in the nineties wrote a book on *Ruskin et la Religion de la Beauté*. The attempt to discover an aesthetic religion, or a religious basis for aesthetics, is different from anything undertaken by the earlier romantic writers. Keats might be said to make a religion of beauty, but he makes no attempt to connect it with traditional religious attitudes: and the religious traditionalism at which Wordsworth and Coleridge ultimately arrived has little connection with their most intense imaginative experiences; one cannot find much to support the establishment in *Kubla Khan* or *Tintern Abbey*. But in their several ways Ruskin, Rossetti, Holman Hunt, Pater and the nineties were fascinated by traditional religious forms. More than that, they found a kinship between religious experience and the practice and appreciation of art. Shelley, in the preface to *Prometheus Unbound*, says that the aim of poetry is to provide "beautiful idealisms of moral excellence"; and this is still in essence the Renaissance view: Shelley enlarges it by the notion that the poet apprehends and expresses in advance the great movements of history: the artist is a man of insight endowed with powers of expression: but he does not suggest that art, by its own nature, has direct access to the ultimate source of metaphysical goodness. He would hardly have sympathised with Ruskin's dictum that all art is worship; or with the story of Fra Angelico painting on his knees; or with Marius's aesthetic conversion to Christianity. For most of the writers we are considering, aesthetic experience is the first thing, religious experience a dimly apprehended desire. For Ruskin, the religious mode of apprehension and the aesthetic one were equally necessary; and this makes his treatment of the matter both untypical, and much deeper than that of his successors.

Ruskin's religious beliefs have been dealt with somewhat .tartly from the biographical point of view by Mr. Wilenski,[25] who has done a valuable service in tracing the origins and defining the extent of the more manic passages in the works. There can be little doubt that much of Ruskin's preaching is the direct outcome of the obsessions which for long periods dominated his life. Beneath these, however, a quite sane and intelligible pattern of religious development is revealed. He began his career as a bigoted Protestant of the Bible Christian type, to whom Scripture reading was the major devotional practice, and the authority of Scripture absolute. He inherited this creed from his parents, and it is the prevailing belief of the period of *Modern Painters*, *The Seven Lamps* and *The Stones of Venice*. The Protestant and anti-Romanist bias is not very evident in *Modern Painters*: we are told that the Roman Catholic religion encourages gloom, idleness and superstition, and that its best points are due to the influence of mountains; otherwise it is little mentioned. This is not surprising, as *Modern Painters* is mostly about the world of nature: but in *The Seven Lamps* and *The Stones of Venice* he has seriously begun the study of European art, has discovered that a great deal of it is Catholic art, and has come especially under the spell of Gothic. He thus combines admiration for an artistic achievement with intense dislike of the faith that produced it, and somehow he has to come to terms with this contradiction.

It is all the more necessary for him to make his position clear, as he is by now deeply committed to Gothic as the only possible model for modern architecture, and this tended to confuse him with the earlier Gothic revivalists who were notoriously tinged with Catholic belief and practice. There was a natural tendency to class Ruskin's architectural writings vaguely with Pugin's, and Pugin was a convert to Catholicism. Ruskin's love for Gothic art had to be dissociated therefore from any such leanings in religion, and that is probably the main reason for the more stuffily sectarian passages in *The Seven Lamps* and *The Stones of Venice*, of which we give an example later on. There is no need to trace in detail the antics by which Ruskin brings about the desired accommodation. Believing as he does that art is the expression of the moral life of man, he cannot say that medieval art is irrelevant to the Catholicism that inspired it: what he does is to attribute all that is best in it to the nascent spirit of Protestantism within the Catholic Church itself. Even if one were disposed to agree with him one might feel that he protests too much: and the violence and silliness of these passages is due not only to a desire to put himself right with the world, but to a very real fear that he is in danger of losing his own religious security. Letters to his father from Venice refer to his doubts and difficulties in religious belief.[26] One of the best-known passages in *The Stones of Venice*, the description of the interior of St. Mark's and the profound impression of awe and reverence which it creates,[27] is succeeded by a curiously ambiguous paragraph in which Ruskin seems unable to make up his mind whether all this physical loveliness and majesty really fosters the spirit of devotion or not. Mr. Wilenski quotes passages from the diaries at the time when *The Seven Lamps* was being written to show that Ruskin was fascinated by the services in French cathedrals and was actually experiencing an intense attraction to that which he abused.[28]

This sort of fascination by the externals of Catholic art and worship had no doubt already had its effect on Tractarian sensibilities, and was to become a common literary attitude in succeeding years. English writers, not least Ruskin himself, are fond of pointing out that it has little to do with real Catholicism. But it is not open to one like Ruskin, with his profound conviction of the essential unity of aesthetic and moral impressions, to take it lightly. Its effect on him was not to turn him to Catholicism, but to cause him to rely more and more on impressions derived from art and the imaginative life which were quite inconsistent with the Bible Protestantism of his childhood. This first development corresponds with his admiration for the Primitives and a devotional ideal derived perhaps from Fra Angelico, in which a purist art seems almost a direct avenue to religious experience. But as he went further in his study of the Venetians he found himself becoming infected with a naturalist sentiment which was not only inconsistent with his early Protestantism, but with religion, as he he had formerly understood it, of every kind. This second phase culminates in his "unconversion" at Turin in 1858, effected partly by the agency of Veronese, and partly by a bad sermon from a Waldensian preacher which suddenly revealed to him the mean sectarian pettiness of much popular Protestantism.

Certainly it seems intended that strong and frank animality, rejecting all tendency to asceticism, monachism, pietism, and so on, should be connected with the strongest intellects. . . . I don't understand it; one would have thought purity gave strength, but it doesn't. A good, stout, self-commanding magnificent animality is the make for poets and artists, it seems to me. . . . Has God made faces beautiful and limbs strong, and created these strange, fiery, fantastic energies, and created the splendour of substance and the love of it; . . . only that these things may lead His creatures away from Him? And is this mighty Paul Veronese, in whose soul there is a strength as of the snowy mountains, and within whose brain all the pomp and majesty of humanity floats in a marshalled glory, capacious and serene like clouds at sunset—this man whose finger is as fire, and whose eye is like the morning—is he a servant of the devil; and is the poor little wretch in a tidy black tie, to whom I have been listening this Sunday morning expounding Nothing with a twang—is he a servant of God? It is a great mystery. . . . It is all very well for people to fast who can't eat; and to preach who cannot talk nor sing; and to walk barefoot who cannot ride, and then think themselves good. Let them learn to master the world before they abuse it.[29]

This experience was followed by a mood of "intense scorn of all I had hitherto done or thought, still intenser scorn of other people's doings and thinkings, especially in religion; the perception of colossal power more and more in Titian and of weakness in purism"; and in this mood he was "seriously, and despairingly, thinking of going to Paris or Venice and breaking away from all modern society and opinion, and doing I don't know what".[30] But this fleeting inclination toward *la vie de Bohème* was not pursued; and for almost twenty years Ruskin adopted a "religion of humanity" which is reflected in his political and sociological writings. The extent of his departure from orthodoxy is obscured, to some extent deliberately, to avoid hurting his parents; to some extent accidentally by his continued use of Biblical language; but his changed attitude to the Bible and its authority is shown cautiously in the introduction to *The Crown of Wild Olive*, and more frankly in Letter VIII of *Time and Tide*.

Yet while studying the frescoes of Giotto at Assisi in 1874, Ruskin again felt the powerful attraction of religious art. "I discovered," he says, "the fallacy under which I had been tormented for fifteen years—the fallacy that Religious artists were weaker than Irreligious. I found that all Giotto's weaknesses (so called) were merely absences of material science. . . . But I found he was in the make of him, and contents, a very much stronger man than Titian: . . . that the Religion in him, instead of weakening, had solemnised and developed every faculty of his heart and hand; and finally, that his work, in all the innocence of it, was yet a human achievement and possession, quite above anything that Titian had ever done."[31] Again we find impressions derived from art affecting his religious attitude, and his writings from this point assume a more distinctively Christian tone. He began to feel a peculiar devotion to St. Francis, and to believe that he was, in some obscure sense, a Franciscan tertiary—a notion that had already occurred to him in a dream three years before. The sacristan at Assisi believed that he was about to be converted, and prayed every day that this might occur. "É una piccola cosa, ma credo che San Francesco lo farà." Thereafter Ruskin had several times to deny rumours that he was about to be received into the Roman Church: and Aubrey de Vere, Patmore and Manning were all interested in his possible conversion. His own attitude in this last phase seems to have been quite consistent. "I was, am, and can be, only a Christian Catholic in the wide and eternal sense. . . . But I am no more likely to become a Roman Catholic than a Quaker, Evangelical or Turk."[32]

To a biographer of Ruskin there would be much else of importance to discuss—perhaps an impressive sincerity which survives uncontaminated under all Ruskin's vagaries and obsessions. It is notable that Ruskin's despairing infatuation for Rose la Touche, though it nearly cost him his reason, had not the power to modify his religious beliefs in the slightest degree, even when a return to his old Evangelical position might have won him all he wanted of her regard. Yet we continually find his religious attitude modified by experience derived from art. The main phases of Ruskin's religious development were all connected with artistic experiences; the first with Gothic architecture, Botticelli and Fra Angelico; the second with Veronese and Titian; the third with Giotto. And beneath all these changes of theological expression there seems to lie a natural religion, having the closest possible connection with Ruskin's aesthetic experience, that remains fundamentally unchanged. This natural religion which underlies all Ruskin's thought and could be illustrated from almost any department of his writings, is exhibited most clearly in *Modern Painters*. It may be thought unjust to illustrate a pervasive attitude of Ruskin's from his earliest book, and one which is usually considered immature. I do not believe that it is immature in any sense that matters. It is true that Ruskin's art-scholarship vastly increased later on; but he is not here writing for the most part on matters where scholarship is of much account: it is true that *Modern Painters* is capricious and unbalanced; but Ruskin's later writing did not noticeably improve in this respect. And there is a freshness about the presentation of the ideas, a sense of working freely, unimpeded by dank fogs from the unconscious, that he did not often manage to recapture. The Oxford lectures, that bible of Ruskinians in the eighties, seems in comparison a rather weary repetition of ideas which by that time had become fixed. There are whole ranges of thought in the later works that are not even foreshadowed in *Modern Painters*, but the ideas that are in *Modern Painters* are commonly expressed there with more spontaneity and life than ever again. This is especially so with the feeling for nature, which has not yet had time to become reminiscent and repetitive. It is even so with the religious aspect of the book. Ruskin at this time was a fervent and untroubled Evangelical, and his religious feeling seems very pure and unforced: in the early volumes especially, sectarian bias is not very evident, for he has not yet been powerfully affected by faiths different from his own: he is not yet up against the necessity of excusing himself for admiring Catholic art: and his own particular version of nineteenth-century Protestantism has a very individual and not unattractive flavour.

Like other Evangelicals of his time Ruskin believed in the absolute authority of the Bible: and the habit of testifying in season and out of season by using the words of Holy Writ remained with him long after he had ceased to believe that they had any supernatural validity. But what gives his piety a different note, and links it with his individual sensibility, is a strong Wordsworthian element. Wordsworth is quoted in *Modern Painters* more often than any other poet, and his conviction of the power of nature over the moral life of man is obviously a dominant force in Ruskin's mind. The result is that his pietism is fused with a sort of nature-mysticism in which all his deepest interests are brought into activity. Ruskin is a religious man to whom the imaginative interpretation of sensuous experience is nevertheless a necessity. Happier in this than such tortured spirits as Gerard Manley Hopkins, there was to him no contradiction between these two modes of experience: the one led naturally to the other, and the connection between them is the most important link in his structure of ideas. His duty as a critic of art is to make this connection clear to other people; and there were not many in the fifties who were inclined to regard the apprehension of beauty as a means of justifying the ways of God to man. To explain to a stiff-necked and uncircumcised generation truths that have always been an intimate and self-evident part of one's own make-up usually leads to over-emphasis and repetition: hence the prolixity and the hortatory tone of *Modern Painters*.

To Ruskin it was all extremely lucid. We have a duty to cultivate all the senses to their highest attainable point of accuracy and power. By most men this is left undone, especially in respect of the sense of sight. Most men do not really see what is around them. The genius like Turner can see truly what he sees by native and instinctive sense of form; for others a laborious training of the visual sense is required. This training Ruskin sets out to provide in *Modern Painters*—to deliver men from the bondage of custom and show them what the world around them really looks like. Some of this trained observation has been systematised in botany, geology and so forth, and these sciences can well be brought in to assist the unseeing eye: but the collection of facts is not the end. The minute and attentive study of natural forms finally reaches a degree of intensity, and a freedom from all utilitarian considerations, at which it can be called Theoria or contemplation: and here Ruskin translates the Greek conception, that of passing from the contemplation of particulars to an underlying principle behind them, into his own evangelical terms. From this contemplation, he says, arise joy, admiration and gratitude, and we are inevitably led to contemplate the beautiful as a gift of God, whom Ruskin thinks of in his peculiarly anthropocentric way as having provided beauty in Nature solely for our delight.

It is the direct literalness of Ruskin's religious beliefs at this period that makes this very simple form of natural religion available to him. Nineteenth-century scepticism and subjectivism have not yet touched him. His experience was the direct contrary of Tennyson's

> I found him not in star nor sun
> Nor eagle's wing, nor insect's eye:

and he would have been violently impatient of Coleridge's attempt to find a foundation for faith in German subjectivist metaphysics. As we have suggested, there are many passages in *Modern Painters* which belong to the same school as Paley's *Natural Theology*, the book which Coleridge constantly attacks. For Ruskin, as for the theologically minded scientists of the eighteenth century, the wisdom of God is manifested in the works of creation, and he finds perhaps the best expression of his belief in a passage he quotes from Linnaeus. The fact that the quotation occurs first in the preface to the 1883 edition of *Modern Painters* goes to show the enduring nature of this aspect of Ruskin's faith. "Deum sempiternum, immensum, omniscium, expergefactus transeuntem vidi, et obstupui"—"As one awaked out of sleep, I saw the Lord passing by—eternal, infinite, omniscient, omnipotent, and I stood as in a trance." To Ruskin this was the justification of art equally with that of science, and it forms the bond that ties his artistic, his scientific and his religious interests into a single whole.

IV. ART AND THE SOCIAL ORDER. THE NATURE OF GOTHIC

From the practical point of view the most important overflow from Ruskin's art-criticism was his sociology, and his sociology as such is outside our field. But it is necessary to follow the process by which he passes from aesthetic to politics and economics. The main extra-artistic interest of *Modern Painters* is in natural history, and the main function of man to adore his Creator by learning to know and love His works. But *The Seven Lamps* and *The Stones of Venice* show a growing interest in human institutions. Ruskin has not yet reached the stage of *Munera Pulveris*, where he is prepared to put the political economists right on their own ground, but he is becoming increasingly conscious of social and economic behaviour and its effects on art. The abandonment for some years of art-criticism is marked by the publication of *The Political Economy of Art* in 1857; but it is foreshadowed long before in the famous sentence in *The Seven Lamps*, "I believe the right question to ask respecting all ornament, is simply this: was it done with enjoyment—was the carver happy while he was about it?"[33] This shift of interest from the work of art to the life of the man who produced it continues in the chapter on

"The Nature of Gothic" in *The Stones of Venice*; and it is in this famous chapter that the political and social consequences of aestheticism are first outlined. Morris reprinted it at the Kelmscott Press, in youth it was his Bible, and it formed the background of all his craft-work. We owe to it a diversity of social effects, some past, some still with us: a form of socialism already obsolete; the arts and crafts movement; such experiments in community life as that of Eric Gill; and also, I fear (among the moral elements of Gothic are Changefulness, Grotesqueness and Redundance), the anarchic riot of modern suburban development.

All these things either by a natural development or by corruption spring from Ruskin's conviction that art is the expression of the ethos of the artist. In the fifth Lamp, the Lamp of Life, he had already reached the conclusion that we do some work that is necessary for our bread, and some also that is not necessary; and that the only reason for the unnecessary work is that it is for our delight. If the worker did not take pleasure in doing it, the spectator cannot rightly take pleasure in contemplating it, and it should therefore never have been done at all. It is not enough to have our art-work designed by men of taste; unless the men who actually execute it take pleasure in the task the work will be dead: you cannot get life by paying for it. If the work is not worth the whole powers, physical and moral, of the workman, it is not worth doing at all. Ruskin describes a new church near Rouen, loaded with rich detail that has been designed with a certain amount of taste and scholarship. "But it is all as dead as leaves in December; there is not one tender touch, not one warm stroke, on the whole façade. The men who did it hated it, and were thankful when it was done."[33] If there were a workman capable of being discontented with this inferior work, he would not in our society remain a workman, but would struggle into being an "artist". We have thus divided our handicraftsmen into slaves and academicians and spoilt both in the process.

The Stones of Venice elaborates this. Ruskin distinguishes between servile ornament, in which the executive mind is absolutely subordinated to the inventive; and the medieval or

Gothic system in which the mind of the inferior workman is recognised and has full room for action but is guided and ennobled by the ruling mind. This is the only truly Christian system. The worst conceivable is the Renaissance system, which is an impossible attempt to make the executive power equal the inventive at every point. The first system is wrong because it fails to recognise the domain of human liberty; the third is wrong because it fails to recognise the limits of human capability. It is equally wrong to make the workman a slave, or to demand that he should be a Michelangelo.

Both Byzantine and Romanesque have in part overriden these illegitimate demands, but the only art to do so completely is Gothic. Gothic becomes therefore for Ruskin the central type of all art, and the chapter on the "Nature of Gothic", perhaps to Ruskin himself, certainly to his followers, becomes more than a piece of historical criticism, it becomes a statement of principles conceived as having universal validity. This universal validity they derive from a correspondence with the real nature and desires of man. The "characteristic or moral elements of Gothic", we are told, are savageness, changefulness, naturalism, grotesqueness, rigidity and redundance. These are the characteristics as belonging to the building; as belonging to the builder they would be savageness or rudeness, love of change, love of nature, disturbed imagination, obstinacy, generosity. Ruskin starts by making this equation between the character of the work of art and the character of the artist. He does not go on to suggest directly that these qualities are the fundamental characteristics of all humanity, but he tries to show that each of them embodies an essential human desire, that each of them must find its appropriate satisfaction in any valid system of art or of society. Naturalism is the appropriate middle course between Purism and Sensualism; changefulness the appropriate middle course between a sterile immobility and a diseased love of novelty. In fact Ruskin is justifying his critical principles in the eighteenth-century way by referring them to what is central and unchanging in human nature, apart from the influence of fashion and individual temperament. Especially he feels that Gothic has estimated man's status rightly, without either presuming on or degrading his real capabilities. The "savageness" of Gothic is not a matter for regret or apology, but a just confession of man's imperfect nature.

That admission of lost power and fallen nature, which the Greek or Ninevite felt to be intensely painful, and, as far as might be altogether refused, the Christian makes daily and hourly, contemplating the fact of it without fear, as tending, in the end, to God's greater glory. Therefore to every spirit which Christianity summons to her service, her exhortation is: Do what you can, and confess frankly what you are unable to do; neither let your effort be shortened for fear of failure, nor your confession silenced for fear of shame. And it is, perhaps, the principal admirableness of the Gothic schools of architecture, that they thus receive the results of the labour of inferior minds; and out of fragments full of imperfection, and betraying that imperfection in every touch, indulgently raise up a stately and unaccusable whole.[34]

The vice of nineteenth-century civilisation is that it has preferred the lower perfection to the higher. The human condition is such that perfection is only possible in lesser things. Animals are more perfect in their kind than man, yet are always held to be inferior to him. We demand mathematical accuracy in details of construction and ornament which can only be achieved by sacrificing all that is specifically human in the nature of the workman. Because we admire a smooth minuteness we make man into a tool.

And now, reader, look round this English room of yours, about which you have been proud so often, because the work of it was so good and strong, and the ornaments of it so finished. Examine again all those accurate mouldings, and perfect polishings, and unerring adjustments of the seasoned wood and tempered steel. Many a time you have exulted over them and thought how great England was, because her slightest work was done so thoroughly. Alas! if read rightly, these perfectnesses are signs of a slavery a thousand times more bitter and more degrading than that of the scourged African, or helot Greek. Men may be beaten, chained, tormented, yoked like cattle, slaughtered like summer flies, and yet remain in one and the best sense, free. But to smother their souls within them, to blight and hew into rotting pollards the suckling branches of their human intelligence, to make the flesh and skin which, after the worm's work on it, is to see God, into leathern thongs to yoke machinery with, —this is to be slave-masters indeed; and there might be more freedom in England, though her feudal lord's lightest words were worth men's lives, and though the blood of the vexed husbandman dropped in the furrows of her fields, than there is while the animation of her multitudes is sent like fuel to feed the factory smoke, and the strength of them is given daily to be wasted into the fineness of a web, or racked into the exactness of a line.[34]

And there can be no half-measures about this. You must either make a tool of your workman or a man of him: you cannot make both. Men are not meant to work with the precision of machines, and if you will have that precision out of them you must dehumanise them. In every man there is the capacity for something better than this machine-like labour, some power of feeling and imagination. If he is to function as a man this power must be used. But as soon as this begins to happen, as soon as the ordinary workman begins to think about form, to invent form of his own instead of merely copying, hesitation and imperfection will inevitably follow; the smooth mechanical minuteness will be gone. But the operative will have become a man.

> Go forth again to gaze upon the old cathedral front, where you have smiled so often at the fantastic ignorance of the old sculptors: examine once more those ugly goblins, and formless monsters, and stern statues, anatomiless and rigid; but do not mock at them, for they are signs of the life and liberty of every workman who struck the stone; a freedom of thought and rank in the scale of being, such as no laws, no charters, no charities can secure; but which it must be the first aim of all Europe at this day to regain for her children.[34]

The degradation of the workman into a machine makes all sympathy and charity from the rich, and all improvement of material conditions, equally vain, and it is this degradation that is the real source of class hatred. It is not Jacobinism or hunger that makes the lower classes hate the upper, it is the sense of their own degradation, felt by the workmen themselves. In the Middle Ages the difference between the noble and the peasant was merely a legal and economic one: in the nineteenth century the difference between rich and poor is almost a difference of metaphysical status. There is nothing wrong in master-ship and kingship. What is wrong is the degrading of those who are not masters below the level of the properly human. And that is what has occurred. The much-praised division of labour is really the division of men, into segments and fractions of men.

Ruskin's thought has a way of accumulating round a few focal points. His ideas on the relation between art and the social structure nearly all cluster round this man-machine antithesis. The problem is still real, but conditions have changed so much that it is perhaps hardly worth while at this late date to discuss his views in detail. It might be pointed out that peasants several times revolted in the Middle Ages, in spite of the meta-physical satisfactoriness of their status; and that however wrong they may be, most men feel freer after a day's light work in a factory than after a day spent in dropping their blood in the furrows of their fields. The greatest contradiction in this argument of Ruskin's is parallel to the one which vitiates a good deal of his aesthetics. Just as he was unable to see (as indeed most people were till after the advent of Cubism) that geometrical form can also express the forms of nature, perhaps in a more fundamental way than "naturalism", so he is unable to see that mathematical precision is not necessarily inhuman, it also is an expression of human faculty. We have become accustomed to the notion that God might be a mathematician: it would almost seem to Ruskin that he could only be so on condition that he got all his calculations a little wrong. And did Ruskin really believe that the sculptures of Chartres were the product of a rude untutored freedom? But for all its incom-pleteness, historically speaking, this train of thought probably proved the most influential part of Ruskin's teaching, because it led him to what was, from the material point of view, the heart of Victorian civilisation, the social situation resulting from the new industrialism.

> And the great cry arising from all our manufacturing cities, louder than the furnace blast, is all in very deed for this,—that we manufacture everything there except men; we blanch cotton, and strengthen steel, and refine sugar, and shape pottery; but to

brighten, to strengthen, to refine or to form a single living spirit, never enters into our estimate of advantages. And all the evil to which that cry is urging our myriads can be met only in one way; ... by a right understanding, on the part of all classes, of what kinds of labour are good for men, raising them, and making them happy; by a determined sacrifice of such beauty, or cheapness, as is to be got only by the degradation of the workman; and by equally determined demand for the products and results of healthy and ennobling labour.[34]

In order that the products of this healthy and ennobling labour might be immediately recognised, Ruskin gives two rules:†

Never encourage the manufacture of any article not absolutely necessary, in the production of which Invention has no share.
Never demand an exact finish for its own sake, but only for some practical or noble end.[34]

The young lady who buys glass beads is engaging in the slave trade, for the workmen who made them work as automata "without the smallest occasion for the use of any single human faculty". Our modern glass is far superior in accuracy of form and cutting to the old Venetian: but we ought to be ashamed of it, for the English workman has become a mere machine for rounding curves and sharpening edges, while the Venetian invented a new design for every glass that he made.

The consequences of these principles become apparent in the next generation, and it is not necessary to say much of them here. The second rule—never demand an exact finish for its own sake—has had a somewhat disreputable history as the illegitimate parent of the more tiresome arts and crafts; and much poker-work and beaten pewter, the strange beliefs that a squiggly line is necessarily more artistic than a straight one, can be laid to its door. It has nevertheless given much innocent happiness; and to justify amateur inefficiency was very far from Ruskin's intention. His own methods of teaching drawing are almost painfully insistent on precision; they begin with practice in drawing straight lines with a pen, that one would imagine, in its dehumanising effect, to approximate

† As a matter of fact he gives three, but the third, a caveat against copying, is redundant, and may be included in the first.

very closely to the manufacture of glass beads. His first rule, on the other hand, leads to the demand that the production of all that immense accumulation of unnecessary objects which neither serve the purposes of life, nor give any creative satisfaction to those who make them, should simply cease. Just as Tennyson had been horrified by the pointless profusion of nature, so Ruskin and his followers were horrified by the pointless profusion of the industrial arts, the sheer waste of human energy involved by such objects as the public-house railings that figure so prominently in the preface to *A Joy for Ever*. Morris carries this idea further: it forms the economic basis of *News from Nowhere*: and it thus transmitted to the early Socialist movement the ideal of simplicity of life and a deliberate limitation of wants, to which the Socialism of to-day only submits under pressure of a hard necessity. But here we pass from Ruskin's teaching to its practical applications, and for these we must turn to pre-Raphaelitism, and the work of Morris.

Chapter II

ROSSETTI AND THE P.R.B.

I. THE AESTHETIC OF PRE-RAPHAELITISM

THE larger English provincial towns are particularly rich in the works of the pre-Raphaelites. Rossetti, Hunt and their fellows sold their pictures to the new business magnates, and now that many of their collections have been dispersed, the public galleries of the North and Midlands contain an exceptionally high proportion of meticulous records (painted on a wet white ground) of foliage and flowers; of excursions into religio-romantic dream worlds, where the Holy Grail and the mythology of the Vita Nuova contrast strangely with the smoke-blackened bricks and mortar outside. From the grimy and tram-berattled centre of Liverpool one can enter the Walker Art Gallery to be confronted by Rossetti's vast canvas of *Dante's Dream*; and its hieratic solemnity, its lavish symbolism, its remote and passion-wasted faces represent one side of the pre-Raphaelite movement: while tucked away in a low corner is John Brett's silvery shimmering little picture *The Stone-breaker*, surely one of the most charming minor works of the English school; and its delicate literalism, every fracture of the flints and every tree on the distant downs exquisitely painted, is equally representative of pre-Raphaelite aims. This is all as it should be—it is indeed an excellent illustration of the paradoxical nature of the movement—for pre-Raphaelitism was in part a protest against towns like Liverpool, yet it was gladly welcomed by them: and it included two very different impulses —one a patient naturalism, the other almost in contradiction to it, a flight from actuality into archaic romance.

For this reason the term pre-Raphaelite stands in general

usage for a number of different things. To some it represents the sophisticated religious simplicity of Rossetti's *Ecce Ancilla Domini* and *The Girlhood of the Virgin*; to some the refined and spiritualised eroticism of his various portrayals of Elizabeth Siddal, or the franker sensuousness of his later work, what William Rossetti, with accurate infelicity, called "female heads with floral adjuncts"; while to others the essence of the movement is the minute representation of natural appearances, exemplified by Hunt's painful studies of a brick wall at midnight and Millais's careful painting of the sedges and dog-roses of an actual stream as a background to his Ophelia. All these strains were present, besides a vein of sincere but rather vague piety in Hunt's middle style, and one of contemporary domestic realism in his *Awakened Conscience*, Rossetti's *Found*, and Martineau's *Last Day in the Old Home*. Indeed the basic mistake of the pre-Raphaelites was in forming a brotherhood at all. There were far too many divergent aims for such a close association, and the actual society began to split up almost as soon as it was formed. The true prototype for pre-Raphaelitism should have been the unorganised literary Romantic movement of fifty years earlier: we can imagine the consequences of trying to fit Scott, Leigh Hunt, Wordsworth and Byron into a pantisocracy. If the original association of the pre-Raphaelites had been less close, its history would be less chequered with recriminations and broken friendships than it is.

Historically speaking, pre-Raphaelitism is a late flowering of the major romantic movement, induced by the new excitement about visual art for which Ruskin was responsible. English art in the nineteenth century presents a confusing picture, but with the notable exception of Blake and his followers, the sense of a new heaven and a new earth that pervades romantic literature had not communicated itself to the painters. Their habits of mind remained either pedestrian or neo-classic. Even a gigantic original like Turner is obsessed with the aim of rivalling Claude. The followers of high art, even a man so closely associated with the new poetry as Haydon, went on painfully pursuing the sublime in the old sense. Their work was still dominated by the canons of the grand style, expounded to England by Sir Joshua Reynolds, while the genre painters were equally attached to the seventeenth-century Dutch tradition. From bòth these Ruskin came to deliver his generation, and the early volumes of *Modern Painters* set out to do much the same job for painting as Wordsworth and Coleridge had done for poetry in the preface to *Lyrical Ballads* and its commentary in *Biographia Literaria*. Rossetti's soundest remark on the painting of his own school was in a letter to Burne-Jones: "If a man have any poetry in him he should paint, for it has all been said and sung, but they have hardly begun to paint it."

Other influences besides Ruskin's were at work. Traditionally, English painters had been craftsmen, almost artisans, in the lower social reaches: the more successful were professional men with an assured position in the genteel classes. But they were not commonly men of much literary culture, and apart from the technicalities of their craft, they were hardly more conscious of their citizenship in the republic of the Muses than surgeons or lawyers. In Ruskin we have a man of great literary powers who devoted himself mainly to art, and this in itself helped to draw literature and painting together. We must remember, too, what is sometimes forgotten, how late it was before some of the most typical romantic literature gained anything like general acceptance. In the forties its influence could still be new and exciting. To Holman Hunt and Millais as young students Keats was a discovery. Hunt picked up his copy of the works of "this little-known poet" in a 4*d*. box, and converted Millais to his enthusiasm. Both they and Rossetti regarded it as part of their mission to deliver painting from vulgarity of thought and triviality of subject by flooding it with ideas from the romantic literature of the earlier part of the century. Rossetti's literary inspiration needs no underlining; but even Hunt, who looked on himself and Millais as *par excellence* the professional painters of the group, regards "the discipleship of the formative arts to that of letters" as "a perennial law". In return, pre-Raphaelitism became far more than a school of painting: it became a movement of thought and feeling whose influence soaked deep into the later nineteenth century, and even spread to the next age. The movement included one brilliant and erratic genius and a sufficient number of determined individualists; with such a composition and with ideals so wide, it is not surprising that it soon outgrew whatever formula it started from; so much so that it would be absurd to try to pin it down to any one determined purpose. With which caution we may begin to examine its origins and to trace some of its contributory streams.

Pre-Raphaelitism is a well-documented affair. Besides the chronicles of the indefatigable William Michael Rossetti we have a fair amount of commentary in the writings of Ruskin, and Holman Hunt's voluminous *Pre-Raphaelitism and the Pre-Raphaelite Brotherhood*. There is also a mass of memoirs and biographies. A great deal of this material, however, is purely biographical, some of it not much more than personal anecdote; though intensely fascinating, as anecdote about such a group could hardly fail to be, it does not throw as clear a light as could be wished on the real ethos of pre-Raphaelitism. Rossetti was not particularly articulate about his aims, and Hunt, who was, wrote about them *ex post facto*; so that one is inclined to suspect that the account of his early aspirations has sometimes been modified to suit the later development of events. William Rossetti not unnaturally assumed his brother's primacy in the movement; Ruskin's criticism supported him in this view; and Hunt's book is pervaded by an offended protest against it, and a desire to claim the whole origin of pre-Raphaelitism for himself and Millais. The attempt to write a history of pre-Raphaelitism omitting Rossetti as far as possible is necessarily rather absurd; but Hunt's writing remains valuable for its full exposition of one aspect of pre-Raphaelite thought: and it is possible to feel a certain sympathy for a single-minded man with a limited aim who finds himself accidentally coupled with a formidable partner who continually steals the limelight by a quite incompatible performance of his own. If Hunt thought less about art in general, he thought far harder about painting in particular than Rossetti, and it is from him that we can learn most about the strictly technical and pictorial development of the creed.

Holman Hunt's father was a moderately unsuccessful city man, and it was with no great willingness and at some personal sacrifice that he permitted his son to become an artist. Naturally enough, Hunt's early career is filled with a determination to become at any rate a successful craftsman, to attain a kind of demonstrable competence that would justify his following art as a profession. His early specimen drawings, sent as tests for admission to the Academy schools, were rejected, as he thought, for slovenliness. "By nature, and the encouragement of my early painting master, slovenliness was my besetting sin, through too great impatience to reach the result." He determined therefore to acquire an exact and undeviating manipulative skill. He learnt by chance from a fellow-student that Wilkie in some of his pictures had abandoned the general practice of an underpainting in monochrome, later glazed with colour, and had finished each part of his picture thoroughly on the day it was begun. Hunt welcomed this practice as requiring clear and decisive handling. About this time his friendship with Millais began. Millais had been the youngest and was still the most brilliant student at the Academy schools. Happy in the possession of adoring parents, great talent and considerable personal charm, he embarked at the age of fifteen on a career of almost uninterrupted prosperity. Hunt, besides perhaps being a little enchanted by the attractive youth, was vastly impressed by the assurance and precision of treatment in his early works. They soon formed the habit of discussing the theory and practice of art, "by no means bound to dogmas that gained general acceptance, but quite ready to re-examine settled views, even though they seemed at first above question".

Some time about 1845 Hunt was lent a copy of *Modern Painters*. It came to him, as to so many others, as a revelation. He sat up all night to get through it, and remarks that "of all its readers none could have felt more strongly than myself that it was written expressly for him". From now on Hunt's budding aesthetic is given a definite direction—a direction indicated in a conversation with Millais soon after. Hunt's record of it was written fifty years later; he does not pretend, of course, to recall the actual words, but he insists on the substantial accuracy of his recollection, and it is probable that we have an only slightly chastened and developed version of the argument of the two young men. The burden of it is that English art had attained a facile proficiency, and that the English masters of the eighteenth century had worked "without the discipline of exact manipulation". Sir Joshua was not interested in form, he was interested in humanity, and this saved him from mere conventionalism: but the rules of art he laid down, and his affection for the Caracci and the Bolognese school, were to lead his successors into the worst kind of picture-making by recipe.

> Under his reign came into vogue drooping branches of trees over a night-like sky, or a column with a curtain unnaturally arranged, as a background to a day-lit portrait; his feeble followers imitated his arrangements so that there are few rooms in an exhibition in which we can't count twenty or thirty of the kind. Is it then premature to demand that the backgrounds of pictures should be representations of nature as well as their more important portions? . . . His lectures were admirably adapted to encourage students to make a complete and reverential study of what art had done in the past, . . . but Reynolds was not then in sight of the opposite danger of conventionalism which has since affected the healthy study of nature; the last fifty years, however, have proved that his teaching was interpreted as encouragement to unoriginality of treatment, and neglect of that delicate rendering of nature, which had led previous schools to greatness.[1]

Millais agrees, and adds his own aspirations toward the completest "finish"; Hunt replies that without fundamental study of form, finish is wasted, and goes on with the question of precedent.

> I would say that the course of previous generations of artists which led to excellence cannot be too studiously followed by us, but their treatment of subjects, perfect as they were for their time, should not be repeated. If we only do what they did so perfectly, I don't see much good in our work. The language they used was then a living one, now it is dead, though their work has in it humanly and artistically such marvellous perfections that for us to repeat their treatment of sacred or historic subjects is mere affectation. . . . Neither of us is sophisticated enough to appreciate the system in vogue, and not to feel that it

ends in insupportable mannerism and sameness of feature that soon pall upon the sense beyond toleration. . . . Let us go on a bold track; some one must do this soon, why should we not do it together? We will go carefully and not without the teaching of our fathers: it is simply fuller Nature that we want. . . . Why should the several parts of the composition be always opposed in pyramids? Why should the highest light be always on the principal figure? Why make one corner of the picture always in shade? For what reason is the sky in a daylight picture made as black as night?†[2]

He concludes with a panegyric on *Modern Painters* which makes it fairly clear that this was the source from which many of these ideas were derived.

So far the case is clear. We are contemplating yet another of these returns to nature with which the course of poetry and painting is diversified, each one to become itself an outworn convention in the course of fifty or a hundred years. Hunt intersperses his remarks with cautions against medieval revivalism, directed, as we shall see, against Rossetti, and probably inserted in retrospect. Dates are absent, but this conversation is supposed to take place about 1846–7, and we can take it perhaps, in conjunction with later evidence, that Hunt establishes his case for a reform of art on Ruskinian lines projected by himself and Millais, before they had had any but the most casual contact with Rossetti.

Hunt exhibited his picture of the *Eve of St. Agnes* at the Academy in 1847. A common enthusiasm for Keats drew Rossetti's attention to it, and from then on the acquaintanceship grew. Hunt infected Rossetti with his ideas, and sub-acidly remarks, "It was pleasant to hear him repeat my propositions and theories in his own richer phrase". The intention of this is presumably to suggest that Rossetti merely provided a literary amplification of what Hunt had already thought out. But this really will not do. It is true that Rossetti in his early days was enthusiastically appreciative of other men's talents and other men's ideas: but he had a less exclusively professional outlook, and a far more generally cultivated mind than Hunt

† These lines afford a fair sample of the conventional rules of composition, inherited ultimately from the eclectic school of Bologna, against which Ruskin and the P.R.B. were in revolt.

46

and Millais. It is also clear that he had other motives to a
pre-Raphaelite revolt than their student talk. In 1847 he
acquired a MS. book of Blake, containing prose, verse and
drawings.

> His ownership of this truly precious volume certainly stimu-
> lated in some degree his disregard or scorn of some aspects of
> art held in reverence by *dilettanti* and routine students, and thus
> conduced to the pre-Raphaelite movement; for he found here
> the most outspoken (and no doubt, in a sense the most irrational)
> epigrams and jeers against such painters as Correggio, Titian,
> Rubens, Rembrandt, Reynolds and Gainsborough—any man
> whom Blake regarded as fulsomely florid, or lax, or swamping
> ideas in mere manipulation. [3]

It is also true that when he set out to be a painter his experi-
ence was more literary than pictorial, and that he was a spas-
modic and dilettante student: so that it may well have seemed
to the industrious and single-minded Hunt that he knew hardly
anything about painting. Rossetti's early reading had been
almost entirely of a romantic and imaginative kind—the
Arabian Nights, Shakespeare, Scott, Byron, Shelley, Keats, and
an assortment of Gothic and terror literature, "brigand tales"
and so forth. At the Academy schools he was constantly making
sketches of "knights rescuing ladies, of lovers in medieval
dress, illustrating stirring incidents of romantic poets". He
displayed no trace of the quasi-scientific interest in nature of
Ruskin and his disciples. What could it matter, he said,
whether the earth moved round the sun or the sun circled
round the earth?

His earliest devotion among painters was to Ford Madox
Brown. He wrote him an enthusiastic letter, and after a pre-
liminary interview in which the laborious and unsuccessful
Brown regarded him with considerable suspicion, managed to
enter his studio as a pupil. Brown set him down to a study of
bottles (Hunt rather unkindly reproduces it): but he could
make nothing of it, being eager to get on with original work
of his own. However, the friendship with Brown was a lasting
one; although Rossetti may have learnt little from him tech-
nically, and Brown never became a P.R.B., his influence on the
society, and in turn theirs on him, was considerable. Brown

had worked mostly in Paris and Rome, labouring and experimenting in several styles. While in Rome he had met Overbeck, the leader of a group of German artists called the Nazarenes, who· combined a species of primitivism in design and treatment with a strong religious sentiment and a life led in semi-religious community. Brown fell under their influence, and some of his work at this period—*Cherubs watching the Crown of Thorns* and *Our Lady of Good Children*—were painted in their manner. Rossetti enthusiastically admired it, and there can be little doubt that Brown's Nazarene phase is partly responsible both for the style of Rossetti's early paintings and for the grouping of the pre-Raphaelites into something called a "Brotherhood". It all fitted in with Rossetti's tendency to dwell on the externals of religion as objects of mainly aesthetic contemplation. No one brought up by Mrs. Rossetti, and in the company of Christina and Maria, could have avoided having the practice of religious devotion constantly before their eyes. The effect on the sons was curious. William became a professed freethinker, while Gabriel casually absorbed what he could see of Christianity into his pantheon of romantic myth. However, this is not the whole story about Rossetti's early work. Tiring of Brown's bottles, he attached himself to Hunt and began to paint *The Girlhood of the Virgin* in his studio and more or less under his direction. Writing, again it must be remembered, a generation later, Hunt deprecates the aureoled dove representing the Holy Ghost and the seven cypresses typifying the "seven sorrowful mysteries",† but takes pride in having induced his pupil to paint the little Gothic screen and the embroidery and draperies of the Virgin from the actual objects. Two of the main streams of pre-Raphaelitism were coming together—the medieval and archaising tendency, and the scrupulous fidelity to fact derived from Ruskin.

The two streams did not mix at all easily or thoroughly.

---

† *Sic.* Whether the confusion between the Seven Dolours of the B.V.M. and the Five Sorrowful Mysteries is Rossetti's or Hunt's does not appear. Quite likely Rossetti's: in 1849, while on a visit to Boulogne, he wrote, "The evening before last I walked about the principal church of the town during Mass or Vespers or whatever they call it". His Catholic leanings, unlike Pater's, did not include much knowledge of ritual or iconography.

It is evident from the start that Millais and Hunt doubted the seriousness of the artistic intentions of the other members of the P.R.B. Beside themselves there were Gabriel, whom Hunt regarded as a pupil to be purged of the pernicious influence of Gothic revivalism; Woolner, a yet untrained sculptor; Collinson, whom on personal and artistic grounds everyone seems to have tacitly despised; Stephens, who was hardly beyond the student stage; and William Rossetti, who was not an artist at all. Gabriel was clearly the only personality in the rest of the group, and according to Hunt, both he and Millais were extremely suspicious of his medievalist tendencies. He developed a habit of referring to the Brotherhood as Early Christian, to which Hunt objected, himself, according to his own account, suggesting the term pre-Raphaelite. Doubts about the other four members are early evident. "Millais would not ratify the initial acceptance of the four candidates without check on their understanding of our purpose, for he feared the distortion of our original doctrine of childlike submission to Nature. The danger we feared at the time was from the vigour of the fashionable revival of Gothic art."[4] We will not enter in detail into the somewhat ungracious controversy about the origin and true nature of pre-Raphaelitism. But if we turn from Hunt's reminiscences to a contemporary document—to the P.R.B. journal kept by William Rossetti—it is clear that both tendencies were present from the start, and that William Rossetti, non-painter and Rossetti as he was, thoroughly understood both the return-to-nature ideal and the dangers of an Early Christian primitivism. He writes of a bas-relief by Tupper, an associate though not a member of the group:

> It is at the extremest edge of P.R.B.ism, most conscientiously copied from Nature. . . . The P.R.B. principle of uncompromising truth to what is before you is carried out to the full.[5]

And of Orchard's contribution to *The Germ*, an extremely Nazarene dialogue on art:

> Orchard sent Gabriel a second portion of his first Dialogue on Art, treating herein chiefly of early Christian (or as he terms it, pre-Raphael) art, and seeming to out-P.R. the P.R.B. The word is impolitic and must be altered.[6]

It was not altered, however, and some sort of primitivist intention remained in the general consciousness, in spite of Hunt and Millais, as part of the connotation of pre-Raphaelitism.

The fact is, of course, that there were whole areas of Rossetti's mind which were quite outside the comprehension of Hunt and Millais. What they put down to a dangerous affectation was the result of a long development of feeling, and one which was in the end to become more important than their own naturalism. The story was plainly enough told, if they had cared to read it, in Rossetti's prose tale *Hand and Soul*,[7] his contribution to the first number of *The Germ*. To anyone brought up in the Rossetti household, intellectual and spiritual activity was the normal stuff of life: nobody had ever supposed that Gabriel would become anything but some sort of artist. Hunt's anxious preoccupation with technical competence was in part the reaction against an environment that could understand nothing else. Rossetti characteristically assumed that technical skill would come when it was wanted, followed his own wayward fancies, absorbed other men's ideas, and beneath all this apparent dilettantism, devoted himself to the development of his own vision. Part of the development is described in *Hand and Soul*, in a prose already accomplished, a new kind of writing in which the rhythm and vocabulary of Pater is already foreshadowed.

> He would feel faint in sunsets and at the sight of stately persons. . . .
> He was weak with yearning, like one who gazes upon a path of stars.

Hand and Soul tells the story of Chiaro dell' Erma, an imaginary early Tuscan painter. As a young unknown student he applies to Giunto Pisano, the foremost artist of his day, to become his pupil.

> He was received with courtesy and consideration, and shown into the study of the famous artist. But the forms he saw there were lifeless and incomplete; and a sudden exaltation possessed him as he said within himself "I am the master of this man". . . .
> After this, Chiaro's resolve was that he would work out thoroughly some one of his thoughts, and let the world know

him. But the lesson he had now learned, of how small a great-
ness might win fame, and how little there was to strive against,
served to make him torpid and rendered his exertions less
continual.

May we not unfairly assume that this takes Rossetti to the
point where Hunt first noticed him, as the idle yet self-confident
student at the Academy schools? Chiaro proceeds to idle and
enjoy himself, until he hears one day of the paintings of a youth
named Bonaventura, who it is said will soon rival the great
Giunta Pisano himself. (Does Bonaventura stand for Millais?)
Chiaro is recalled to his ambition and settles down to a course
of steady work. Here the material parallel with the career of
Rossetti ceases, though the parallel in the realm of ideas does
not. In three years Chiaro becomes famous, yet for all his fame
he remains unsatisfied. With all that he had done in these
three years, even with the studies of his early youth, there had
been a feeling of worship and service. "It was the peace-
offering he had made to God for the eager selfishness of his
aim." At this point we begin to find a curious fusion of ideas
from Dante with Rossetti's own nascent religion of art. Chiaro's
mistress, nine years old, like the Beatrice of the beginning of
the *Vita Nuova*, becomes identified in his mind with "his own
gracious and holy Italian art". Chiaro, like Dante, dreams that
she is destined to die: and it seems to him that when she has
"passed into the circle of the shadow of the tree of life", and
been seen of God and found good, he and others engaged
in the like devotion will be permitted "to gather round the
blessed maiden, and to worship her through all ages of ages,
saying Holy, Holy, Holy". So, by a strange transposition of
Dantesque ideas, Chiaro's Beatrice, instead of becoming the
symbol of Theology, becomes the symbol of Art, yet is equally
accepted by God, and becomes a citizen of Heaven as Dante's
Beatrice had been.

But when Chiaro looks more closely into himself, it becomes
apparent that he had misinterpreted his own cravings, and that
what he had mistaken for faith was no more than the worship
of beauty. So he determines to discipline himself more strictly,
and take another aim for his life. He enters on a period of cold

symbolism, personification of abstract virtues, eschewing the action and the passion of human life, and aiming only at the presentment of some moral greatness. Still he does not find happiness or fulfilment. He paints a moral allegory of Peace in the porch of the church of San Rocco. One day he is looking at it from a distance, and a faction fight breaks out in the church porch itself; swords are drawn; "and there was so much blood cast up the walls of a sudden, that it ran in long streams down Chiaro's paintings". His moral allegories seem useless and worse than useless; does not their dull ineptitude even turn men away from the right path?

> Am I not as a cloth drawn before the light, that the looker may not be blinded; but which showeth thereby the grain of its own coarseness; so that the light seems defiled, and men say "We will not walk by it". Wherefore through me they shall be doubly accursed, seeing that through me they reject the light.

At this moment, when Chiaro, convinced of the rootlessness of his earlier faith and the mischievousness of his moral fervour, is in a state of bewildered despair, a vision appears to him. It is the vision that appears some time or other to most romantic poets—that of a woman who turns out to be the image of his own soul. She addresses him:

> Fame sufficed not, for that thou didst seek fame; seek thine own conscience (not thy mind's conscience but thy heart's) and all shall approve and suffice.

Chiaro has been mistaken in thinking that his faith had failed him. How can he distinguish between faith and love which must interpenetrate each other? Who is he to turn upon God and withdraw his own offering as unworthy because it was contaminated by the love of beauty? God is wiser and will accept the love of beauty as also a faith.

> What he hath set in thine heart to do, that do thou; and even if thou do it without thought of him, it shall be well done; it is this sacrifice that he asketh of thee, and his flame is upon it for a sign.

It was not his earlier faith that had failed and proved unworthy, it was his cold abstract moralising. It is not for him,

as a man, to say coldly to the heart what God has said to the
mind warmly. God does not demand that men shall be
moralists; he demands that they shall work from their own
hearts, as he works from his. Finally, his soul lays a charge
upon him:

> Chiaro, servant of God, take now thine art unto thee, and
> paint me thus, as I am, to know me: weak, as I am, and in the
> weeds of this time; only with eyes which seek out labour, and
> with a faith, not learned, yet jealous of prayer. Do this; and
> so shall thy soul stand before thee always and perplex thee
> no more.

This is a new kind of pre-Raphaelite creed—not fidelity to
external nature, but fidelity to one's own inner experience,
which is to be followed even if it contradicts formal morality,
just as in Hunt's belief nature is to be followed even if it contra-
dicts the precepts of Sir Joshua Reynolds. This fidelity to
experience is all that God demands of the artist, it is as accept-
able to him as a formal religious faith, and an art carried on in
this spirit is itself a worship and service of God. There is also
the germ of a later creed here; the ethic of Pater and the
immoralism of the nineties might both trace their origin to
this source; and one is reminded of what Yeats said later, in
conscious discipleship, most probably, to Rossetti—that the
poet's church is one in which there is an altar but no pulpit.
Ruskin had tried to show that the right practice of the arts was
also a sort of religious worship; Rossetti is announcing a new
phase, in which the emotions that had before belonged exclu-
sively to religion are transferred bodily to art.

Most people, looking prospectively into Rossetti's later
career, have not unnaturally assumed that the religious sym-
bolism of *The Blessed Damosel* and of his early paintings is
mere ornament, used as part of a romantic *décor* and little else.
We may now begin to suspect that this is something less than
the truth. It is true that Rossetti uses a good deal of Christian
symbolism; and there is nothing to suggest that he does so
with any Christian meaning. When Rossetti paints the
Annunciation he is not depicting one of the mysteries of the
Christian faith in any theological sense. But he is not merely

painting it as he might paint a theme from Keats: he is depicting something that has really been a content of his own soul—a sense of awe, of humility and of revelation, in which many of the emotions that attach to the Christian mystery are included. It is needless to remark that the heaven of *The Blessed Damosel* has little in common with the heaven of theology, and includes an evidently erotic element which could not possibly find a place there: but it remains true that Rossetti's heaven arouses in him many of the emotions that belong to the Christian heaven for the ordinary unsophisticated believer. The suspicion with which the Rossettian religion of art was greeted by many contemporaries was awakened not only because it was a religion of art, but because it was a religion of a kind more common among the notoriously lax and emotional Italians than among Englishmen—one in which strong feelings of devotion and worship exist without any obvious effect on moral conduct. Pre-Raphaelitism could include a good deal of orthodox religious sentiment, often of a High Church or Catholic cast, because it dealt in a good many of the same emotions, although they were directed by the more aberrant brethren to very different objects. But we must return to this theme in discussing Rossetti and Dante.

The principle of fidelity to inner experience was evidently accepted as one of the pre-Raphaelite canons, for it forms the subject of a sonnet (a very poor one) by William Michael Rossetti, specially written to express the aims of the movement and printed on the cover of *The Germ*.

> When whoso merely hath a little thought
> Will plainly think the thought which is in him,—
> Not imaging another's bright or dim,
> Nor mangling with new words what others taught—

"What I meant," William explained later, "is this: a writer ought to think out his subject honestly and personally, not imitatively, and ought to express it with directness and precision: if he does this, we should respect his performance as truthful, even though it may not be important. This indicated for writers much the same principle as the P.R.B. professed for painters—individual genuineness in the thought, reproductive genuineness in the presentment."[8] The sub-title of *The Germ* was "Thoughts towards Nature in Poetry, Literature and Art", and was the invention of Dante Rossetti: a phrase which, according to William Michael, "indicated accurately enough the predominant conception of the Pre-Raphaelite Brotherhood, that an artist, whether painter or writer, ought to be bent upon defining and expressing his own personal thoughts, and that they ought to be based upon a direct study of Nature, and harmonised with her manifestations".[9]

The advertisement repeats the aim of encouraging "an entire adherence to the simplicity of Nature", and adds to it that of directing attention, "as an auxiliary medium, to the comparatively few works which art has produced in this spirit". This auxiliary aim takes us directly to the name pre-Raphaelite itself. Why was this name chosen? Why was it in the painters before Raphael that the simplicity of Nature was to be found? And how much did the pre-Raphaelites really know about painting before Raphael? The answer often given to the last question is that the Brotherhood knew nothing about early Italian painting, and that the pre-Raphaelite label was quite unwarrantably assumed. But this does not, on investigation, prove to be altogether true. It is certainly true that at the formation of the Brotherhood, in 1848, they had seen the originals of only very few early paintings. But if the inspiration of English art students was to be confined to works of which they had seen the originals, English art would be more provincial than it is. They had, of course, seen engravings: and early Italian painting was in any case not entirely unknown to English artists. Dyce in the previous generation had been a student of the *quattrocento*, and had been neglected for his divergence from the convention of brown trees and canvases smothered in asphaltum. Hunt had seen a picture by Van Eyck. (This must have been the portrait of Jan Arnolfini and his wife, which was acquired by the National Gallery in 1848.) Reproductions of Ghiberti's gates from the Baptistery at Florence were available in Somerset House and the Royal Academy, and both Hunt and Rossetti drew from them. Hunt and Millais studied a book of engravings of the frescoes of the

Campo Santo at Pisa, in Millais's studio.[10] And F. G. Stephens's
article on "The purpose and tendency of Early Italian art" in
No. 2 of *The Germ* refers to Masaccio, Benozzo Gozzoli,
Orcagna, Fra Angelico, Ghirlandaio and Ghiberti, whose works
he knew, as he says in a footnote, from reproductions in
D'Agincourt's *Histoire d'Art par les Monumens*, Rossini's
Storia della Pittura, Otley's *Italian School of Design* and his
130 facsimiles of rare prints. It seems then that even before
any of the Brotherhood had been abroad, their knowledge of
early painting was not wholly negligible. In 1849 Hunt and
Rossetti went on a trip to France and Belgium: in the Louvre
they saw Fra Angelico's *Coronation of the Virgin*, and in
Belgium looked at the Memlincks and made a careful study of
the work of Jan and Hubert Van Eyck. It was immediately
after this journey that Rossetti began *Ecce Ancilla Domini*.
Giotto is mentioned in *The Germ*, but there is no evidence that
they knew anything of him besides the name; and Botticelli
remained unknown until he was popularised later by Ruskin.
By the standards of modern connoisseurship no doubt the
knowledge of the pre-Raphaelites was very slender; but it will
hardly do to represent them as affecting a primitivism of which
they knew nothing.

There is the further and more interesting question of what
such early painting as they knew meant to them, with what
motives they gave the Brotherhood that particular label.
Clearly the influence of Ruskin counted for much. Hunt had
read the early volumes of *Modern Painters*, and knew all about
the corruptness of Guido and the Caracci. Contributions to
The Germ by Stephens and Orchard reveal that the Ruskinian
Anschauung was already more or less common property. But
it must be remembered that the references to Raphael in
Volumes I and II of *Modern Painters* are uniformly respectful:
the diatribes against the "clear and tasteless poison" of his
art and the corruption and pride of the Renaissance do not
appear in full force until Volume III, in 1856, seven years or so
after the P.R.B. had begun to make its impact on the public
mind. Hunt's account of the first use of the name looks like a
natural continuation of the passage from *Modern Painters* on

the art of Raphael quoted on page 7; but in fact the incident preceded the Ruskin passage by a good many years. One may suspect a back-reaction of P.R.B. ideas on Ruskin himself. Hunt says that the name pre-Raphaelite was flung at him and Millais as a joke, before the foundation of the Brotherhood, by a group of students who were amused by their objections to Raphael's *Transfiguration*. Hunt and Millais attacked it "for its grandiose disregard of the simplicity of truth, the pompous posturing of the Apostles, the unspiritual attitudinising of our Saviour. . . . In our final estimation this picture was a signal step in the decadence of Italian art."[11] Hunt elaborates his attitude to Raphael in a passage which we might compare to some modern technical judgments on Milton. The burden of his argument is that it is not Raphael, but the practice of Raphael hardened into convention by his imitators, against which he and Millais were in reaction.

> Pre-Raphaelitism is not pre-Raphaelism. Raphael in his prime was an artist of most original and daring course as to convention. . . . He tacitly demonstrated that there is no fast rule of composition to trammel the arrangement dictated to the artist's will. Yet indeed it may be questioned whether, before the twelve glorious years had come to an end after his sight of the Sixtine chapel ceiling, he did not stumble and fall like a high-mettled steed tethered in a fat pasture who knows not that his freedom is measured. . . . There is no need here to trace any failure in Raphael's career; but the prodigality of his productiveness, and his training of many assistants, compelled him to lay down rules and manners of work; and his followers, even before they were left alone, accentuated his poses into postures.
>
> They caricatured the turns of his heads and the lines of his limbs, designed their figures in patterns; and they built up their groups into formal pyramids. The master himself, at the last, in the *Transfiguration*, was not exempt from such deadly artificialities and conventions. The artists who thus servilely travestied the failings of this prince of painters were Raphaelites. . . . the traditions that went on through the Bolognese Academy (which were introduced at the foundation of all later schools and enforced by Le Brun, Du Fresnoy, Raphael Mengs, and Sir Joshua Reynolds to our own time) were lethal in their influence, tending to stifle the breath of design. The name pre-Raphaelite excludes the influence of such corrupters of perfection, even though Raphael, by reason of certain of his works, be in the list.[12]

The root of Hunt's and Millais's objection to post-Raphaelite art, then, was its convention and mannerism in design, the famous principles of composition of the grand style. Their admiration for the earlier painters was mainly for their un-stereotyped and unconventional presentation of their subjects. Hunt writes of the engravings from the Campo Santo of Pisa:

> The innocent spirit which had directed the invention of the painter was traced point after point, with emulation by each of us who were the workers, with the determination that a kindred simplicity should regulate our own ambition, and we insisted that the naive traits of frank expression and unaffected grace were what had made Italian art so essentially vigorous and pro-gressive, until the showy successors of Michael Angelo had grafted their Dead Sea fruit on to the vital tree just when it was bearing its choicest autumnal ripeness.

On the other hand Hunt was elaborately anxious to guard himself against any accusation of primitivism in technique, and both he and Millais were determined that their pre-Raphaelitism should include all the accomplishments of the later schools, though it was to abandon their affectations.

> As we turned over the prints of the Campo Santo designs in Millais' studio, we remarked Benozzo Gozzoli's attentive observation of inexhaustible Nature, and dwelt on all his quaint charm of invention. . . .
> Yet we did not curb our amusement at the immature per-spective, the undeveloped power of drawing, the feebleness of light and shade, the ignorance of any but mere black and white differences in the types of men, the stinted varieties of flora, and their geometrical forms in landscape; these simplicities, already out of date in the painter's day, we noted as already belonging altogether to the past and to the dead revivalists, with whom we had resolved to have neither part nor lot.

Rossetti, however, was more unreservedly attached to the primitives, probably for more complex reasons. We have already his admiration for Brown's quasi-Early Christian style, of which Hunt was so suspicious. On the journey to France and Belgium in 1848, Rossetti's enthusiasm and Hunt's reserve are equally noticeable.

> The Adoration of the Spotless Lamb did not satisfy my expectations, although there was much suggestion derived from

the Apocalypse which affected Rossetti to write of it. The same applies notably to Memmeling; he was led to love these paintings beyond their artistic claim by reason of the mystery of their subjects.[13]

Indeed, Rossetti's two sonnets on pictures by Memlinck dwell exclusively on their interpretation of religious mysteries. But the sonnets on Old and New Art (LXXIV–LXXVI in *The House of Life*), written in the dawn of the pre-Raphaelite movement, reveal the aspirations of this period more clearly, and show how Rossetti related this mystic sentiment to the history of art. The early painters knew

> How sky-breadth and field silence and this day
> Are symbols also in some deeper way.

Art in those early days "looked through these to God and was God's priest". And the young artist, alone in a Philistine world "where never pencil comes nor pen", is exhorted not to pride himself on his superiority to the mediocrities of mere technical accomplishment, but to compare himself humbly with the great lights of the distant past, who are also an illumination for the future. A good deal of the typical young artist's contempt for that art which is of no immediate use to him mingled with this sentiment. Rossetti, with how much of Hunt's connivance is not clear, in a sort of journal of their Continental journey, dismissed the contents of the Louvre as "slosh", and all painters from Rembrandt to Rubens as "filthy slosh". In later years these unpremeditated strains were tactlessly exhumed by Mr. Hueffer, much to the annoyance of Hunt, who would have been glad to have such youthful extravagances forgotten.

Madox Brown, who was never a member of the Brotherhood, but was so closely associated with them that he cannot be left out of account, seems to have occupied a middle position between reliance on unsophisticated nature and the conventions of the grand style. Writing of "constructive beauty", he says:

> It is a feature in art rather apt to savour of conventionality to such as would look on nature as the only school of art, who would consider it but as the exponent of thought and feeling; while on the other hand, we fear it to be studied to little effect

by such as receive with indiscriminate and phlegmatic avidity all that is handed down to them in the shape of experience or time-sanctioned rules.[14]

This is what we should expect from his big picture of this date, *Chaucer at the Court of King Edward II*, which, in spite of a good deal of Gothic trimming and some naturalism of detail, is by no means neglectful of the convention of formal composition.

There is yet another attitude towards pre-Raphael or Early Christian painting which must be taken into account as one of the ingredients of pre-Raphaelitism—a quasi-religious feeling, most evident among the epigoni of the school, but not without its effect on Rossetti. F. G. Stephens's essay on "The Purpose and Tendency of Early Italian Art"[15] does not add a great deal to what we have already heard; it is in fact mainly Ruskinian in aim and substance. Its main tendency is to tie up the Ruskinian ethic not only to Nature but also to early painting. We learn that the modern English school is characterised by "an entire seeking after originality in a more humble manner than has been practised since the decline of Italian art in the Middle Ages. . . . This patient devotedness appears to be a conviction peculiar to, or at least more purely followed by, the early Italian painters"—a feeling, we are informed, which caused many of them to retire to a monastery. The modern artist does not retire to a monastery, but he may show the same high feeling by firm attachment to truth in every point of representation. The discourse ends portentously with a warning against voluptuousness and sensuality, a vice most repugnant to youth, and the most infallible agent of the degeneration of art.

This vaguely Franciscan piety is more strongly marked in the dialogue by Orchard in the fourth number of *The Germ*. Orchard was quite unconnected with the P.R.B., but he conceived a great admiration for Gabriel's *Girlhood of the Virgin*, and he and the Rossettis met once or twice. The dialogue in its turn was much admired by Stephens and Gabriel, though William thought it forced ideas of purism beyond all due bounds. Christian, who is the mouthpiece of Orchard in the dialogue, insists that "fine art absolutely rejects all impurities of form: not less absolutely does it reject all impurities of passion and expression". The fault of the Dutch and English schools is that they have painted "merely from the animal side of man". Kosmon and Kalon, the worldly man and the aesthete, attempt a defence of the animal side of man, but they are overborne. All perfect art is Christian art. Kosmon objects that "Medieval or pre-Raffaele art" is characterised by "youthful and timid darings, unripe fancies oscillating between earth and heaven, . . . everywhere is seen exactness, but it is the exactness of hesitation, and not of knowledge—the line of doubt and not of power". Mature art comes into being when all these rude scaffoldings are thrown down. But Christian replies:

> Kosmon, your thoughts seduce you; or rather, your nature prefers the full and rich to the exact and simple: you do not go deep enough—do not penetrate beneath the image's gilt over-lay, and see that it covers only worm-devoured wood. Your very comparison tells against you. What you call ripeness, others, with as much truth, may call over-ripeness, nay, even rotten-ness. . . . And the art which you call youthful and immature—may be, most likely is, mature and wholesome in the same degree that it is tasteful, a perfect round of beautiful, pure and good. . . . What an array of deep earnest and noble thinkers, like angels armed with a brightness that withers, stand between Giotto and Raffaele; to mention only Orcagna, Ghiberti, Masaccio, Lippi, Fra Beato Angelico, and Francia. Parallel *them* with post-Raffaele artists? If you think you can, you have dared a labour of which the fruit shall be to you as Dead Sea apples, golden and sweet to the eye, but, in the mouth, ashes and bitterness.

For all its overstrained and feverish purism (Orchard was an invalid, and died just after writing it) the dialogue is energetic and sincere. The most curious thing about it, in view of Rossetti's later development, is that it won so much of his admiration. We must recognise, however, that this kind of objectless devoutness was very much part of Rossetti's mind at this period. *Ecce Ancilla Domini* and *The Girlhood of the Virgin* were painted under its influence. Whatever theological interpretation Rossetti put on them, he painted them when fresh from the experience of real medieval religious painting, and with the idea of transmitting some of its spirit. In a vague way, and with more precaution against primitivism and ritualism, the same sentiment pervaded the movement. Hunt, years later, unconsciously echoes the words of Orchard's dialogue to describe the real relation of the Brotherhood to early art. "True judgment directed us to choose our outflow from a channel where the stream had no trace of the pollution of egoism, and was innocent of pandering to corrupt thoughts and passions."† At which point we can leave the confused genesis of the pre-Raphaelite aesthetic, and proceed to trace a little further its development in practice.

The Brotherhood was founded in 1848, with what internal strains we have already seen. The resultant social atmosphere is clearly enough revealed in the P.R.B. journal. There is evidently much good fellowship, and we see the growth of esoteric standards and a private dialect, usually delightful to a youthful coterie. "Sloshy" is the word used for such objects as weather, waitresses or works of art that are found to be fluid, shapeless or ill-realised: the beauties of art, nature or the human form are "stunners"; and they all seem to have enjoyed themselves very much. But Brown appears far more often in Rossetti's company than Hunt and Millais: Millais in particular seems to stand aloof—probably regarding himself as already a successful painter of some years' standing among a group of novices. Both Hunt and Millais had exhibited before, but the first specifically pre-Raphaelite pictures, all bearing the mystic initials P.R.B., were shown in 1849. They were Millais's *Lorenzo and Isabella*, Hunt's *Rienzi* and Rossetti's *Girlhood of the Virgin*. The original intention was that all should exhibit at the Royal Academy. Hunt and Millais did so; Rossetti, by an act which might be considered at least uncomradely, decided not to risk rejection at the Academy, but to show his picture at the Free Exhibition at Hyde Park Corner, where he could buy a place on the walls. The effect was unfortunate. The Free Exhibition opened a week before the Academy, and Rossetti's picture was hailed as the dawn of a new school.

† Orchard: "Because the stream at that point is clearer and purer, and less polluted with animal impurities, than at any other in its course."

ROSSETTI AND THE P.R.B.

It was very favourably reviewed in the *Athenaeum*, the sincerity and earnestness of feeling being compared to that of the early Florentine monastic painters. Hunt's and Millais's works met with a cooler, though by no means unfriendly, reception from the same periodical, and were criticised for archaism and the imitation of imperfect models. This was peculiarly bitter to Hunt, who regarded Rossetti as his pupil, and the *fons et origo* of an archaism in the P.R.B. of which he strongly disapproved. Nevertheless the friendship survived, and Hunt and Rossetti had their happy journey together in France and Belgium in the autumn of 1849. Then, in 1850, the storm broke, partly precipitated, one must admit, by another tactless action of Rossetti's. The initials P.R.B. were supposed to be kept secret, and had so far attracted no attention. But Rossetti, who liked mysteries, yet also liked to make them the topics of general conversation, told several people about the Brotherhood; and an outraged English art criticism found itself confronted, not with a few young and experimental artists, to be alternately reproved and encouraged, but with an organised movement of manifestly revolutionary intentions. In the 1850 Academy Millais exhibited his *Christ in the House of His Parents*, Hunt his picture of *Priests and Druids*. Rossetti showed his *Ecce Ancilla Domini*, again at the Free Exhibition. The *Athenaeum*, so favourable the previous year, launched a full-scale assault on the principles and practice of the Brotherhood. They were accused of every moral and aesthetic vice—affectation, sensationalism, wilful distortion—*und so weiter*. To the reader of English art-criticism the indignant recitative is sufficiently familiar. Dickens's attack in *Household Words* on Millais's picture is also notorious. Millais and Hunt bore the brunt of the attack, but Rossetti was not exempt. Other journals and the general public joined in, and the term pre-Raphaelite became a hissing and a byword, very much as post-Impressionist did sixty years later. Rossetti, always morbidly sensitive to criticism, was so affected by this rancorous attack that he resolved never to exhibit in public again—one of the few resolutions he ever kept. Hunt and Millais were left to face the music alone, and Hunt's resentment at this is still perceptible in the memoir written in his old age. Nevertheless he and Millais exhibited again in the 1851 Academy—Millais *The Return of the Dove to the Ark*, *The Woodman's Daughter* and *Mariana*, Hunt his *Valentine and Silvia*. Brown's *Chaucer* appeared in the same exhibition. The *Athenaeum* returned to the charge; and *The Times*, including Madox Brown in their condemnation, analysed the principles of the group as "an absolute contempt for perspective and the known laws of light and shade, an aversion to beauty in every shape, and a singular devotion to the minute accidents of their subjects, including, or seeking out, every excess of sharpness or deformity". They went on to remind the Academy that "the public may fairly require that such offensive jests should not continue to be exposed as speci-mens of the waywardness of these artists who have relapsed into the infancy of their profession". Academy professors lectured against the Brotherhood and Millais was cut in the streets.

However, effectual aid was at hand. Patmore, a friend of the Brotherhood and a contributor to *The Germ*, suggested that Ruskin should write something about the P.R.B. Early in May Ruskin wrote two letters to *The Times*, exerting all his per-suasive power and his growing authority to defend the prin-ciples of pre-Raphaelitism and to rebut the attack on faulty drawing. He gives an explanation of the name pre-Raphaelite in accordance with the general sentiment of the Brotherhood, though he finds it necessary to deprecate their supposed Romanist and tractarian tendencies.

> They intend to return to early days in one point only—that, as far as in them lies, they will draw either what they see, or what they suppose might have been the actual facts of the scene they desire to represent, irrespective of any conventional rules of picture making: and they have chosen their unfortunate though not inaccurate name because all artists did this before Raphael's time, and after Raphael's time did *not* this, but sought to paint fair pictures rather than represent stern facts; of which the consequence has been that, from Raphael's time to this day, historical art has been in acknowledged decadence.[16]

He denies the charge of bad perspective, and says that in treatment of detail "there has been nothing in art so earnest or so complete since the days of Albert Dürer''. A further letter a fortnight later adds a good deal of particular criticism, quite severe enough to remove any suspicion of complicity in the P.R.B. conspiracy. In the same year he published a pamphlet on pre-Raphaelitism, which indeed contains little about the pre-Raphaelites, being mostly about Turner, as Ruskin's writing was apt to be at this time; but it seriously compares the painting of the P.R.B. with that of Turner, and proclaims the conformity of their practice with his own principles.

This was the turning-point in P.R.B. fortunes. Soon after the letters to *The Times*, Ruskin made the acquaintance of Hunt and Millais: a little later, that of Rossetti, who remarked ''he seems in a mood to make my fortune''. Later relations between Ruskin and the various Brothers belong to biography rather than to criticism; the main point here is that although his interest had first been aroused by Hunt and Millais, Ruskin's later determined championship of Rossetti tended to increase the impression that he was the leader of the group:† as, in imagination and intellectual force he obviously was. What is to be said on the other side may be read at length in Hunt's *Pre-Raphaelitism*.

This was the turning-point in P.R.B. fortunes, but it was also in a sense the end of the Brotherhood. From now on, Rossetti tended to separate himself more and more from the others. Hunt and Millais show an increasing censoriousness about the non-painting members of the society. But they were soon rewarded by their own success. Hunt's *Hireling Shepherd* and Millais's *Ophelia* in the 1852 Academy had a markedly favourable reception. Rossetti sold his *Girlhood of the Virgin* to the Dowager Marchioness of Bath, and *Ecce Ancilla Domini* to McCracken. Brown's work showed increasingly pre-Raphaelite tendencies, and the influence of the school on Martineau and others was already becoming apparent. Pre-Raphaelitism was becoming respectable. By January 1853 William Michael Rossetti writes in the P.R.B. journal:

† To do Rossetti justice we should emphasise that he did not attempt to claim this position for himself; and apart from the separate exhibiting, did all he could to see that equal justice was done to his colleagues. The evidence for this can be seen in his correspondence with William Michael and Ruskin.

I should not have forgotten to premise that, though both pre-Raphaelitism and Brotherhood are as real as ever, and purpose to continue so, the P.R.B. is not and cannot be so much a matter of social intercourse as it used to be. The P.R.B. meeting is no longer a sacred institution—indeed is, as such, well-nigh disused.[17]

It is outside the plan of this book to follow the later careers of these artists. Pre-Raphaelitism itself was by now fully mature, though its impact on English life was only beginning. Most of the later painting it produced was a disappointment. The pre-Raphaelites were a cultural and aesthetic force, but not a great school of painters, and indeed their pretensions to be a school at all ceased about this time. Hunt pursued a long course of respectable fidelity to his original ideals, producing two distressingly successful pictures—*The Light of the World* and *The Scapegoat*, and at least one that seems to me original and beautiful—*The Triumph of the Innocents*. Millais, always a superb technician, after a few lovely early paintings such as *Autumn Leaves*, made progressively more concessions to the popular taste, degenerating in middle life into a producer of well-painted anecdotal pot-boilers. Rossetti, technically perhaps the least remarkable, painted his exquisite gem-like water colours, among the masterpieces of nineteenth-century romantic art; and his long series of voluptuous "female heads with floral adjuncts", often beautiful in their way, and with effects which it would be hard to exaggerate on the sensibility of the coming generation; but strictly as painting, exploring no new territory. The torch of early pre-Raphaelite enthusiasm now passed to other hands—to those of Rossetti's younger disciples, Morris and Burne-Jones; and it is to their work that we must go to see the further development of pre-Raphaelite principles.

It is hard to sum up their importance as a school of painters, and in any case it is not my business. There is still room for a full history of pre-Raphaelite painting in the light of modern taste. I suspect that the large subject pictures would do little to relieve the general sense of disappointment, but that many exquisite minor works would be revealed, besides a pervasive and beneficial effect on book-illustration and the smaller arts of design. Perhaps it is not unfair to say that their most important contribution was to the spirit in which painting was undertaken. "Literary" they may have been; their justification is that they brought English painting again into touch with the most vivid imaginative life of their time; and their "Early Christian" affiliations brought almost the odour of sanctity into the practice of the arts. This may have led to preciosity, but it also led to a real ennobling of the attitude towards the visual arts. If we can see the figure of Bunthorne on the horizon, those of Frith and Landseer at least are disappearing into the shadows. The attitude of the cloistered and devoted aesthete is healthier for art than that of the rank commercial populariser; and if the English people after this date were again to regard art with indifference and sometimes with hostility, at least they were never again to regard it as the comfortable apotheosis of their own commonest tastes and sentiments. To that extent at least the history of the P.R.B. is something more than a chronicle of unfulfilled promise.

II. ROSSETTI'S POETRY. ROSSETTI AND DANTE

In many poets there is one complex of ideas that is central to their experience. They may write much on other themes, may even write better on other themes, but their deepest experiences are all concentrated more or less closely round one theme :

Et tout le reste est littérature.

There is a good deal of literature in the bad sense in Rossetti's poetry. The decorative romantic poems, the ballads, the modern Browningesque monologues—all have easily recognisable literary models: they add something of their own to their several conventions, but not perhaps very much. And it is difficult to feel in them that Rossetti is following the principle enjoined in his own tale of Chiaro dell' Erma—that it is the artist's business to paint his own soul, regardless of convention or external precept: he is doing these things because he has admired things of the same kind in the works of other people, not because of a new experience in himself. The central core of Rossetti's work is in the poems written under the influence of Dante—and that is of course a literary influence too. But it is so in a different way. In the first place it is inbred and hereditary. He writes in the introduction to his *Early Italian Poets*:

> The first associations I have are connected with my father's devoted studies, which, from his own point of view, have done so much toward the general investigation of Dante's writings. Thus, in those early days, all around me partook of the influence of the great Florentine; till, from viewing it as a natural element, I also, growing older, was drawn within the circle.

More important, the Dante of the *Vita Nuova* acquired a relevance to Rossetti's own nature and his own life that makes the inspiration received from him something far more than literary. Thus *The Blessed Damosel*, *The House of Life* and the translations of the early Italian poets stand apart in Rossetti's work.

Perhaps the first thing to say of the other poems is how well, with few exceptions, they are written. Rossetti is far more instinctively and naturally a poet than a painter, and from his earliest works, *Hand and Soul* and *The Blessed Damosel*, to the later *King's Tragedy*, his writing, however frail and overwrought its sentiment, has an assurance, precision and directness of attack that we do not often find in his painting.

> Our Lombard country girls along the coast
> Wear daggers in their garters, for they know
> That they might hate another girl to death,
> Or meet a German lover—[18]

> Mother of grace, the pass is difficult,
> Keen as these rocks, and the bewildered souls
> Throng it like echoes, blindly shuddering through.
> Thy name, O Lord, each spirit's voice extols,
> Whose peace abides in the dark avenue,
> Amid the bitterness of things occult.[19]

> The Queen sat idle by her loom:
> She heard the arras stir,
> And looked up sadly: through the room
> The sweetness sickened her
> Of musk and myrrh.

Her women, standing two and two,
In silence combed the fleece.
The pilgrim said, "Peace be with you,
Lady"; and bent his knees.
She answered "Peace."[20]

The first is an example of Rossetti's not very frequent vigorous directness; the second of his more customary intense elaboration; the third of his languid romantic manner. In their several ways it is hard to imagine anything better done.

These non-Dantesque poems fall into three main groups—those in the manner of Browning, the decorative romantic poems derived from Keats, and the ballads. The dramatic monologues *A Last Confession* and *Jenny* are as good as anything of Browning's of the same kind, with perhaps the evidence of a less commonplace mind behind them. *Jenny* is an isolated attempt at dealing with contemporary life. The intention of treating modern subjects formed a rather transient part of the pre-Raphaelite programme, and *Jenny* has its pictorial analogues in Hunt's *Awakened Conscience* and Rossetti's *Found*. The decorative Keatsian poems *Rose Mary*, *The Bride's Prelude* and *The Staff and Scrip* are the least adapted to modern taste. They seem overloaded and too merely poetical, without relevance to anything but previous literature. They bring up in an acute form the whole question of what is called poetry of escape, poetry that seems to do nothing to interpret the experience of its author or the life of its time. This sort of charge is often laid against pre-Raphaelite work, and is felt by many people to be damaging. Its relevance to Rossetti is obvious. He had no interest in science, little in politics, and not much in what most of his serious-minded contemporaries would have called religion.

They spoke of progress spiring round,
And light, and Mrs. Humphrey Ward.

When conversation ran on these lines Rossetti was not likely to be of the company. There is of course no particular reason why he should have been. To provide an escape from actuality is one quite legitimate function of poetry. But if poetry is going to take us out of the world we know, we may demand that it shall create a world of its own, complete in itself, answerable to its own laws, or happy in its own anarchy. The most successful romantic art, from *Daphnis and Chloe* to the surrealists, has always done this. *Aucassin et Nicolette*, *Twelfth Night*, the landscapes of Claude, *The Ancient Mariner*, the fantasies of Paul Klee, all, at their different levels, call in new worlds to redress the balance of the old. If instead of this we are taken merely into some literary suburb we may justifiably feel dissatisfied. Rossetti, it is to be feared, often gets no farther than this. His dream world is built up out of easily recognisable properties, most of which have been used before, and its hushed stillness is due not so much to a real remoteness from this vale of tears as to an extremely efficient sound-proofing system.

But let us take Rossetti's case where it is stronger—in the ballad poems. Criticism has tended to circle round the question of how far they reproduce the manner of the old ballads. It is clear that one of the best of them does not. *Sister Helen* is based on the cumulative dramatic ballads of the *Edward* pattern; and the harsh, bitter feeling, the use of dialogue and repetition with gradually increasing intensity are all closely followed. But the personifications ("Hate, born of Love, is blind as he"), the decorative metaphors ("With the loud wind's wail her sobs are wed"), and the over-subtle refrain changing from stanza to stanza all combine to produce quite a different effect. *The King's Tragedy* is closer, but it is dramatic in the wrong way. It has the note of an individual voice, as the ballads never do. On the other hand *Stratton Water*, in diction, in narrative method, in everything except the happy ending, is perhaps the nearest thing to an old ballad (or shall we say an old ballad edited by Scott?) that a modern writer has produced.

> O many's the sweet word, Lord Sands,
> You've spoken oft to me;
> But all I have from you to-day
> Is the rain on my body.
>
> And many's the good gift, Lord Sands,
> You've promised oft to me;

But the gift of yours I keep to-day
Is the babe in my body.

They told me you were dead, Janet,—
How could I guess the lie?
They told me you were false, Lord Sands,—
What could I do but die?

Now keep you well, my brother Giles,—
Through you I deemed her dead.
As wan as your towers are to-day,
To-morrow they'll be red.

But when we have said this, what have we said? Rossetti
rarely wrote so wholly successfully elsewhere as in these
ballads, but for all their good workmanship, they are pastiche:
and though pastiche may be the result of a real imaginative
experience, it is imaginative experience on a level that is fairly
near the surface.

The intense appreciation of an earlier literature that led
Rossetti to this kind of imitation has of course its proper sphere
of activity: it is translation. It is not very important to do in
English as a literary exercise what has already been done in
English as the expression of a first-hand experience. But to
reproduce a poetic experience that belongs to another language
and that English has never known may be extremely important.
From Tudor times to half-way through the eighteenth century
this was generally acknowledged. North's *Plutarch* and Pope's
Homer were among the most influential books of their own
periods. From the emergence of the vernaculars to the break-up
of European civilisation in our own day translation was one of
the most important means of maintaining a common culture.
To no country has this been more important than to England,
always liable to long spells of insular solitude. Alfred brought
to England a selection of Latin Christian literature; Chaucer
brought French romance; the Tudor translators a vast col-
lection of classical and Renaissance texts; the Augustans yet
more classics, treated with more understanding of their formal
qualities; and each of these in its turn fertilised native pro-
duction. The nineteenth century continued the process; but

with the decay of the neo-classic ideal and the arrival of romantic standards of originality and inspiration, the prestige of translation declined. Good poets were no longer willing to spend their powers on recreating foreign classics for their own age. Yet the task remained as necessary as ever, and nineteenth-century letters suffered from the fact that it was not done. Tennyson would have been far better employed in translating Vergil's Eclogues than in writing English Idylls. Rossetti, as we have suggested, was particularly fitted for this sort of work, and it can be argued that his *Early Italian Poets* is his most valuable contribution to poetry.

In the first place the job needed doing. Dante, his predecessors and contemporaries, by some accident, had never made their impact on English poetry. Chaucer had had little or no contact with the Dantesque influence, and in any case his temperament was more inclined to making *gemütlich* adaptations from Boccaccio than to the sweet subtleties of the *dolce stil nuovo*. The Elizabethans were interested in a later Italian literature, and to the Augustan age Italy for the most part meant the Italy of the High Renaissance. Later English misjudgments of the Middle Ages were partly due to a relative ignorance of its most refined literary expression. The Provençal troubadour poetry, too, was little known. In translating the earlier poets of the Sicilian school Rossetti gives a version of that, for the Sicilians wrote under Provençal influence; while in the translations from Dante and his circle he is introducing his readers to one of the great formative phases of European poetry of which they knew almost nothing. The code of ideal love inaugurated by Guido Guinicelli's famous canzone *Al Cor gentil ripara sempre amore* (of which Rossetti's translation is a masterpiece) has had a profound effect on European sensibility and continual echoes in English poetry: but until the appearance of Rossetti's book few English readers had had the opportunity of referring to the original sources of the creed. Textual and critical information about these writers was very incomplete in Rossetti's day; Rossetti worked hard at digging out what was known; and in the event virtually created early Italian poetry for the general English literary consciousness.

ROSSETTI AND THE P.R.B.

The merits of these translations have been discussed by Mr. R. D. Waller in his valuable book *The Rossetti Family*, with infintely greater knowledge of the originals than I can claim. The slightest acquaintance with the pre-Dantesque poems, however, is enough to show the fantastic difficulty of rendering this often obscure and fine-spun verse, and the astonishing fidelity that Rossetti achieves. It has been said that he throws too much of a Rossetti colouring over the whole; but against this we should note his success in a variety of manners; from the sentimental-satirical playfulness of Ciullo d'Alcamo's tenzone "Thou sweetly-smelling fresh red rose" (*Rosa fresca aulentissima*), and the unabashed Epicureanism of Folgore da San Geminiano's sonnets on the Sienese *brigata*, to the sweet exaltation of Guinicelli and Dante. One of the examples quoted by Mr. Waller is the translation of Giacomino Pugliese's poem on his dead lady (*Morte perche m'hai fatta si gran guerra*), in one stanza of which we find such Rossettian phrases as "her sweet motion when she walked", and "the soft fall of her hair", which have no counterpart in the original. There are others too; the first stanza ends:

> And in my heart dost bid the bird not sing
> That sang so sweet.

In the Italian there is no bird and no singing, only *la gioia e'l'allegranza* that have been taken away. Mr. Waller points out that Rossetti was not aiming at a literal rendering; we might add that Rossetti himself gave as the first rule of translation that a good poem shall not be turned into a bad one; and in the original, for all the beauty of general effect, there is some monotony of phrasing, alleviated in the Italian by a playing on the sounds *allegranza*, *tristanza*, *speranza* and so forth—an effect which would be impossible to reproduce in English. When there is a piece of inspired simplicity in the original Rossetti renders it with pre-Raphaelite faithfulness.

> *Membro e ricordo quand'era con meco*
> *Sovente m'apellava dolce amico,*
> *Et or nol face.*

> I do remember that while she remained
> With me, she often called me her sweet friend;
> But does not now.

Rossetti has given himself a comparatively easy time with Guido Cavalcanti, by not translating the most obscurely scholastic of the canzoni; and with Dante and his circle generally he is on a better-trodden track than with the earlier poets. With the *Vita Nuova* especially, Rossetti's success is almost complete. His fault, it has been pointed out, is a tendency "to screw Dante's note up a little higher". I should rather say the occasional introduction of a note of Keatsian languor and lusciousness: *Saria innanzi lei piangendo morta* appears as "Must fall aswoon, feeling all life grow weak". Sometimes there are unnecessary ingenuities: *Fuggon dinanzi lei superbia ed ira* is rendered "Hate loves and pride becomes a wor-shipper". But such cases are neither very damaging nor very numerous; and the tact with which Rossetti navigates, in the prose of the *Vita Nuova* especially, between an incongruous modernity and an affected archaism is very rare.

It would be hard to overrate the effect of these translations, made when he was very young, on Rossetti's sensibility. They must of course have involved close study, and the feeling of these poems seems to have become a part of his mind more than that of any other poetry. The prevailing impression derived from them, in spite of much variety in detail, is an idealisation of love—a love that was constant, enduring, and hardly conscious of any physical origin. Rossetti could also find there a recurrent split between this and another kind of love. As he himself remarked in a note:

> It is curious to find these poets perpetually rating one another for want of constancy in love. Guido is rebuked . . . by Dino Compagni; Cino da Pistoia by Dante; and Dante by Guido, who formerly had confided to him his doubts about Lapo Gianni.

On the one hand he would find the kind of love celebrated in Guido Guinicelli's *Al cor gentil ripara sempre amore*:

> The fire of love comes to the gentle heart
> Like as its virtue to a precious stone;

To which no star its influence can impart
　　Till it is made a pure thing by the sun;
　　　　For when the sun hath smit
From out its essence that which there was vile,
　　The star endoweth it.
And so the heart created by God's breath
　　Pure, true, and clean from guile,
A woman, like a star, enamoureth.

On the other hand, Cino da Pistoia's half-cynical justification for his dereliction of the ideal:

　　One pleasure ever binds and looses me;
　　That so, by one same beauty lured, I still
　　Delight in many women, here and there.

Or the unabashed candour of Cecco Angioleri:

　　I'd pick the nicest girls to suit my whim
　　And other folk should get the ugly ones.

He must have found a still deeper dichotomy in the sonnet of Guittone d'Arezzo, where he prays to the Blessed Virgin for help against the terrors of earthly love; or even in the gentle idealist conclusion of Guido's ode, where he imagines himself before the bar of Heaven, pleading for forgiveness for having given to love a worship that was due only to God and the Mother of God.

　　Then may I plead: "as though from Thee he came,
　　　　Love wore an angel's face:
　　Lord, if I loved her, count it not my shame."

Any attempt to explain Rossetti's poetry must take this train of feeling into account. The *Vita Nuova* especially is a central part of Rossetti's experience. Its mythology and some of its leading motives are omnipresent in *The House of Life*, and he made designs to illustrate it all through his career. What Rossetti draws from it is chiefly the idea of a continuing relation to a dead love; and its aptness to his situation after the death of Elizabeth Siddal needs no remark. What is more remarkable is that he seems to have been possessed by this complex of ideas while she was still alive, even before he had met her. A hint of it appears in *Hand and Soul*, and Rossetti

75

singles out for special mention the canzone of Giacomino Pugliese on his dead lady. It is almost as if Elizabeth Siddal had to die in order to fulfil her role in his poetic myth. It is obvious enough that in spite of the Dantesque inspiration and colouring, Rossetti's conception of this relation is totally unlike Dante's. Rossetti does not at any time show the slightest symptom of understanding the central ideas of the *Purgatory* or the *Paradise*, or even of knowing that they exist. Perhaps he knew more about Hell. It can be argued that one who is incapable of understanding the Beatrice of the *Paradiso* must have been equally unable to understand the Beatrice of the *Vita Nuova*: but it would be necessary to modify that too simple statement: and it is in the modifications that most of the essentials of the Rossettian ethos are to be discovered.

The split between ideal love and the exigencies of day-to-day life does not seem to have caused any profound disturbance to the medieval mind. A Catholic culture has never found it difficult to accept the gulf between ideal and achievement. *Video meliora proboque, deteriora sequor*: and both the better and the worse are accepted as inevitable part of human experience. The ultimate vanity of ideal love itself is expiated in periodical recantations—in Guittone's sonnet referred to above, in Petrarch's *Padre del ciel, dopo i perduti giorni*; of which we have the English counterpart in Sidney's "Leave me, O love which reachest but to dust". While failure to maintain the purity of ideal love is expiated in the reproaches of friends—almost a convention in Dante's circle—and a not too difficult return to the ideal. In any case no attempt was made to domesticate ideal love. It existed in a world of its own, marriage and lighter loves in another world. The system had its internal strains, but behind it all was the vast Catholic structure in which love of another order was the central fact, and in which all contradictions could be reconciled. So that it was no impossible feat for Dante to transform the Beatrice of the *Vita Nuova* into the Beatrice of the *Paradiso*. When, at the summit of the Purgatorial mount, he is commanded to look again on his lady's face—

Guardami ben: ben son, ben son Beatrice—

he feels again "the great power of an old love", and recognises that the Florentine girl of his youth and the radiant embodiment of Divine Wisdom are the same.

But for one like Rossetti, a denizen of Charlotte Street in the forties, there is considerable danger in the confused half-acceptance of this exquisite and austere mythology. In Puritan England the ideal had not been permitted to remain in its own sphere, it had had to descend into the market-place: and if this had led to some ennoblement of the market-place, it had also led to a great debasement of the ideal. The dichotomy between ideal love and daily conduct was no longer socially recognised; but ideal love had degenerated into a negative code of sexual ethics combined with a romantic sentimentalism. There is no need to suppose that when Dante wrote the *Vita Nuova* he was a virgin: when Rossetti first read it he almost certainly was. But Dante knew where both his ideal love and his lechery fitted into the total scheme of things: Rossetti had no scheme of things into which they could fit. The young Rossetti took sincerely and wholeheartedly from the *Vita Nuova* the idealisation of a love still virginal: but he had no idea of how this was to be accommodated to the demands of the senses, or to the demands of the soul for something that would last beyond life. Hence the tragedy of his marriage and the bitter remorse of his later years; hence in his poetry the mere romantic confusion of unrelated notions that could only have made sense if fitted into some coherent scheme of belief.

In spite of a vivid and acute intelligence and a great deal of patience in working out imagery and technique, Rossetti had not the spiritual energy to relate the several orders of his experience to any consistent structure. So he takes the way out that is the besetting temptation of romantic literature, mixes the different orders of his experience together, mistakes analogy for identity, and ends in an emotional and spiritual mist. *The Blessed Damosel* shows the beginning of this process. The idea of a continuing relation between a lady in heaven and her lover on earth is Dantesque: but one is surprised to find the lady still sufficiently material for her bosom to make the bar she leaned on warm. The idea of justifying an earthly love in heaven comes perhaps from Guido Guinicelli's canzone: but the result is startlingly different; the damosel finds no need to ask pardon for having confused the "love that reachest but to dust" with the love of God. When her knight comes to heaven

> He shall fear, haply, and be dumb
> Then I will lay my cheek
> To his, and tell about our love,
> Not once abashed or weak:
> And the dear Mother will approve
> My pride, and let me speak.

The Queen of Heaven herself brings them before the throne of God.

> Thus will I ask of Christ the Lord
> Thus much for him and me:—
> Only to live as once on earth
> With Love,—only to be
> As then awhile, for ever now
> Together, I and he.

The relation of the damosel and her knight in heaven is conceived simply as a continuation of their love on earth, a procedure, it appears, which the heavenly host warmly approves. This is clearly not Christian: but are we certain how far Rossetti intended it to be? Many people have been disturbed by an inconsistency between the Christian symbolism of the poem and its purely romantic emotional orientation. Analogies could of course be found in greater poetry. One is disturbed by finding that Milton's Lycidas, after being received by "the solemn troops and sweet societies" of the saints above, becomes in the next few lines the genius of the shore, a classical nature deity. Milton, one supposes, is using a piece of classical myth as somewhat incongruous decoration to a fundamentally Christian poem. Rossetti is perhaps doing something less traditional—using Christian symbols as mythological decoration to a romantic love-poem. In the same connection Mr. Waller quotes the penultimate stanza of *A Portrait*, and remarks that it "inconsequently telescopes Dante's tenth heaven into a perfected heaven of human love". The lover looks forward to the time when he will rejoin his lady in heaven:

> How shall my soul stand rapt and awed,
> When, by the new birth borne abroad
>   Throughout the music of the suns
>   It enters in her soul at once
> And knows the silence there for God.

Mr. Waller then pertinently asks "Had Rossetti been questioned about the last two lines of this otherwise very beautiful stanza, could he have explained them in terms of literal belief or metaphorical imagination?"[21] We are here approaching a more important question about Rossetti's symbolism. Admitted that this is not Christianity, is it sense?

In the long sonnet-sequence, *The House of Life*, more or less deliberately based on the medieval and Renaissance sonnet-sequences, Rossetti develops a whole mythology and a whole *mystique* of love. It would not be correct to call it either his own or an adaptation from Dante; it is rather a continual use of imagery and ideas from Dante for his own not very clear purpose. He is like a man using sculptured fragments from some ancient building to make a picturesque ruin of his own design. It is sometimes true in both cases—in that of Dante no less than that of Rossetti—that imagery drawn from religion is used to express an earthly love. In the *Vita Nuova* (XXLV) the lady Primavera who comes before Beatrice is compared to John the Baptist who comes before the true light. Similarly the lady of *The House of Life* undergoes oblique transformations into the likeness of the sacred personages. In the second sonnet she gives birth to love, yet is born of him; that is she becomes *figlia del suo figlio*, like the Blessed Virgin. In the sestet of the third sonnet she harrows hell, like Christ. Other resemblances to the Dantesque mythology are constant. Love appears in *The House of Life* as the "lord of terrible aspect" of the *Vita Nuova*; Passion of Love (Sonnet IX) is flame-winged, as the Love of the *Vita Nuova* came wrapped in a cloud of flame. As in the *Vita Nuova*, forebodings of death appear, before there is any overt reason to fear it. Like Dante, Rossetti excuses himself sophistically for an infidelity, using the same argument as Cino da Pistoia to Dante himself.

But all these resemblances are on the surface, for Dante has in mind a perfectly clear distinction between his imaginative mythology and what he regards as theological truth. Rossetti has no such distinction in and we therefore never know what status to give to his images. We have quoted the end of *The Portrait*, where the lover enters the soul of his beloved "and knows the silence there for God". Whether he knew what he meant by this or not, Rossetti meant it sufficiently to say it more than once. In Sonnet V of *The House of Life*—

> Thy soul I know not from thy body, nor
> Thee from myself, neither our love from God.

Perpetually tormented by the irreconcilability of the unsensual love he had idealised and the love of the senses, he tries to identify them. Knowing that Dante's ideal love became in some way identified with the highest spiritual values, but blankly unaware of the austere scholastic method, the exact analysis and definition by which the transformation was accomplished, he simply turns his own confused and all too human conception of love into the highest value, and calls it God.

Yet his conception of love has no unity: there is the Flame-winged and the White-winged, Passion of Love and Love's Worship (IX). There is Soul's Beauty (LXXVII), to be followed

> How passionately and irretrievably,
> In what fond flight, how many ways and days:

There is Body's Beauty (LXXVIII), who weaves a web

> Till heart and body and life are in its hold:

and no real reconciliation between them is ever achieved. The ultimate blind alley is described in the fine sonnet *Lost on Both Sides*.

> So separate hopes, which in a soul had wooed
> The one same peace, strove with each other long,
> And Peace before their faces perished since:
> So through that soul, in restless brotherhood,
> They roam together now, and wind among
> Its bye-streets, knocking at the dusty inns.

It is for the biographer to trace Rossetti's passion for

Elizabeth Siddal, how it failed to satisfy his senses, and the bitter unhappiness, culminating in the final tragedy, that his defections and infidelities were to cause. It is only too easy to relate most of the sonnets in *The House of Life* to some stage or other in the progress of this unhappy story. The most powerful are the later ones of bitter remorse and self-reproach; *Known in Vain*; *The Heart of the Knight*, which can be compared to the traditional sonnets of recantation; *Lost Days*; *Vain Virtues*; and *Look in my face, my name is Might-have-been*, painfully evocative of Rossetti's later years—

> Mark me, how still I am! But should there dart
> One moment through thy soul the soft surprise
> Of that winged Peace which lulls the breath of sighs,—
> Then shalt thou see me smile, and turn apart
> Thy visage to mine ambush at thy heart
> Sleepless with cold commemorative eyes.

The one clear hope that recurs constantly among this mass of sultry and tormented feeling is the hope that what was frustrated in life may be fulfilled after death. Here *The House of Life* joins hands with much of the most typical Victorian poetry, with *In Memoriam*, for instance, and reflects in Rossetti's extremely individual way the general religious perplexities of the time.

> Ah! when the wan soul in that golden air
> Between the scriptured petals softly blown
> Peers breathless for the gift of grace unknown,—
> Ah! let no other alien spell soe'er
> But only the one hope's one name be there,—
> Not less nor more, but even that word alone.

The significance of Rossetti's work for the sensibility of the *fin-de-siècle* is very great. It inaugurates that period of emotional unrest in which satisfaction in sought in the traditional religious symbolism, but is not found, since the symbols have been emptied of almost all their traditional religious content. We begin to discern for the first time the figure of the conscious aesthete, deliberately pursuing beauty—

> . . . how passionately and irretrievably
> In what fond flight, how many ways and days.

His confused and partial return to the medieval concept of an ideal love, dominating the whole of life, is a genuine enrichment of the content of poetry. The bread-and-butter treatment of sexual themes, the "passionless sentiment" of Tennyson, is replaced by something which, for all its divagations, is a more adequate version of experience. The concept of a love which can never be satisfied by its simple bodily objects is not absorbed by Rossetti as it was by Dante into any total scheme of life: and this, together with the association between love and death, and the conflict between "soul's beauty" and "body's beauty", have often been written off as ethical eccentricities of the decadence. We must acknowledge in post-Freudian days that their psychological significance is more permanent. Rossetti is attacking some of the central neuroses of our culture. It is true that his progeny in the nineties did not amount to much: but the impasse in which he ultimately found himself provided the starting-point for the work of Yeats. Rossetti's turning away from science, sociology and progress into the analysis of his own soul led him into a *selva oscura* from which the only outlet is a dim, half-earthly, half-religious hope: in Yeats this faint hope gives rise to a tireless exploration of new possibilities of experience.

Chapter III

WILLIAM MORRIS

Rossetti's friendship with Burne-Jones and Morris began in 1856. This virtually marks the break-up of the earlier pre-Raphaelite movement. From then on, Rossetti's associations were more and more with the younger men—Rossetti's undergraduate followers, as Hunt acidly called them. They were, of course, never members of the P.R.B. But Morris and Burne-Jones at Oxford intended to form a brotherhood on pre-Raphaelite lines; the *Oxford and Cambridge Magazine* was started in imitation of *The Germ*, and while Hunt and Millais were developing on their divergent lines, what to the general public still seemed to be pre-Raphaelitism was continued and developed in the Morris circle. The medieval-romantic side of pre-Raphaelite painting is developed in the work of Burne-Jones, with an additional decorative slant, a use of linear rhythm derived from a wider knowledge of the *quattrocento*— particularly perhaps from Botticelli. Morris alone of the group was deeply affected by Ruskinian social ideals, and by their influence was led to extend pre-Raphaelitism into fields which the Brotherhood itself had never trod. Morris's craftsmanship, his success as a business man, and his political work all made an impact on English life as a whole that pure pre-Raphaelitism could never have achieved. He has thus escaped the allegations of romantic unrealism that have attached themselves to the P.R.B.: a selection of his works has been edited by G. D. H. Cole: he has been accorded a creditable place in English communist literature, and he is treated with general respect in circles which have little liking for the detached palace of art.

Yet the sympathy with which Morris is regarded in our own day is not based on any real agreement with his ideas. He is the prophet of a kind of socialism that is no longer active; many of his economic notions are patently illusions; hardly anyone nowadays practises handicrafts, and none believe that they will save society; contemporary taste has not much room for the Morris style of decoration; nobody reads his poetry; and of the few people who have ever handled a copy of the Kelmscott Chaucer, probably none has ever really read in it. Yet many who find both the personal and the literary aspects of Ruskin quite intolerable feel drawn to Morris and find in him a sympathetic campaigner against industrial hideousness, even now that the failure of his campaign has been assured. The failure may well seem so complete that there is little left to be said; and indeed there is little, except to define the moment of nineteenth-century culture when Morris's endeavour could seem a practical one. If Sir Kenneth Clark had found it possible to include Morris in his study of the Gothic revival there would be no need to deal with his craftsman's work here; for it is in this context that it really belongs. We tend to look at him prospectively, as the ancestor of arts and crafts, the reformer of domestic taste, an early example of the bourgeois Marxist. But for an understanding of Morris there is much to be said for seeing his work as part of a movement that had been going on, with many changes of sentiment, since Horace Walpole built Strawberry Hill.

Perhaps the most striking characteristic of nineteenth-century romantic medievalism is that what began as a fashionable antiquarian pastime developed into a comprehensive and determined set of beliefs with serious social and religious consequences. The history of the Gothic revival illustrates this particularly well. The first phase is dilettante and literary; its imaginative expression is *The Castle of Otranto*, highly successful in producing slightly factitious shudders, but a work which no one, least of all its author, could take *au grand sérieux*. The architectural monuments of the period are Strawberry Hill and Fonthill Abbey; and, in a more modest way, the gates and lodges of innumerable country houses. But in the next age this limpid and amiable trickle is wholly overborne by the turbid waters of religious revival. Emotions far more powerful than any within Horace Walpole's ken begin to attach themselves to the Middle Ages; Gothic becomes not an amusement but an article of faith. It is from then on that the Gothic revival begins to make its real impact on English life. The amusing dilettantism of a cultivated class is not likely to soak in very far; and even serious aesthetic considerations do not commonly affect the heart of England very much. But when these motives can be captured by religious or moral fervour the case is different. Pointed arches, blue china, negro sculpture, become (what, indeed, I suppose they are) the outward and visible signs of inward and spiritual states, and are revered or execrated accordingly. As Morris himself wrote, many years later:

> The first symptoms of change were brought about by the Anglo-Catholic movement, which must itself be considered as part of the Romantic movement in literature; and was supported by many who had no particular theological tendencies, as a protest against the historical position and stupid isolation of Protestantism. Under this influence there arose a genuine study of medieval architecture. . . . [1]

The dominant figure of this phase of the Gothic revival is Pugin, a Victorian whose achievements and influence have been strangely neglected by our age. His name is barely known to the thousands who daily see his work on the façade of the Houses of Parliament; and an immensely influential range of ideas of which he was undoubtedly the originator is commonly attributed to other people. Son of a distinguished draughtsman and student of Gothic ornament, Pugin early made contact with Gothic architecture in a mainly technical and archaeological spirit. From childhood he had made painstaking drawings of whatever medieval buildings he could get at, and soon was doing independent work as a draughtsman and designer. His studies of English churches filled him with disgust at the general neglect of ancient art and the iniquities of restorers; still more with disgust at the Anglican churchmen who sanctioned them. Soon he came to suspect that his reverence and his indignation were not only inspired by the monuments of medieval art themselves, but had something to do with the religion that lay behind them. Long afterwards he wrote:

> I learned the truths of the Catholic religion in the crypts of the old cathedrals of Europe. I sought for these truths in the modern churches of England, and found that since her separation from the centre of Catholic unity she had little truth and no life; so, without being acquainted with a single priest, through God's mercy, I resolved to enter His church.[2]

There are many roads to Rome, and without in the least impugning the propriety of Pugin's ultimate motives, we may remark that he was perhaps the first man to be led to Catholicism by architecture. From then on his work as an architect and designer was almost entirely in the service of the Church. *Domine, dilexi decorem domus tuae.* The results, alas, were disappointing: Pugin was obliged to build skimped churches with inadequate means in grimy manufacturing towns; and there was little real sympathy with his work, even among his own communion. Pugin's passionate zeal for archaeological accuracy and exact rubrical correctness were almost as disturbing to the conservative and unaesthetic Old Catholics as to the blackest of Protestants. His feelings about the visible edifice of the Church were suffused with a rich clerical unction which many Catholics never experience at all. The reader can conveniently observe both this phase of Gothic sentiment and the reaction it provoked, in "Romanist Modern Art", Appendix XII to the first volume of *The Stones of Venice*. Ruskin quotes from Pugin's *Remarks on Articles in The Rambler*.

> Those who have lived in want and privation are the best qualified to appreciate the blessings of plenty; thus to those who have been devout and sincere members of the separated portion of the English church; who have prayed and hoped and loved, through all the poverty of the maimed rites which it has retained—to them does the realisation of all their longing desires appear truly ravishing. . . . Oh! then, what delight! what joy unspeakable! when one of the solemn piles is presented to them, in all its pristine life and glory! The stoups are filled to the brim; the rood is raised on high; the screen glows with sacred imagery and rich device; the niches are filled; the altar is replaced, sustained by sculptured shafts, the relics of the saints repose beneath, the body of our Lord is enshrined on its

consecrated stone; the lamps of the sanctuary burn bright; the saintly portraitures in the glass windows shine all gloriously; and the albs hang in the oaken aumbries, and the cope chests are filled with orphreyed baudekins; and pix and pax and chrismatory are there, and thurible, and cross.

Ruskin, of course, regarded it as part of his mission to de-Catholicise the Gothic revival, and here he sets about it by amiably remarking: "Of all the fatuities, the basest is the being lured into the Romanist Church by the glitter of it, like larks into a trap by broken glass; to be blown into a change of religion by the whine of an organ-pipe; stitched into a new creed by gold thread on priests' petticoats; jangled into a change of conscience by the chimes of a belfry. . . . One might have put this man under a pix, and left him, one should have thought." And he goes on to some rancorous if not wholly unjustified abuse of Pugin's architectural practice.

This unedifying fragment of the *odium theologicum* might well have been left unremarked, if it were not that it points the way to a new development in the Gothic movement that was soon to become of the greatest social and aesthetic importance. As long as the Gothicists based their artistic preferences on religion they could hope all things and believe all things. The possibility of a religious revival can never be wholly ruled out. However unlikely it may seem, humanly speaking, this is not a matter where, for the believer, to speak humanly can ever be the last word. And even on the plane of actuality, the revival of Catholicism in England in the thirties and forties was visible enough. So that in spite of all the frustrations and disappointments of his life Pugin was always buoyed up by the hope that "the present revival of Christian architecture" in England was due at any time for a resounding victory. Furthermore, Pugin was no bigot; he had worked hard for a *rapprochement* between the High Anglicans and the Catholics; for him the English churchmen were separated brethren, and Catholicism in England had been robbed and despoiled, not killed. England was still at heart a Christian country, and it was therefore manifest to him that it should have a Christian, *scilicet* Gothic architecture.

> While we profess the creed of Christians, whilst we glory in the being Englishmen, let us have an architecture the arrangement and details of which remind us alike of our faith and of our country.[3]

He realises that nothing can be gained but by "a restoration of the ancient feeling and sentiments: 'tis they alone can restore Gothic architecture". But there was no reason why the ancient sentiments should not revive; indeed they were reviving, they had done so in his own belief and practice and in that of many others. Hence there is nothing inconsistent or absurd in the attempt to use Gothic in nineteenth-century England.

> There is no reason in the world why noble cities, combining all possible conveniences of drainage, water-courses and conveyance of gas, may not be erected in the most consistent and yet Christian character. Every building that is treated naturally, without disguise or concealment, cannot fail to look well.[4]

O blessed exercise of hope and joy! The mind goes back to the encaustic tiles, the terra-cotta tracery and the cast-iron columns of the buildings actually erected in this faith; the sheer unserviceability of the style would have finished it before long. But the intellectual weapon that was to put an end to Pugin's hopes, and to turn the minds of the more thoughtful medievalists in quite another direction, was Ruskin's Protestantism. Determined to free the glories of medieval art from all taint of Romish error, Ruskin is forced to inquire into the nature of Gothic from a new point of view. If the essence of Gothic is religious, it must owe nothing to the historic church, it must be the expression of his own peculiar combination of Wordsworth, botany, and Evangelical devotion. The piety of the Gothic craftsmen is shown in their patient naturalism; and their inspiration is not derived, as Pugin would have it, from a loving submission to ecclesiastical proprieties, but from a free exercise of their own creative powers. This is the Protestant and naturalistic interpretation of Gothic: and it is of course worked out with far more philosophical fullness than any of Pugin's notions. The emphasis on the free use of the workmen's faculties introduces a new range of ideas into nineteenth-century medievalism—that the nature of art is determined by the condition of the man who produces it. Gothic is different from Renaissance art because in the former the workman is a free man, in the latter he is a slave. And in nineteenth-century conditions the workman is not even a slave but is reduced to the status of a machine. So that as early as 1853, the date of the second volume of *The Stones of Venice*, the emphasis of neo-Gothic thought is shifted from religion to sociology and economics. This means at once that the atmosphere is less hopeful. A religious revival might occur at any time; for a good deal of his life Pugin was inspired by the hope of the conversion of England. But if the spirit of Gothic depends not on this, but on the status of the workman, there is obviously a long and weary way to tread before any change can be expected. Art is at least partly bound by the iron chain of economic necessity. The whole social order of England must be changed before a revival of the spirit of medieval art can be looked for. Naturally this was not perceived at once: the growth of Ruskin's conviction is seen in his work after 1857—in *The Political Economy of Art* and *Unto this Last*. And with the growth of Ruskin's sociological interests a new note of depression and sometimes of hopelessness appears in his view of the prospects of art. The one Gothic building constructed directly under his auspices, the Science Museum at Oxford, disgusted and dis-illusioned him before it was finished. The necessary conditions for a true revival of art were more complex than had been suspected, and the struggle was to be a longer and harder one than it had seemed to sanguine neo-Catholics. It is at this point that the work of Morris begins to make its contribution; it belongs to this last phase of the Gothic revival, the sociological one. But Morris was of a robust and sanguine temperament; his pugnacity and practical energy carried the struggle into fields that Ruskin never reached.

A glimmer of Anglo-Catholic medievalism had flickered on his boyhood. Like many another young man in the fifties, he was confirmed in his sympathy with medieval art by his High Church leanings. It did not last; Morris's link with the already failing Oxford Movement was shortlived, and in later life he professed the orthodox godlessness of Marxism. But even in his socialist period, in the passage quoted above, he continued to acknowledge the influence of Catholic idealism on the revival of Gothic art. His real awakening, however, came with the reading of Ruskin at Oxford. The "Nature of Gothic" chapter became his Bible, and many years later, in 1892, a reprint of it was one of the earliest books produced by the Kelmscott Press. The preface to this reprint states clearly enough his view of Ruskin's teaching. "To my mind this chapter is one of the most important things written by the author, and in future days will be considered as one of the very few necessary and inevitable utterances of this century. To some of us when we first read it now many years ago, it seemed to point out a new road on which the world should travel." And indeed there are few of Morris's artistic principles which do not spring from this source.

On the more practical matters Morris's ideas are surprisingly close to Pugin's; it is worth remarking on this, if only to do justice to a man so much of whose work has been appropriated by others. I have found only two references to Pugin in Morris's writing, neither of them complimentary, and it is not likely that there was any direct influence. The influence may, however, have been indirect. Quite early in Ruskin's career it was suggested that he had learnt from Pugin; and indeed it is difficult to believe that his studies of Gothic architecture could have failed to feel Pugin's influence. However, Ruskin always denied it, explicitly in Appendix III to the third volume of *Modern Painters*. The rancour of the attack on Pugin in *Romanist Modern Art* might lead one to suppose that he protests too much, and he seems to have displayed embarrassment over the business on other occasions. The recently published material on Ruskin's private life has shown him as a pathological liar when his self-esteem was concerned, and it may well be that Pugin's influence was greater than he cared to admit. At the least we may say that part of Ruskin's path had been fairly well trodden beforehand: that the historical and archaeological side of his work was in the main the natural continuation of what Pugin had done before; and that the essential continuity of the movement is witnessed by the curious way that the career and principles of Morris the disciple reproduce those of Pugin the unacknowledged forerunner.

No doubt a good deal of the resemblance between the two men was personal and accidental. They were similarly careless of the trappings of gentility, and were both accused of looking more like merchant seamen than artists. Both were pugnacious and could be sublimely rude to people who were insensitive to their ideals. Each accomplished more work in a lifetime than five ordinary men could contrive to get through. What is more significant, however, is the close resemblance between their aesthetic principles. They were both essentially applied artists who regarded architecture as the mistress art: Pugin actually made it his profession, while Morris worked largely on its confines. Their differing inspirations have already been remarked: what they had in common was that their feeling for Gothic was not purely aesthetic but was heavily mixed with motives that we can broadly call moral. Both continually play off medieval splendour against shabby modern vulgarity, and the antithesis is not simply an artistic one. Pugin's most powerful weapon was his "Contrasts": a set of engravings executed in pairs, showing the medieval side by side with the modern way of doing things. In this effective piece of propaganda the emphasis is partly aesthetic, partly religious, but at least partly social and moral as well. No. IX, Contrasted Conduits, shows not only an ugly and undignified modern erection, surmounted by a gas-lamp, contrasted with a beautiful Gothic design: in the modern conduit the pump is locked and guarded by a policeman, while in the medieval one a passer-by is drawing water freely. The Contrasted Towns show the Gas Works, the Lunatic Asylum and the Socialist Hall of Science in place of St. Mary's Abbey, All Saints and St. Olave's. Morris's *Art and Industry in the Fourteenth Century* points a similar contrast between the squalid and oppressive modern town and the surviving Gothic cathedral standing above it.

Over there the railway works, with their monotonous hideousness of dwelling houses for the artisans; here the gang of field-labourers; twelve shillings a week for ever and ever, and the workhouse for all day of judgment, of rewards and punishments;

on each side and all around the nineteenth century, and rising solemnly in the midst of it, that token of the "dark ages", their hope in the past, now grown a warning for our future.[5]

Their common hatred of the Renaissance is inspired by a similarly small modicum of aesthetic considerations. For Pugin, St. Peter's was "the upas-tree of Christendom", "a humbug, an abortion, a mass of imposition and a sham constructed even more vilely than it was designed". Morris, more temperately, merely described it as the ugliest building in Europe before the nineteenth century, and adds that art has been in prison from the time of its building to his own day. The eighteenth century is for Morris a Slough of Despond, from which he hopes that the art of his age has arisen. Georgian houses are "not oppressively ugly and base, and it is possible to live in them without serious disturbance to work or thought", but this is about all that can be said for them. By Morris's time the wickedness of neo-classical architecture was so firmly established that it was no longer necessary actually to look at the buildings at all.

It is noticeable that Morris is not much interested in pure painting, and beyond an admiration for medieval illumination shows little sensibility to it. He is contemptuous of Rubens, which is perhaps a good test case; he has none of those flirtations with the Venetians that threatened to upset Ruskin's moral balance; and his taste in modern painting is restricted. He had an admiration, later somewhat qualified, for Rossetti, and a whole-hearted devotion to Burne-Jones; but his attitude to Whistlerian impressionism was essentially that of Ruskin. "You will find clever and gifted men at the present day who are prepared to sustain as a theory that art has no function but the display of clever executive qualities, and that one subject is as good as another." The pictures produced by these men seem "intended to convey the impression on a very short-sighted person of divers ugly incidents seen through the medium of a London fog". Of French impressionism he does not seem to have heard.

The fact is that Morris is not much interested in art as the mere expression of visual sensibility; he sees it as that which gives beauty and dignity to other parts of life. Where the interests of the earlier Gothicists were mainly ecclesiastical, Morris's were mainly domestic, and his craftsmanship began as a response to a purely personal need—the need to decorate his own house. When Philip Webb built the Red House at Upton for Morris it was soon found that suitable furniture and hangings for it were simply not to be had; the work of Morris and Co. began with Morris's personal efforts to make a home that he could bear to live in. The settles, the cupboards, the embroidered cloths were made for the excellent reason that Morris wanted the things. Throughout his life he worked best when he was closest to an immediate practical need; his principles are less interesting than his practical hints. Indeed, his principles are mainly Ruskin's, and are often presented simply as such. Scattered throughout *Hopes and Fears for Art* and the *Lectures on Art and Industry* we have the orthodox Ruskinian view of the history of architecture, the proper relation of the craftsman to the artist, and of the handicrafts to the rest of life. Nor, for such a vigorous and explosive mind, is there any great freshness in the expression. Morris pounds away at the old doctrines till the reader is inclined to give them an almost mechanical assent. The argument is sound and effective enough, but it has none of the arresting and eccentric vivacity of Pugin's attack on contemporary aesthetic errors. Morris complains that the genuine style of his era "is exemplified in the jerry-built houses of our suburbs, the stuccoed marine parades of our watering-places, the flaunting corner public-houses of every town in Great Britain, the raw-boned hideousness of the houses that mar the glorious scenery of the Queen's Park at Edinburgh", but he cannot make a grotesque satirical invention like Pugin's superb description of the new cemetery.

This is generally Egyptian, probably from some association between the word catacombs, which occurs in the prospectus of the company, and the discoveries of Belzoni on the banks of the Nile; and nearly opposite the Green Man and Dog public-house, in the centre of a dead wall (which serves as a cheap medium of advertisement for blacking and shaving-strop manufacturers), a cement caricature of the entrance to an Egyptian temple, $2\frac{1}{2}$ inches to the foot, is erected, with convenient lodges for the policeman and his wife, and a neat pair of cast-iron hieroglyphical gates, which it would puzzle the most learned to decypher; while, to prevent any mistake, some such words as "New Economical Compressed Grave Cemetery Company" are inscribed in *Grecian* capitals along the frieze, interspersed with hawk-headed divinities, and surmounted by a huge representation of the winged Osiris bearing a gas-lamp.[6]

Morris immediately becomes more lively and individual the closer he comes to the practice of a particular craft and the use of a particular material. The Gothic revivalists generally tended to find material circumstances an inspiration rather than a handicap.

In pure architecture the smallest detail should *have a meaning or serve a purpose*; even the construction itself *should vary with the material employed*, and the designs should be adapted to the material in which they are executed.[7]

Eschew all vagueness. . . . Hold fast to distinct form in art. . . . Try to get the most out of your material, but always in such a way as honours it most. Not only should it be obvious what your material is, but something should be done with it which is specifically natural to it.[8]

The first of these passages is by Pugin, the second by Morris; but they are almost interchangeable. The firm stand on respect for material and frank revelation of construction became Morris's basic practical rule: and it is perhaps the most lasting legacy that the Gothic revival has left behind.

The natural accompaniment of this is a great respect for utility. "In matters of ordinary use a man must go out of his way to make something bad," Pugin remarked: and we may compare Morris's verdict on the objects in a rich man's house —that the only tolerable ones are to be found in the kitchen. Morris in particular has a strong prejudice for solidity and simplicity. He writes of some of the exhibits in the South Kensington Museum:

Now, consider, I pray you, what these wonderful works are, and how they were made; and indeed it is neither in extravagance nor without due meaning that I use the word "wonderful" in speaking of them. Well, these things are just the common household goods of those past days, and that is one reason why they are so few and so carefully treasured. They were common things in their own day, used without fear of breaking or spoiling —no rarities then—yet we have called them "wonderful".[9]

This is leading rapidly to the view that real art means peasant pottery and rush-seated chairs, and that other mani-festations of the creative spirit are tainted with luxury and pride. One may suspect the presence of some muddle in Morris's mind. Some of his statements on the matter are unexceptionable. After giving a list of the things required in a healthy man's house he adds: "This simplicity you may make as costly as you please or can"—hang the walls with tapestry or cover them with mosaic—"all this is not luxury, if it be done for beauty's sake and not for show: it does not break our golden rule: have nothing in your house which you do not know to be useful or believe to be beautiful."[10] But when he says "the greatest foe to art is luxury, art cannot live in its atmosphere", he is saying what as a matter of historical fact is remarkably untrue. And when he says "a stout table, a few old-fashioned chairs, a pot of flowers, will ornament the parlours of an old English yeoman's house far better than a wagon-load of Rubens' will ornament a gallery in Blenheim Park",[11] well, it is fairly obvious that he is not thinking about art at all, though of course he may be thinking about something else equally important. The lecture on *The Prospects of Archi-tecture* similarly suggests that architecture for Morris is largely a matter of slum-clearance and garden suburbs. It is evident throughout that his aesthetic judgments are profoundly affected by this moral and social preference for simplicity of life, a preference which crops up again as an essential element in the Morris kind of Socialism.

Morris's motives in all this are profoundly worthy of respect. He is trying to recreate an art that shall be not the appanage of a class but shall really spring from the life of the people: and any later dislike for the limitations of arty-crafty aesthetics should not blind us to the fact that they constitute one of the few sincere attempts to solve this problem in recent times.

The peasant-pottery, rural-crafts side of Morris's belief was at least matched by a continual effort at working the thing out in practice. At the Merton Abbey works, when it became necessary to train men for a new craft, Morris did not attempt to find people with special gifts or background. He made a point of taking any boys who happened to be about the place, and they appear to have done all that was required of them. The demand for simplicity was meant in the first place to bring about an art that the people as a whole might be expected to consume; but perhaps even more important, that the people might be expected to produce; an art that "will be the gift of the people to the people".

This insistence that every man shall be an artist brings about some curious inconsistencies. If there was one thing that was essential to the Ruskin-Morris aesthetic it was the iniquity of the division of labour: more than anything else it was the division between gentleman-designer and mechanic-executant that had brought about the final degradation of art. Yet Morris's practice in fact brought back the same old dichotomy in another way. Morris sincerely tried to reduce social and economic division among his workmen by a system of profit-sharing, and though he saw that in existing society he could not undermine his own position as capitalist entrepreneur without destroying the whole business, he sacrificed a great deal of his personal fortune to the Socialist movement that was to make such fortunes impossible. However, this does not go very far towards proving that all men are artists. He did go a long way to show that, given decent conditions, a share of individual responsibility and a pride in their work, most men could become good handicraftsmen and be the happier for it: but the old split between artist-designer and mere executant still went on; in fact it is seen particularly clearly in Morris's own work. He himself never gained any real skill in drawing the human figure or animal forms. The birds and animals in his wallpaper designs were commonly drawn by Philip Webb. The successful Morris tapestries and stained glass were always from designs by Burne-Jones, though Morris generally provided the verdura backgrounds and borders and arranged the leading for the stained glass. The results are often beautiful, for Burne-Jones is a romantic artist with a unique, if tenuous, personal gift, and Morris was in the closest sympathy with both the man and his work. But this is something very different from the Ruskin-Morris ideal of a work conceived and executed throughout by the mind and hand of the same man.

This brings us to the difficult question of the aesthetic value of Morris's own work—difficult because it was so varied, and because in decorative and domestic art of this kind it is particularly hard to get away from the influence of fashion. We should perhaps clear the accidentals out of the way first. The social importance of Morris's work in making the huge British middle-class public realise, probably for the first time, the mere existence of aesthetic values, would be hard to over-estimate. The growth in the normal bourgeois family of some sort of care, however rudimentary, for colour and design in their everyday surroundings, is largely due to the diffusion of Morris's ideas. And the cumulative effect of this in mitigating the daily ugliness of an industrialised world has undoubtedly been very great. Such alliances between art and industry as there are—the employment by manufacturers of good designers, the use of decent and lively posters by the railways and the London Passenger Transport Board—all these leavenings of the normal urban squalor are in great measure the fruit of Morris's propaganda and practice. If he had done nothing else he deserves an honourable niche in English cultural history for this. But we have still to look at his own actual designs; and when we do so it is hard to avoid the conviction that they suffer, as his poetry does, from his feeling that anyone could do it, with training and practice, that art is a craft, in fact. There is a sense in which he did not believe in art enough. With his relative lack of interest in "intellectual art", as he calls it, his own art becomes purely decorative, and there is inevitably a thinness and tedium in decorative art that has no real roots in personal vision, in tradition, or in social utility. His work seems to lack emotional significance; which may seem an illegitimate demand to make of decorative art. But the best decorative art does seem to have it, does seem to convey something of the ethos of the designer or of his age. Morris's decoration offers pleasing colour, as the verse of Jason makes a pleasing noise, but they are both opaque: they give none of those glimpses, as through a translucent material, into a world of experience below the manifest surface; and it is this which makes the difference between art and mere good workmanship. The exception is when he is interpreting the work of Burne-Jones: but Burne-Jones, whether one likes him or not, was an original artist; and Morris here is only the translator of his vision. In practice, too, the claims of utility and those of beauty seem to have been imperfectly adjusted in many Morris products. In his furniture Morris seems to feel that the demands of utility are satisfied by making something immensely heavy and solid; and those of beauty by getting Burne-Jones to paint something on it. The result is not an organic unity.

In fact, for all Morris's personal sincerity, there is a basic inconsistency in his position. The goods turned out by the firm were sheer luxury products; they found their way only into the hands of rich men. Immense though the indirect effects of Morris were, his actual works did almost nothing towards the art of the people that he desired. The prestige that Morris products acquired was in the end a snob prestige: it owed nothing to popular taste, but a great deal to the ultimate acceptance by the *haute bourgeoisie* of the work of the pre-Raphaelites. The frank rapacity of Whistler and Rossetti, selling art for what it would fetch to Lancashire manufacturers, was far more consistent than the policy of Morris. What a popular nineteenth-century art could have been like, one can hardly imagine; but it would have been something very different from the products of Morris and Co., and it would have found no place for a delicate exotic like Burne-Jones. Should one praise Morris for backing his own aesthetic fancy and making a successful attempt to put pre-Raphaelitism on the commercial map; or for making a propaganda for the revival of a true art of the people? It is not altogether easy to praise him for doing both at the same time.

As Morris becomes more deeply involved in practical Socialism, his artistic position seems to become increasingly hopeless. He wants beautiful and well-made things: yet he is committed to the belief that art can only be the expression of the society that produces it. The society of his own time can produce no real art: his own products grow up in hot-house isolation and are quite hopelessly out of touch with the real spirit of the age. In later life Morris realised this.

> The genuine style of our era is exemplified in the jerry-built houses of our suburbs, the stuccoed marine parades of our watering places, the flaunting corner public-houses of every town in Great Britain, the raw-boned hideousness of the houses that mar the glorious scenery of the Queen's Park at Edinburgh. These form our true Victorian architecture. Such work as Mr. Bodley's excellent new buildings at Magdalen College, Mr. Norman Shaw's elegantly fantastic Queen Anne houses at Chelsea, or Mr. Robson's simple but striking London board schools, are mere eccentricities, with which the public in general has no part or lot.[12]

He even faces, at moments, the possibility that art under these conditions may not survive, or ought not to survive.

> Sirs, I believe that art has such sympathy with cheerful freedom, open-heartedness and reality, so much she sickens under selfishness and luxury, that she will not live thus isolated and exclusive. I will go further than this and say that on such terms I do not wish her to live.[13]

What he will not face is that the kind of work he desires is out of touch with any conceivable modern society. He never tackles the problem of machine production and its relation to the life of the artist; he assumes always that the sort of gimcrack mechanical luxuries he does not himself desire are desired by nobody; he idealised the taste of the working class and indulges, without any obvious justification, a belief that if left to themselves they would produce nothing but what was useful or beautiful. The point will recur in discussing Morris's Socialism: here we may remark that it is quite unhistorical to assert, as he constantly does, that all good art is the expression of the life of the people. Some art has been so, at some periods: but for the most part art has been precisely what Morris says it cannot be—a luxury product—either the indulgence of a leisured class, or the expression of the private sensibility of an artist who has been in some way sheltered from the economic struggle. When Morris says that the art of the future "will not be an esoteric mystery shared by a little band of superior beings . . . it will be the gift of the people to the people",[14] he is stating an article of faith, a noble faith, but alas, one without any positive evidence to support it.

As the world at present probably contains a number of people who are convinced at the same time of the necessity of art and of the inevitability of social revolution, Morris's principles remain important. The topics he discusses are constantly discussed to-day; the reviews are full of dissertations on the economic position of the artist; and more than in Morris's day the artist is faced with either some form of servitude to the industrial machine or professional liquidation. Morris's generosity of spirit has gone; but a new realism has come into the discussion, since we can now see a little way round the corner that Morris was only approaching. Poverty and destruction from two world wars, the arrival of a measure of Socialism, of one kind or another, over most of Europe, have meant that the private patron has almost disappeared. Morris would note with satisfaction that, however the artist may misuse his gifts, he is rarely employed to-day in making objects for rich men's houses. But alas, the results that Morris expected from this liberation have not followed: art has not found a new place in the life of the people: it has not moved into the marketplace from the residence of the merchant prince: it has moved if anywhere into the museum. Most contemporary discussion suggests that if what we call the fine arts are to survive it can only be by some sort of state patronage: which means in the end, as Herbert Read has pointed out, that they will have to become the sort of thing that some civil servant thinks the public ought to want.

For a private patron the artist used to paint with a definite notion of what was expected of him—he knew that the painting would be hung in a living-room, that it would be lived with, that it would have to please a specific "taste". But the painter who aims at State patronage—with what preconceptions shall he paint? The picture will be hung in some bleak or pompous gallery—he cannot be sure where it will be hung: it must please the taste of some obscure or unknown official before it is offered to the appreciation of a wandering, indifferent public. Not exactly an inspiring prospect for the painter.[15]

It is true that it was not with painting that Morris was most concerned: but in the applied arts with which he was concerned his programme has proved hardly more realistic. His attempts to revive the decorative arts without relating them to contemporary industrial techniques was foredoomed to failure. To try to restore handicraft as the basis of production could only intensify the split between 'artistic' hand-made goods and commercial ones made by the machine: and the resultant arts and crafts movement, for all the innocent joy it gave to many, turned out one of the most disappointing children of the Ruskinian doctrine. The people who really bridged the gulf between art and commerce were the plagiarists and imitators, the manufacturers who copied Morris's designs and used them for their machine-made goods. It was Morris's success in the luxury trade that made manufacturers realise that good design was worth having, even in the end worth paying for; and it was the ordinary course of commerce that really distributed the Morris reform in taste throughout the social system. The odd result is that Morris's most lasting and useful effect has been on a kind of production that he himself despised and wanted to abolish. It was not part of Morris's intention, but it was as a result of his work that a place was found for the decorative artist in the mechanised commercial system: and in spite of just complaints about the decline in the higher kinds of taste, it would be absurd to underrate the importance of this in alleviating common everyday ugliness.

What may yet prove to be the most fruitful of Morris's ideas is that art may become, as in *News from Nowhere*, the alternative occupation of people whose ordinary employment is elsewhere. All Morris's efforts to build the arts into the social fabric broke down, and it is difficult to see a happier fate for most modern attempts in the same direction. What cannot break down is the fact that art of some kind will continue to be produced because there will always be some people who wish to produce it. The principle has long been accepted by writers; nobody tries to extract a living from a stony world by writing poetry. Painting and sculpture to-day have similarly lost most of their economic and social justification. What may save them is Morris's principle that art is man's pleasure in his work. It need not be the work society pays him for. If Morris's kind of Socialism could find no place for the disengaged artist, working without consideration of social utility, it is hardly likely that the less aesthetic Socialism of the twentieth century will do so. But if among the many promises of Socialism, that of increased leisure is not wholly vain, art may yet survive, and escape the surveillance of the government inspector, as a thing that a few people do because they want to do it; not perhaps a joy in widest commonalty spread, or the gift of the people to the people, but an underground movement of the spirit that may yet, in some remote future and in some unforeseeable way, rescue human life from total mechanisation.

II. MORRIS AND SOCIALISM

It is from this point, from an eventual despair at the prospects of art under capitalism, that a consideration of Morris's Socialism ought to begin. Because Morris wrote a Utopian romance, was an artist and a medievalist, it is sometimes thought that his Socialism was of a gentle and cloudy kind. This is of course far from true. His attempts to revive the arts in an industrial society came up against a blank wall; and the only way out he could see was through an explosion. By the time Morris came to Socialism he was in no mood for half-measures: his programme was the Marxist one, its motive force was the class war, its culmination was to be a violent revolution. He conceives the contemporary social struggle in terms of power politics, because he is fighting a society based on material power, and believes that it must be fought with its own weapons. But it was mainly because he was an artist that he became a revolutionary. Some kind of reform or Fabianism would have been the obvious policy for fulfilling his material aspirations: short of a complete break with the traditions of industrial civilisation he can see no hope for art. So he adopts the austere revolutionary orthodoxy for the duration of the struggle: the fulfilment of his private vision must be postponed till after the victory.

English Socialism before Morris's day had been either Utopian or strictly economic, but not as a rule both. Coleridgian pantisocracies on the banks of the Susquehanna, Owenite villages of co-operation, come in the first class: the various Socialist deductions from Ricardo's labour theory of value, culminating in the acceptance of Marxism, come in the second. On the whole they had little to say to each other; their ultimate destinations may not have been far apart, but their methods and temperaments were. There is a similar contrast between the middle-class thinkers who approach a kind of idealist Socialism from the philosophic and humanitarian aspect—Coleridge, the Christian Socialists, Ruskin; and those who approached it as a fighting working-class movement, like the Chartists. The one side is pacific, co-operative, and attempts to reduce the area of class conflict: the other is militant and aggressive, and relies for its results on the intensification of the class war. Morris is one of the few people to attempt the combination of both influences, influences which, by the time he became politically active, we may sum up as the Ruskinian and the Marxist.

Although the influence of Ruskin had pervaded Morris's work since his Oxford days it had not led him into any kind of political activity. In Ruskin's case, the nature of Gothic took him directly to politics and economics: the efficient cause of Morris's entry into political life was different. He acquired the habit of lecturing, organising, mobilising public opinion in his Society for the Protection of Ancient Buildings: he had no particular love for the work as such, but he wanted the results. Then, in 1877 the indignation of a Liberal minority to which Morris belonged was aroused over the famous Eastern question. The crux of this was Disraeli's policy of condoning an oppressive régime in Turkey to offset the dreaded power of Russia.

A hands-off Russia agitation was started, not unlike some that we have become familiar with since; the Eastern Question Association was formed; Morris became active in it, and in 1877 wrote a manifesto on the subject addressed to the working men of England. Even at this early stage he appeared to feel that it was only to the working classes that an appeal could usefully be made; and by the time the Eastern crisis was over he was thoroughly in touch with the Radical working-class leaders all over London. The feebleness of Liberal support for the Eastern Question Association had thoroughly disgusted him with what he called the cowardice of middle-class politics, and the disgust rapidly came to include the Liberal programme of social reform. He soon came to feel that "disaster and misfortune of all kinds . . . will be the only things that will breed a remedy".[16] His contempt for Whiggery and his movement towards Socialism progressed rapidly from this time on, though he still hoped for some kind of Radical wing of the Liberal party which should force the hand of the Whigs.

About the actual crisis in Morris's political development there is some element of mystery. Later he said that he was converted, against the intention of the author, by Mills's posthumous papers on Socialism: but this has all the air of a *post facto* explanation. What was probably happening was that a latent Socialist tendency derived from Ruskin was fusing in his mind with a hope in the workers, and a contempt for the bourgeoisie, derived from his recent political experience. After the process was complete, Morris set about to prove his convictions, and ground away unhappily at Marx and the economists. But it was the revolutionary hope, not the logic of economic analysis, that brought about the change. In 1883 he joined the Social Democratic Federation.

The moment was propitious for a man of Morris's temperament. Socialism in England was in a mood of apocalyptic fervour. The old working-class hostility to Socialist doctrine was disappearing. London workmen were reading Marx, and the influence of revolutionary exiles from the Continent was becoming powerful. Ill-organised, and split by the usual doctrinaire dissensions, the small body of English Socialists nevertheless believed that capitalism was in its last phase and the revolution was at hand. The hint of violence was in the air, and the historical parallel between the destruction of feudalism by gunpowder and that of capitalism by dynamite was not infrequently employed. A very short time after his conversion from middle-class Radicalism Morris adopted this revolutionary orthodoxy pretty completely. His Oxford lecture of 1883, *Art under a Plutocracy*, at which Ruskin took the chair, is completely Socialist in tone and completely contemptuous of all Liberal and reformist measures. In *Whigs, Democrats and Socialists* (1886), the only future he can see for a constitutional Parliament is "a perpetual Whig rump, which will yield to pressure when mere political reforms are attempted, but will be quite immovable to any real change in social or economic matters".

> One and all, then, we are responsible for the enunciation of Socialist principles. . . . This responsibility to Socialism cannot be shaken off by declarations against physical force and in favour of Constitutional methods of agitation; we are attacking the constitution with the very beginnings, the mere lispings of Socialism.[17]

About the same time he writes:

> It is impossible to see how destruction of privilege can stop short of absolute equality of condition; pure Communism is the logical deduction from the imperfect form of the new society, which is generally differentiated from it as Socialism.[18]

In sharp contrast to the Ruskinians and Christian Socialists he completely accepts the class war as the motive force of social change.

> You think that individuals of good will belonging to all classes can, if they be numerous and strenuous enough, bring about the change: I on the contrary think that the basis of all change must be, as it has always been, the antagonism of classes: I mean that though here and there a few men of the upper and middle classes, moved by their conscience and insight, may and doubtless will throw in their lot with the working classes, the upper and middle classes as a body will by the very nature of their existence, and like a plant grows, resist the abolition of

classes: neither do I think that any amelioration of the condition of the poor on the only lines which the rich can go upon will advance us on the road.[19]

Many passages in Morris's writings have precisely the note of twentieth-century Communist tracts; particularly in a hatred and contempt for Social Democrats and reformists, to use present-day terminology, far more bitter than that for professed Tories. There had been a revival of the Christian Socialism of Kingsley and F. D. Maurice: William Morris comments: "The Christian Church has always declared against Socialism; its mainstay must always be property and authority. . . . Of course as long as people are ignorant, compromise plus sentiment always looks better to them than the real article." We find in fact little that is original in Morris's Socialist lectures: they are honest and straightforward expositions of the Marxist position, and they differ only from many later utterances of the same school by being written in better English.

Equally, when he approaches the matter as a craftsman rather than a revolutionary he adds little to the Ruskinian doctrine. This had by now become the orthodoxy of those generous spirits who were disgusted with industrial civilisation. Morris's individual contribution is the attempt to tie the Ruskinian and the Communist positions together. If there is no logical reason for being led to Catholicism by a concern for art there is surely still less for being led to Marxism. The paternal feeling and avuncular tone of Ruskin's dealing with the social order are odd companions for the historic mission of the proletariat; and the attempt to get Marx and Ruskin into the same basket leads Morris into some queer manœuvres. At the time Morris joined the English working-class movement it was long past its frame-breaking days. Instructed by the Marxian analysis the workers looked forward to taking over the capitalist world at the height of its technical powers. With his interests, Morris did not and could not do so. Modern technology was at least as much his enemy as modern social organisation. Remove the capitalist class, turn the organisation of industry over to the workers—and the world would still be little nearer to Morris's ideal. Having overcome wage-slavery it would still be necessary to overcome the slavery to the machine, and the social revolution in itself would do little or nothing towards that end. It is impossible for Morris to admit this; so with a more or less wilful blindness he consistently plays it down; he steadily suggests, and he does it so often that in the end it acquires an almost hypnotic force, that it is solely the greed of the masters that accounts for the mechanisation of modern life. The whole drift of his propaganda makes it necessary for him to identify the breakdown of the capitalist system with the breakdown of the machine age.

He proceeds to do this by the concept of unnecessary production. Much of the work done in the world appears to Morris as merely the production of stuff that is not wanted, turned out by capitalists for the world market in order to make profit. Ploughing, fishing and sheep-tending are delightful and dignified occupations:

> No, it is not such labour as this which we need to do away with, but the toil which makes the thousand and one things which nobody wants, which are merely used as the counters for the competitive buying and selling, falsely called commerce, which I have spoken of before—I know in my heart, and not merely by my reason, that this toil cries out to be done away with.[20]

He elaborates the point in *News from Nowhere*:[21]

> It is clear from all that we hear and read, that in the last age of civilisation men had got into a vicious circle in the matter of production of wares. They had reached a wonderful facility of production, and in order to make the most of that facility they had gradually created (or allowed to grow, rather) a most elaborate system of buying and selling, which has been called the World-Market; and that World-Market, once set a-going, forced them to go on making more and more of these wares, whether they need them or not. So that while (of course) they could not free themselves from the toil of making real necessaries, they created in a never-ending series sham or artificial necessaries, which became, under the iron rule of the aforesaid World-Market, of equal importance to them with the real necessaries that supported life. By all this they burdened themselves with a prodigious mass of work merely for the sake of keeping their wretched system going.

It seems to be the heart more than the reason that is at work. Just as the moral passion for simplicity of life affects Morris's judgment on art so it does his judgment on society. When he says that "nobody wants" the products of industrialism he can only mean that nobody ought to want them. Clearly they do want them in some sense, or the things would not be sold. In part he is suggesting that the demand has been artificially stimulated; and in other places he seems to mean that the goods have been forced in some way on unwilling purchasers. In fact all experience goes to show that people living in the state of ideal simplicity that Morris desired are only too ready to welcome the shoddy products of industrialism as soon as they can get them.

Morris averts his eyes from these considerations because they are fatal to his scheme. The real problem of his ideal society is how the large population of a modern state is to be supported at a decent level without wholesale industrialisation. His answer is, by doing without things. But it is also an axiom of Morris's belief that in a Socialist state no one would have to do without anything that he wanted. The solution is plain: people don't really want all the things they would have to do without. They simply stop making them, and relieved of the burden of useless labour, return to the handwork that they really enjoy. The old gentleman who expounds the social system of *News from Nowhere* has no difficulties about planning or consumer's choice:

> The wares which we make are made because they are needed: men make for their neighbours' use as if they were making for themselves, not for a vague market of which they know nothing, and over which they have no control: as there is no buying and selling, it would be mere insanity to make goods on the chance of their being wanted; for there is no longer anyone who can be *compelled* to buy them. So that whatever is made is good, and thoroughly fit for its purpose. Nothing *can* be made except for genuine use; therefore no inferior goods are made. Moreover, as aforesaid, we have now found out what we want, so we make no more than we want; and as we are not driven to make a vast quantity of useless things, we have time and resources enough to consider our pleasure in making them. All work which it would be irksome to do by hand is done by immensely

improved machinery; and in all work which it is a pleasure to do by hand machinery is done without.

How the machinery is made and how the power is generated without irksome and inartistic work on the part of somebody does not appear. And here it becomes plain that Morris is talking a good deal of nonsense. It is possible that what advertises itself as a Utopian romance should not be challenged on the score of probability; but I do not think so. There is no sense in discussing Utopias unless one asks how far they are possible, and one cannot write an effective moral fable by faking the physical conditions. It is incontrovertible but also pointless to say that if everything were quite different from what it is everything would be quite different. A Utopian romance may legitimately be over-optimistic about human nature under changed conditions, but it may not divide a pound between twenty people and give them half a crown each. That is what is happening in *News from Nowhere*. There is not enough work done to keep life going at the standard there described. Foreign trade has apparently ceased; the economy is a purely regional one; agriculture and the greater part of manufacture is carried on by hand labour alone; yet there is leisure and plenty for all. With the population of England reduced to about a tenth of its present level some of it might be possible. But Morris nowhere suggests that the new age is inaugurated by a pogrom or controlled by contraception. At the best, the infinite leisure, the absence of all pressure or urgency is more suited to an island in the South Seas than to the northern coasts of Europe.

The rapid unscrambling of the psychological eggs of the nineteenth century must probably be granted. It is in the nature of a Utopia to suggest that if certain external conditions were changed, human nature would change more than we should expect. There is always a chance that this may be true. But Morris hardly realised how much he was alone in the demand for a simple life of manual toil, handicraft, and home-bred entertainment. Socialism has long given up its dreams of love in a cottage and set up a marriage of convenience with technocracy. One of the few serious threats to the absolutism of the

Communist *Anschauung* in Russia was the discovery by Russian soldiers that the workers in capitalist Europe had far more of the mechanised luxuries than they had ever seen: and the long-term objective of Socialism to-day is a braver and newer world than capitalism could supply. Even in Morris's day there was no desire among the workers to turn themselves into four-teenth-century guildsmen. The appetite for mechanical clutter is not so easily overcome. This is Morris's real enemy at least as much as the capitalist world, and there is no evidence that the one would cease to be without the other. If the mechanisa-tion of life were merely a bosses' manœuvre as Morris suggests, the problem would be relatively simple, but in a deeper sense than he suspects the machines have become the masters of men.

Alas, his position is not really tenable. For all his deter-mination to renounce his class, and in spite of much practical success, he is already afflicted with the basic schizophrenia of the modern intellectual. His analysis of the contemporary social situation does not really lead to the conclusion that he wants to reach. The chapter on "How the Change Came" in *News from Nowhere* is a sober account of a social revolution in the Marxist manner. Much of it we can see happening around us to-day.

> That machinery of life for the use of people who didn't know what they wanted of it, and which was known at the time as State Socialism, was partly put in motion, though in a very piecemeal way. But it did not work smoothly; it was, of course, resisted at every turn by the capitalists; and no wonder, for it tended more and more to upset the commercial system I have told you of, without providing anything really effective in its place. . . . For a long time matters went on like this. The power of the upper classes had lessened, as their command over wealth lessened, and they could not carry things wholly by the high hand as they had been used to in earlier days. So far the State Socialists were justified by the result.

Much of it has been seen, with technical improvements, in the Europe of the last twenty years.

> Bands of young men, like the marauders in the great strike of whom I told you just now, armed themselves and drilled, and began on any opportunity or pretence to skirmish with the

WILLIAM MORRIS

people in the streets. The Government neither helped them nor put them down, but stood by, hoping that something might come of it. These "Friends of Order" as they were called, had some successes at first, and grew bolder; they got many officers of the regular army to help them, and by their means laid hold of munitions of war of all kinds.

The course of events is all planned to show the utter futility of any constitutional or gradualist measures; and whether one accepts this view or not, the story as Morris tells it is clearly the result of serious analysis of actual social conditions. As soon as the revolution has occurred, however, we find ourselves in a wholly different world, not only a different England, but a different universe of discourse.

People flocked into the country villages, and, so to say, flung themselves upon the freed land like a wild beast upon its prey; and in a very little time the villages of England were more populous than they had been since the fourteenth century, and were still growing fast.

England became a garden, a new art sprang up spontaneously out of men's natural pleasure in their work; "a craving for beauty seemed to awaken in men's minds, and they began rudely to ornament the wares that they made"; a leisurely but not stupid country life became normal—but why go on? The whole picture is in almost every detail the exact antithesis of the regimented megalopolitan ant-hill which is all the future actually seems to offer, under whatever régime.

Had I the plantation of this isle, my lord,
I' the commonwealth I would by contraries
Execute all things: for no kind of traffic
Would I admit; no name of magistrate;
Letters should not be known; riches, poverty,
And use of service, none; contract, succession,
Bourn, bound of land—

The England of *News from Nowhere* is a modern reshaping of the ancient myth, in legend named the Golden Age, in political philosophy the state of nature. Morris has provided it with a realistic prelude, but his real distinction is that in a period of domestic realism in fiction, private fantasy in poetry, his

111

romance has the validity of an image from a deeper level, one of the archetypes from the collective unconscious of mankind. To political thinkers the life of man in a state of nature has appeared in various lights: on the one hand, nasty, brutish and short; on the other, a state of primitive equality more like the pastoral world of the poets. Socialist sentiment has often owed a great deal to these political or poetical myths of a time of unfallen simplicity before the institution of civil society or private property. *News from Nowhere* springs from the same emotional source. Morris's immersion in the political flux and his propaganda for rapid and catastrophic change did nothing to alter his deep longing for a stable and changeless order, such as we see portrayed, in a variety of different guises, in his poetry and his pure romances. The England of *News from Nowhere* is another Earthly Paradise, but one that is attached to the contemporary world by a slender thread of social analysis. Morris is trying to present his dream in the light of waking knowledge, and the most surprising feature of the book is not its unreality, but how nearly he succeeds. It is doubtful whether the social analysis contributes much to this. The book derives is strength from another source—it has the reality of a myth. Myths are after all fundamental to the psychic life: no demonstration of what is merely possible can fill the minds of men unless it can draw energy from these underground sources: and no merely personal or fashionable fantasy can do so, except for a limited time and class. The romantic writers had been working since the late eighteenth century for a revival of mythology, and the pre-Raphaelites had transferred some of the same motives to art; but most of the fantasies remained obstinately private and rarely achieved the status and validity of myth. Morris achieves it in *News from Nowhere* alone. This tenuous sketch of an idealised suburban life, in which there is no painfully hard work, no poverty, no passion that cannot be fairly contained by the social organism; this world where labour is an art, and the ordinary things of use are works of art, has really very little to do with modern Socialism or the result of an economic revolution. It is the nineteenth-century restatement of one of the most persistent visions of mankind.

WILLIAM MORRIS

From the point of view of this discussion it is also something else. Morris's Socialism is almost the only attempt to embody the Ruskin-pre-Raphaelite ethos in an actual political programme. It was a brief and transitory phase of the Socialist movement; and when Morris is cited to-day as one of the Labour pioneers it is by people who have a strictly qualified sympathy with his ideas. Nor would it be true to say that his work has had even an indirect effect on the development of Socialist thought. By the end of his life the relative failure of his attempt to ally politics and the arts was already evident. Morris's historic importance is that he made this clear. He made his attempt and it failed; and the next inheritors of the aesthetic tradition gave up the attempt. Art falls back on its own aristocratic seclusion. "As for living, our servants will do that for us." The concern of Yeats with popular art serves as a personal inspiration; socially it is little more than a pious hope. If art is not to have its way with society, it will have its way in a private world of its own.

III. MORRIS'S POETRY

Morris's poetry presents something of a problem to the twentieth century. This large body of romance literature includes a number of the most famous stories of Europe, told in verse that is never less than adequate, and often extremely beautiful. It belongs to a still larger body of quasi-medieval nineteenth-century romance, a kind of poetry which for more than a century has contributed one of the dominant strains to English literary sensibility. Morris's own contribution to this literature is both in bulk and quality very considerable, and up to about 1914 the number of cheap reprints indicate that it was also extremely popular. Yet to the common reader of to-day it is "a legend emptied of concern"; and the student of poetry finds it so remote from most that seems of significance to him that he is far more likely to give his attention to the obscurest Elizabethan than to this respectable but vaguely obsolete interlude in literary history.

The fact is that our attitude to romantic poetry is badly in need of overhaul. Not so many years ago (it is well to remind ourselves), romantic, in the categories of the prevalent criticism, nearly always meant good, and classical, in the sense in which it is opposed to romantic, as often as not meant bad, artistically, and sometimes rather bad morally too. Dryden and Pope were not classics of our poetry, they were classics of our prose; and if Johnson's critical judgments were sometimes found to be right, it was necessary to announce the fact with an air of slightly defiant paradox. To the ordinary unspeculative literary consciousness, to write about skylarks or Lyonesse was both poetical and virtuous, while to write about urban civilised society was prosaic and slightly despicable. The eighteenth century existed for the purpose of being reacted against in 1798, and was otherwise a regrettable gap in the English literary tradition; and the notorious fact that it spelt Gothick with a k showed that its attitude towards the Middle Ages was trivial and complacent. It is necessary to repeat these outmoded tenets, for many people still more or less alive were brought up in this creed; and now that it has decayed it has left a deep stain on literary self-esteem, so that in good society it is not considered right to mention it any more.

However, if we do not mention it, recent literary history makes very little sense. Somewhere in the dead ground just out of our present line of fire advanced actions against the romantic values were fought, by T. E. Hulme, Wyndham Lewis and others. Yearnings, aspirations, covert alliances with the unconscious and the ideal were decisively put down, and a new classicism emerged, under the banner of T. S. Eliot; so new that it carried connotations that we had never suspected of belonging to classicism at all. For one thing it was surprisingly in alliance with the revised version of Catholic Christianity: for another, it had lost its concern with lucidity and disciplined and symmetrical form. While it insisted on precision of imagery in detail, and paid critical tribute to logical arrangement (Marvell's *Coy Mistress* derived some of its merit from being arranged in the form of a syllogism), it was in practice tolerant of a purely impressionistic arrangement of images, so that narrative structure and the more evident continuities of feeling disappeared. The result in Mr. Eliot's work was a new kind of poetry, technically exacting, yet formally very free and unstereotyped, in which the twin demands of the twentieth century, for order and for liberation from most of the existing orders, were reconciled. This poetry has now become classical in another sense—in the sense that it is a permanent part of our literary tradition. We are concerned here with the critical attitude that accompanied it.

In Mr. Eliot's criticism of poetry we find a constant concern about imprecision of feeling and the resultant vagueness of expression. He detects these inadequacies in nineteenth-century poetry in particular, but not exclusively there: Hamlet, for instance, is an "artistic failure" because the cause of Hamlet's emotion is not explicit in the play—it exists only in his or Shakespeare's unconscious. Poems which merely evoke a mood are gaseous and inexact. Seventeenth-century lyrics are approved because their emotions are clearly and precisely realised. The result is an extremely guarded attitude towards much of the poetry that the nineteenth and early twentieth century had accepted without question. Enthusiastic camp-followers carried this tendency further. Rather, one must suspect, to the embarrassment of their master, they sought to establish a strict surveillance over all forms of literary expression; an index was prepared of books which the faithful were forbidden to read with enjoyment; to meditate before a sunset or to express an undefined desire for some non-existent or not clearly realised state of affairs became an indictable offence. This last canon provided a link with a rather different school of criticism, a sociological one. Eliot had been careful not to imply that the merit of a poem depended on its application to contemporary actualities: but there were others who had stronger social and political interests, and for them, to write poetry that was not in some way a reflection of the contemporary social situation was to be suspect. The term escapist came into fashion and was applied to poetry about nature (since we are mostly town-dwellers now), or about remote historical epochs (since we ought to be concerned with our own stage in the class struggle). Thus the wheel came full circle, and to write poetry about skylarks or Lyonesse was now both artistically negligible and morally wrong.

The second war—and of course the peace—upset the political foundations of this kind of criticism: and since a younger generation no longer clearly knows what its literary polemics were directed against, their clarity of outline is somewhat dimmed. Apparently defunct romantic practices are breaking out again. A good deal of modern English painting, for instance, draws inspiration from nature and the appeal of the past: the influence of Yeats has counted for more with younger writers than that of Eliot: and Sidney Keyes, before he was killed at the age of twenty, announced his literary creed as romanticism, quite without panache, as though it were the normal literary attitude for one of his generation. But criticism has hardly caught up with this tendency yet. No new orthodoxy has established itself, and we are now in a good position to survey the canons of the inter-war years. This is not the place to do it: but we can make a summary attempt at placing a scheme of critical values, by seeing what it leaves out.

The romantic orthodoxy failed to give any adequate account of the Augustan age, which was held to have virtue only so far as it anticipated its own demise: the new "classical" taste failed to give any adequate account of the nineteenth century. Some writers obtain honourable mention for occasionally exhibiting qualities that are in general uncharacteristic of themselves: Byron, for instance, comes in strong as a satirist; while those like Shelley who are regrettably all of a piece are unconsidered or summarily dismissed. The kind of writing that has been most steadily ignored is the decorative romantic poetry on quasi-medieval or mythological themes, most of which derives ultimately from Keats. I have collected no dicta of the neo-neo-classical school on *La Belle Dame sans Merci* or *The Eve of St. Agnes*, and the student of poetry brought up on inter-war criticism will probably, if he is candid, confess to some bewilderment in knowing what to say about them. Yet to the general reader of a slightly older generation poetry meant pre-eminently poetry of this kind.

We shall find little enlightenment in going back to the

116

standards of late romantic criticism itself. To murmur something about the renaissance of wonder or strangeness added to beauty will not help us much. And to say, as was often said, that Keats, Rossetti, Morris or whoever it may be "recaptures the spirit of the Middle Ages" is not only unhelpful but untrue. Nineteenth-century romance is excessively conscious of being medieval, which makes it something quite different from that of the Middle Ages itself. (There is alleged to have been an early Cecil B. de Mille film in which the hero said, "Men of the Middle Ages, let us go on the Hundred Years War.") Archaism is finding a place as a definite literary value; and though we have had hints of this in Malory and Spenser, poets had never before thought of making it a fundamental part of their creed. The eighteenth century had justified its flirtations with the Gothic ages because, although strange, they were fundamentally natural; Sir John Witherington in Chevy Chase was as brave as the Marquis of Granby, and brave in the same way. The prime necessity for nineteenth-century romantic poetry was to be extremely different from anything in modern experience. Why should this happen just at this time? Why should "La Belle Dame" become the type of what poetry was expected to be, while the "Prologue to the Satires" becomes very doubtfully poetry at all?

The obvious and unphilosophical explanation, in which there is nevertheless a great measure of truth, is that it was a novelty. The familiar story of the change in taste in the latter years of the eighteenth century in fact says little more than this. No doubt changes in taste are sometimes brought about by no profounder motive. However, the revival of medievalism was very prolonged; and after the turn of the century it attracted to itself so much emotional energy that we may suspect something deeper than a mere change of fashion. The pursuit of the neglected past was not all of the same kind; some of it was scholarly and archaeological, the result of improving technique in antiquarian investigation. This was the impulse behind Percy's *Reliques* and the work of the ballad collectors. Much that looks like mere fantasy or romance to-day was actually inspired by this motive. Scott's non-medieval novels show this clearly enough—those on seventeenth- and eighteenth-century Scotland are a genuine and well-informed attempt at depicting the manners of a bygone age. The sub-title of *Waverley*, "'Tis Sixty Years Since", emphasises the sense of change and the passage of time, and all the novels of this group make much of the contrast between the life of the past and that of Scott's own day. More surprisingly, the same motive is found in his metrical romances, whose objects were partly historical and anthropological. *The Lay of the Last Minstrel* was intended "to illustrate the customs and manners which anciently prevailed on the borders of England and Scotland"; and the object of *Marmion* was "to paint the manners of the feudal times". But a good deal of romantic fiction and most romantic poetry was not intended to do anything of the kind. Its object was not to fill in gaps in our knowledge or to create a consciousness of history and its changes. On the contrary, its object is to take us out of the historical process altogether.

Most poets of the Romantic age were deeply concerned with the process of historic change going on before their eyes. Wordsworth as a young man watched entranced the birth of a new social order: for Shelley the poet is to be "the mirror of the gigantic shadows which futurity casts upon the present". Romantic liberalism became a dominant intellectual force and poets begin for the first time in history to look upon themselves as the *avant-garde* of a new world. Indeed after 1789 it was no longer possible for anyone of lively sensibilities to avoid the constant pressure of the sense of historic change. Hard on the heels of the Revolution came industrialism and a technical development more rapid than any the world had ever seen; and to follow that came evolutionary thought, replacing the old picture of life arranged in static categories by that of an animate world in a state of perpetual flux. In the pre-Reform Bill years this was not completely realised, and many of the most representative figures—Wellington and the later Wordsworth for example—were stoutly resolved to preserve the forms of a changeless society. By the middle of the nineteenth century the sense of change has reached the level of general consciousness, and there are few Victorian writers in whom the awareness, enthusiastic or dismayed, of being rapidly bustled along by science and history is not constantly evident. But even in Keats, who comes early in the period and was little concerned with politics and speculative thought, change is almost an obsession. *Hyperion* was to have been a poem about evolution —the supersession of one order by another which is superior to it; and the great odes are all about transience and its problem.

The fear of change, and the need to fight against this fear, are probably quite fundamental elements in the human psyche. One of the main results of the speeding up of the rate of change in the nineteenth century is the emergence of a vast compensatory longing for a changeless order, a world outside the historic process where this eternal hurry could be stilled. This in itself of course is nothing new. "All things are a flowing, sage Heraclitus said"—and men have always sought refuge from the flux in the changeless realm of the Ideas, or tried to defeat it by the philosophy of *carpe diem*. Now, however, the rate of flow was becoming so fast that the need for compensation was correspondingly greater. While culture and society were seen as largely static, or only moving very slowly, the inevitable change and decay was something to be regretted, but still to be accepted with resignation. Now that change is felt so much more violently in every part of life, resignation is no longer possible. The eager search for new sensations is one pole of romantic literature; but the other pole is this huge nostalgia for a timeless and unchanging order.

It is this pervasive emotion that attaches itself to most nineteenth-century medievalising, and unless we realise it, this large body of poetry is bound to seem mere aimless and rootless fantasy. Actually it has this very large and powerful tap-root running right through contemporary circumstance to the deepest levels of the psychic life. The insulation of some particular area in time or space from the ordinary processes of history is not in itself new. In Bannister Fletcher's history of architecture building is divided into "historical" and "non-historical" styles, the non-historical styles being those of China and Japan. They are of course only non-historical if you believe that all history comes from the Greeks and Romans: but traditionally our culture has believed this. In eighteenth-century literature the East generally appears as a fantastic realm, of which one can predicate ideal wisdom, unruffled contentment or impossible topsy-turvydom, simply because it is outside the well-charted stream of European civilisation. But the eighteenth century was pretty satisfied with European civilisation and did not find it changing uncomfortably fast: so it had little need to develop this line of thought except as a playful indulgence. The nineteenth century, which needed it much more, was just becoming aware of that large neglected tract of European history between the barbarian invasions and the fifteenth century: so it had its Shangri-la ready to hand, and one which had the advantage of being European, and of having left visible monuments behind. The progress of historical and archaeological scholarship vastly increased the knowledge of the actual Gothic ages, and the medievalism of Morris is a solid and well-informed affair compared with the gimcrack fancies of Horace Walpole; but the spirit informing it is still mainly that of the fairy-tale. The social philosophy of Ruskin and Morris shows a very different Middle Age from that in *Religion and the Rise of Capitalism*, where we see a society continually evolving new forms of government and economic organisation. The chapter on "How the Change Came" in *News from Nowhere* is a picture of a real society in the process of revolutionary ferment. Once the revolution has happened we find a society medieval in atmosphere and most externals, in which history seems to have stopped—for all the ordinary motive forces of history, want and misery, the desire for power, technical discovery and speculative curiosity, have all ceased to exist. The same world reappears, without the definite sociological purpose, in most of Morris's romances.

But even in an idealised medieval world men must still grow old and die (though in *News from Nowhere* they do it as infrequently as possible, and we are never actually allowed to see or hear of anybody dying): and the longing for a changeless society easily becomes fused with the longing for a world in which the life of the individual is eternal and unchanging. The Odes of Keats are a series of lovely casuistries on this theme, attempts to make the facts of change, old age and death tolerable—by finding a quasi-permanence in art, by making the individual nightingale immortal because the collective song of all nightingales has persisted, by showing autumn, not as the prelude to winter, but as a pause in time, a still phase where ripeness is all. Perhaps the fundamental reason why *Hyperion* was abandoned was not anything to do with "Miltonic inversions", but that its leading motive, "That first in beauty must be first in might", implies a continual supersession of lower by higher forms, and Keats's genius can only be satisfied in portraying static and rounded achievement. But at this rate we shall soon be talking about the death-wish, and it is probably safer for the literary critic to stay on this side of the pleasure principle.

One of the chief concerns of romantic poetry, then, is to come to terms in some way with change, old age and death. Since the romantic age is not one of an assured religious belief, the solutions are personal, sometimes eccentric, and more often than not in the nature of palliatives for an incurable world.

> But is there any comfort to be found?
> Man is in love and loves what vanished.
> What is there more to say?

There is comfort, however, in saying, with desperation or a pious hope, what with another part of the mind one knows to be untrue.

> Love's not Time's fool, though rosy lips and cheeks
> Within his bending sickle's compass come. . . .

> A thing of beauty is a joy for ever,
> Its loveliness increases; it will never
> Pass into nothingness. . . .

> I mock Plotinus' thought
> And cry in Plato's teeth,
> Death and life were not
> Till man made up the whole,
> Made lock, stock and barrel
> Out of his bitter soul.

These are the most energetically creative moments of romantic poetry. A more frequent source of comfort is to create a world that is only a shadow of the real world, in which its passions and affections appear in such pale colours that they are no longer exciting or painful, and death itself, being a passage from such a shadowy world, is attenuated to a shadow. This is the method of Morris's *Earthly Paradise*.

> Of Heaven or Hell I have no power to sing,
> I cannot ease the burden of your fears,
> Or make quick-coming death a little thing,
> Or bring again the pleasure of past years. . . .
>
> The heavy trouble, the bewildering care
> That weighs us down who live and earn our bread,
> These idle verses have no power to bear;
> So let me sing of names remembered,
> Because they, living not, can ne'er be dead. . . .
>
> So with this Earthly Paradise it is,
> If ye will read aright and pardon me,
> Who strive to build a shadowy isle of bliss,
> Midmost the beating of the steely sea. . . .

And it is not only here, in this prefatory lyric, that this aim becomes evident—it enters into the structure of the work itself. The poem is primarily a collection of tales, but they are set in a framework. A group of Norse wanderers set out from their plague-devastated home and come ultimately to a western island where live the descendants of an ancient Greek colony. The tales are alternate medieval and classical legends told by the wanderers and their hosts in turn. But the wanderers did not set out with the intention of holding a story-telling festival. Among them is a Swabian student of alchemy who is in search of the philosopher's stone and the elixir of life; and under his guidance they set out on their journey to find the fabled Earthly Paradise, the land of eternal youth where death never comes. They do not find it; they pass from land to land, and an elder of the island city tells them that their quest is hopeless. Yet they are received with honour and gratitude, because they bring tales of unknown lands and ages, of a Europe that the islanders have forgotten. The elder addresses them again:

Such, sirs, are ye, our living chronicle,
And scarce can we be grieved at what befell
Your lives in that too hopeless quest of yours,
Since it shall bring us wealth of happy hours,
Whiles that we live, and to our sons' delight,
And their sons' sons.

The only Earthly Paradise there is is the paradise of the tale-teller, the realm of art. The story-telling in the Earthly Paradise has the same symbolic function as the Grecian Urn in Keats's ode—it represents art in general, the only deathless land that actually exists: the only immortality is the kind of immortality predicated of Keats's nightingale. And at the end death has to be faced after all. The Epilogue does not carry the story of the wanderers any further—

Since each tale's ending needs must be the same:
And we men call it death. Howe'er it came
To those, whose bitter hope hath made this book,
With other eyes, I think, they needs must look
On its real face, than when so long agone
They thought that every good thing could be won
If they might win a refuge from it.

And here it seems to cross Morris's mind that the mere attempt to win a victory over change and death is an ignoble one. Is it not possible that the wanderers doubted the value of their quest, even as they set out? When they first saw the land that they believed to be the Earthly Paradise, might not some sense of shame have mingled with their exultation?

Did no shame blot the victory over fear,
(Ah, short-lived victory!) that, whate'er might grow
And change, then changeless were they fettered now,
And with blind eyes must gaze upon the earth,
Forgetting every word that tells of birth,
And still be dead-alive, while all things else
Beat with the pulse that mid the struggle dwells?

Morris is haunted by the fear that there is something despicable in the longing to escape the ordinary human lot, and with a part of his mind, as we shall see, is determined that the only honourable course is to face it stoically. But then the romantic protest comes uppermost, and he replies to his own question by saying that only those have the right to call the quest for the Earthly Paradise shameful who have no need of a prolongation of life "to right the blindness and the wrong" of the ordinary earthly course.

> Think scorn of these, ye, who are made so strong
> That with no good-night ye can loose the hand
> That led you erst through Love's sweet flowery land.

But those who accept with stoic or epicurean resignation the happiness that life can give, without any fear or revolt against its brevity, have not really understood much of life: some of the most significant moments of their experience have passed them by.

> Yet mid your joyous wisdom and content
> Methinks ye know not what those moments meant—

when in the middle of childish pleasure, or of love, would come sudden flashes of dejection and fear. They too are a part of experience, and the ideal of ataraxia that fails to take them into account must be a sham. Poetry, we may here interject, has never failed to note these moments—

> Fallings from us, vanishings,
> Blank misgivings of a creature
> Moving about in worlds not realised.

Medio in fonte leporum surgit amari aliquid. Even the urbane classical moralist, the perfection of whose verses outfaces death itself, realises that its shadow falls inevitably on the roses and the Falernian wine. For the romantic poet of Morris's stamp these intimations of mortality become signposts, directing all experience to the same end,

> The End, forgotten much, remembered yet
> Now and again, that all perfection mocks.

But we must strive to disobey their monitions as best we may. The wanderers were engaged on a quest that all who really love the loveliness of life must also follow, that all poets therefore must follow. Because the wanderers are also tale-tellers they stand as symbols of the poets and their function in the world.

And these folk—these poor tale-tellers, who strove
In their wild way the heart of death to move,
E'en as we singers, and failed, e'en as we—
Surely on their side I at least will be,
And deem that when at last, their fear worn out,
They fell asleep, all that old shame and doubt
Shamed them not now, nor did they doubt it good
That they in arms against that Death had stood.

They set out to find a literal emancipation from change and death. They did not find it: but found instead a relatively happy island, where they are honoured because they are tale-tellers, and where their tales, "all these images of love and pain", cheat the mind of the inevitable end for a time at least. So the romantic poet, through the idealisation of love, the assertion that beauty is eternal, or that he out of his own heart has created all things, including death—tries to evade death and transcend the common human lot: to find in the end that he has only cheated it for a time, that the shadowy isle of bliss has to be abandoned and the steely sea to be faced. The romantic poet is inevitably "the idle singer of an empty day", but it is no small thing to be; men will always need this refuge from the steely sea of mutability; the poetry is more than a refuge, for it is also the protest of man's nature against the conditions of his natural existence. The Envoi to the *Earthly Paradise* is addressed to Chaucer: for he and his compeers at least will understand its purpose:

Yet he and his shall know whereof we cry,
Shall call it not ill-done to strive to lay
The ghosts that crowd about life's empty day.

Morris implies that it is only stark insensibility or a pompously affected composure which can pretend that the ghosts do not exist or do not need laying.

Thus for Morris to collect the old stories, to accept them as they come, and to tell them again in a style that removes them as far as possible from the troubled actuality of life, is to perform the proper function of the poet. It is a curiously incomplete aesthetic. It would exclude tragedy and emotional realism. It explains some of Morris's odd but persistent views about poetry—that anybody who is any good ought to be able to compose it while weaving a tapestry at the same time, that the writing of poetry is a relaxation from the arduous practical business of life. This equally excludes all technical research and experiment, *les affres du style*. The rippling unemphatic rhythm of Morris's verse is explained: it is not due to a defect of energy, it is part of the quality he wants to attain—a state of suspended animation in which we trace the adventures of Jason or the knight of the Hill of Venus with just so much emotional engagement as to take us away from our own daily preoccupations, but not so much as to bring back "the agony and strife of human hearts" with anything like its real force. This has of course been the aim of a good deal of poetry. It is not absent from the *Odyssey*; it is the aim of late Greek and much medieval romance, besides Keats's *Endymion* and *The Eve of St. Agnes*, and the whole body of modern romance that derives from these sources, to which Morris's work belongs. It is not a poetic purpose which will arouse much sympathy at the moment; but we cannot be sure that this is anything more than mere fashion; a taste which has recurred so often may well recur once more.

This shadowy romance poetry may regain its popularity at any time; but it can never of course provide a sufficient poetic ideal; and it does not often provide a sufficient poetic ideal even for an individual poet. Keats was perpetually trying to work his way through it to something else, and it did not satisfy even Morris. The bulk of his work belongs to this genre—many of the lyrics in his early volume, *Jason*, *The Earthly Paradise*, *Love is Enough*; also the series of late prose romances—*The Water of the Wondrous Isles*, *The Sundering Flood*, and so forth, which in tone and spirit can be classed with his romance poetry. Needless to say, this does not represent all of Morris's nature, and he was only able to spend so long in this realm because so much of his active life was spent in a vigorous and polemical attempt to set the crooked straight. And there was present in his earliest verse a very different strain, a harsh stoical acceptance of pain and death, evident in many of the poems in the *Defence of Guenevere* volume, and continued in later life in his various adaptation and translations from the Norse.

The Defence of Guenevere itself and *King Arthur's Tomb* are attempts at the presentation of violent and bitter feeling, derived from Browning. They are not unsuccessful attempts but I am not sure how far they do anything that Morris permanently wanted to do. Browning's dramatisations of figures from the Renaissance and the Middle Ages often seem informed by the wish to show that although they lived so long ago these people felt just as we do. Possibly true enough, but not such a remarkable discovery as Browning seems to think it, and certainly not enough as the basis for a whole poetical philosophy. As a result the historical trappings often seem irrelevant, and Browning is most natural and most adequate in poems that frankly accept the commonplaces of modernity, like *Waring* and *A Portrait*. Possibly *The Defence* and *King Arthur's Tomb* suffer from a similar injection of close-range emotional realism into figures from Malory, whose original beauty lay largely in the fact that they belonged to a dream-world that could not be seen too close. But in such poems as *Sir Peter Harpdon's End*, *Shameful Death*, and *The Haystack in the Floods*, which have their source in Froissart, Morris is trying to take us into a world where cruelty and violent death are normal, and by doing so, to give himself the courage to face them, curtly and without comment.

> Godmar turned grinning to his men,
> Who ran, some five or six, and beat
> His head to pieces at their feet.
>
> .   .   .   .   .
>
> She shook her head and gazed awhile
> At her cold hands with a rueful smile,
> As though this thing had made her mad.
>
> This was the parting that they had
> Beside the haystack in the floods.

We need no travelling in time to-day to remind us of this aspect of experience: when the Victorians wished to bring it home to themselves they had to go back to the fourteenth century, or some other pre-liberal, pre-humanitarian age.

Morris felt a peculiar satisfaction in doing so. It was a compensation for the deficiency of nineteenth-century life.

Just as he felt that contemporary liberalism was based on a wilful blindness to the realities of the class war, so he felt intermittently that contemporary bourgeois comfort and security was based on a similar blindness to the inexorable harshnesses of life. Commonly he was glad enough to neglect them himself: his tastes were normally domestic, and, as he said, bourgeois. The world of *News from Nowhere* is an idealised suburban world. And the world of his romances attenuates fear, violence and death till they are only puppets to be played with. This evasion of the tragic and the terrible, and even of the inevitably unpleasant, was very much part of Morris's nature. Warrington Taylor, for a time the business manager of Morris's Bloomsbury workshops, remarks bitterly in a letter to Rossetti: "I know well the tendency at Queen Square to make life comfortable; anything rather than face death or a fact." But from time to time the compensating need to face death, bitterness and conflict makes itself felt. Hence Morris's adoption of revolutionary rather than reformist Socialism; hence the presence of *The Haystack in the Floods* next to *Two Red Roses across the Moon*: and hence in the end the powerful attraction for him of Icelandic literature.

The first appearance of this new interest is in *The Earthly Paradise*, where *The Lovers of Gudrun* is a version of the Laxdale Saga, significantly different in tone and temper from the purely romantic tales. It is doubtful how far at this stage Morris realised the difference. Medievalism to him was an inclusive and widely extended term. It included such different elements as the Eddas and Sagas, Chaucer, Froissart, Malory and the Border Ballads, even the whole cycle of Greek myth, for Morris deliberately treated it according to the medieval convention of the *Roman d'Alexandre* or the *Knight's Tale*. In 1869, however, he began the serious study of Icelandic, and from then on it occupied an increasingly large place in his mind. In 1871 he made his first journey to Iceland, and after that the soft scenery of Southern England and the Ile de France which had hitherto been the implied setting of most of his romances had to share its place in his imagination with the iron-hard desolation of the North. These two poles of his imaginative experience may be illustrated by two prose passages, one from the lovely description of Kelmscott at the end of *News from Nowhere*; the other from the diary of his first Iceland journey. Here is Oxfordshire:

> The river came down through a wide meadow on my left, which was grey now with the ripened, seeding grasses; the gleaming water was lost presently by a turn of the bank, but over the meadow I could see the mingled gables of a building where I knew the lock must be, and which now seemed to combine a mill with it. A low wooded ridge bounded the river-plain to the south and south-east, whence we had come, and a few low houses lay about its feet and up its slope. I turned a little to my right, and through the hawthorn sprays and the long shoots of the wild roses could see the flat country spreading out far away under the sun of the calm evening, till something that might be called hills with a look of sheep-pastures about them bounded it with a soft blue line. Before me, the elm-boughs still hid most of what houses there might be in this river-side dwelling of men; but to the right of the cart-road a few grey buildings of the simplest kind showed here and there.

And here is Iceland:

> I could see nothing at all of the gates we had come out by, no slopes of grass, or valleys opening out from the shore; nothing but a terrible wall of rent and furrowed rocks, the little clouds still entangled here and there about the tops of them; here the wall would be rent from top to bottom and its two sides would yawn as if they would have fallen asunder, here it was buttressed with great masses of stone that had slipped from its top; there it ran up into all manner of causeless-looking spikes; there was no beach below the wall, no foam breaking at its feet; it was midnight now and everything was grey, and colourless, and shadowless, yet there was light enough in the clear air to see every cranny and nook of the rocks, and in the north-east now the grey sky began to get a little lighter with the dawn.[22]

Love of the visible world was always the dominant sentiment in Morris's mind, and his imaginative experience is most beautifully expressed through that medium. To modern taste, the great defect of the verse tales is their diffuseness. *The Life and Death of Jason* began as one of the stories for *The Earthly*

Paradise, but soon grew out of all proportion, and had to appear
as a separate work. It is not padded or inflated, but every
scene and every incident serves Morris as a theme for profuse
descriptive embroidery, not dream-like in the Shelleyan manner,
and not in the least out of control like the descriptive passages
in *Endymion*, but deliberately elaborated like the detail of a
pre-Raphaelite painting.

> So still she stood, that the quick water-hen
> Noted her not, as through the blue mouse-ear
> He made his way; the conies drew anear,
> Nibbling the grass; and from an oak-twig nigh
> A thrush poured forth his song unceasingly.

This is charming, and Morris shared the medieval feeling
that you cannot have too much of a good thing. Visual effects,
and the life and movement of physical objects are admirably
conveyed.

> But as she spoke, rattling the cable slipped
> From out the hawse-hole, and the long oars dipped
> As from the quays the heroes pushed away,
> And in the loosened sail the wind 'gan play;
> But e'en as they unto the stroke leaned back,
> And Nauplius, catching at the main-sheet slack
> Had drawn it taut . . .

But there is no speculative thought, no background of ideas,
and the expression of emotion is hardly more than a token
payment. Medea has killed Pelias in the presence of his
daughters, under the pretence of rejuvenating him:

> But as she said these words, the luckless three
> Stared at her glowing face all helplessly,
> Nor to their father's corpse durst turn their eyes,
> While in their hearts did fearful thoughts arise.

The insipid effect is at least partly deliberate. Yeats called
Morris the happiest of the poets, and said that his happiness is
always a mainly bodily happiness. These romance poems are
reflections of Morris's ideal world, full of the multitudinous
beauty of physical things, which to be felt at its fullest intensity
must be undisturbed by passion and intellectual curiosity.

Even in the Norse poems, where the harshness and violence

WILLIAM MORRIS

that was excluded from the romances was meant to find its place, Morris's decorative and pictorial tendencies are in fact more evident. In *The Lovers of Gudrun* the powerful outline of the saga story remains, but the verse is still placid and unemphatic, and a great deal of it descriptive. *Sigurd the Volsung* changes to a more energetic metre deliberately, to suit the ferocity of the story, but Morris's natural tendencies are not much changed. He makes no attempt to reproduce the stark brevity of the original eddic lays, probably the most compressed and elliptical of all poetry. He takes his version from the relatively loquacious Volsunga Saga. But even this is immensely expanded, and for all the physical vigour of the verse, emotionally diluted; as can easily be seen by comparing such a passage as the lamentations of Gudrun in the verse of Sigurd with its counterpart in Morris's own prose rendering of the original saga.

It is possible that there were emotional reasons which led Morris to make two renderings of the Sigurd story, besides one of the Laxdale Saga, which has almost the same plot as the Sigurd-Brunhild episode, transferred to another setting. If so they remain part of his intimate biography and are not available for criticism. Morris seems to have been haunted by the story of the husband despised for a more brilliant lover, and to have taken a sombre pleasure in giving the story a heroic setting and tragic results. Morris loathed introspective poetry, and to all appearances his verse remains resolutely the poetry of the old objective world, the telling of traditional stories for nothing but their own sake. I am doubtful how far this attitude is ever really whole-hearted in the modern poet. We often hear with reference to the novel that the old aim of simply "telling a good story" has disappeared. Does not this mean that with the opening up of the inner landscape at the dawn of the romantic age, the earlier purely objective story-telling, about events and characters which are received as given by authority or tradition, has ceased to satisfy both writers and readers? What appear to be such are either symbolical expressions of the writer's own experience, or compensations for its inadequacies. Morris's narrative poems are mainly of the

131

latter kind; the romances supply the lack of serenity and beauty in the life he knew, the Norse poems the lack of heroism and tragic dignity.

What are we to say of this poetry that is not so much an interpretation of the poet's experience as a compensation for it? First, perhaps, that a good deal of this element exists in most poetry.

> By the help of an image,
> I summon to myself my own opposite,
> All that I have least handled, least looked upon.

But we should still be right in feeling that Morris's poetry is unrelated to contemporary experience in a way that medieval romance and earlier epic is not. Medieval romance took its contemporary readers, no less than us, into a dream-world. But it dealt with ideas—about love, chivalry, and super-natural forces—in which its readers really believed. *The Romance of the Rose* or the Grail story had a symbolic signi-ficance for their own times that can in consequence survive in a sense for ours. Even stories like *Amis and Amiloun* or *Aucassin and Nicolette* were using values that to medieval readers were real. Morris's *Jason* or *The Water of the Wondrous Isles* mean nothing beyond themselves; they show us figures on a tapestry, in which it would be idle to look for any further significance; and they have no more relation to nineteenth-century life than Morris's tapestries have to nineteenth-century methods of industrial production. It is the same with Morris's epic. *Beowulf* and the *Iliad* are interpretations of the heroic age, not indeed for the heroic age itself, but at least for a world in which much of the heroic ethos survived. The *Aeneid*, as an example of the literary epic, uses the old heroic themes but relates them to its own time by a conscious contemporary political purpose. Morris's Sigurd simply takes a heroic theme and restates it in his own idiom, but only as an example of a world that no longer exists and of values that have passed away.

What can we say of romance and epic of this kind, divorced from their age as romance and epic have never been before? Only, perhaps, that there are times when such poetry is neces-sary. Ancient epic and romances made poetry out of the sublimated ideals of a special class in society; but there are times when none of the prevailing social ideals can offer any permanent satisfaction to poetry. The period that had just had the Great Exhibition and was soon to have the Boer War was one of these. The attempt to adapt ancient heroic legends to the contemporary atmosphere could hardly result in more than the painful snuffle of Tennyson's blameless king. In such an age, if poetry is not to lose a great deal of its range of subject and emotion, it can hardly do other than accept a frank archaism, the treatment of themes from age past, unrelated to any modern reality, as samples of what mankind has been, or has dreamed about, and may perhaps again. So Yeats believed; and the modern poets who have not thought as he did have achieved excellence at the cost of a painful restriction both of themes and rhythms. Morris as a narrative poet is in much the same position as he is as a craftsman—one who keeps alive an obsolete skill, which seems hardly likely to mean much to the world he lives in, but which may nevertheless be keeping the door open for some necessary re-expansion of the artist's range, in some future that we cannot at the moment foresee.

Chapter IV

WALTER PATER

I. MARIUS THE LATITUDINARIAN

Burning with a hard gemlike flame has not been a popular practice in recent years; and we think of the aesthetes of the end of the last century, if we think of them at all, in terms of Yeats's brilliant dismissal of the nineties in the introduction to the *Oxford Book of Modern Verse*; or of Mr. Eliot's essay on *The Place of Pater*.[1] This last has the peculiarity of being largely about Matthew Arnold; but that is because its purpose is "to trace a direction from Arnold, through Pater, to the nineties, with, of course, the solitary figure of Newman in the background". This may seem a somewhat arbitrary direction; but appearing in this way between Newman and the nineties, Pater and Arnold are sufficiently placed for Mr. Eliot's attitude to become recognisable. His concern is with Pater as a moralist and writer on religious themes, and the most significant point about the essay is the close association of Pater with Arnold; or rather the reason given for this collocation—that they are members of a joint conspiracy whose object is to usurp the throne of religion and put culture in its place.

Let us begin then by considering a little the position of the cultivated agnostic in Arnold's and Pater's day. Mr. Eliot begins by considering *Culture and Anarchy*, and invites us to "raise an eyebrow to admire how much Culture has arrogated from Religion"; and he later suggests that Pater's attitude merely provides an individual variant of the same process. If he had begun with the essay on *The Study of Poetry* it would have been necessary to raise the eyebrow higher still, for there Arnold is much franker about what he is doing. He says quite simply that since belief in religious dogma has decayed, values derived from imaginative literature must take its place. A process whose total effect, Mr. Eliot says, is "to divorce religion from thought", "to set up Culture in the place of religion and to leave Religion to be laid waste by the anarchy of feeling". I do not think it can be seriously disputed that this was the tendency of Arnold's writing, if not its total effect; nor would it perhaps have been disputed by Arnold himself, except for the assumption that feeling is necessarily anarchic. It is, however, extremely misleading to attribute specifically to Arnold what was in fact the main tendency of nineteenth-century religious development. The breakdown of the argument from design, the mainstay of eighteenth-century orthodoxy, under pressure of evolutionary ideas (an unnecessary break-down, but still, it occurred); the similar breakdown of the traditional cosmology; the historical disintegration of the scriptures, had all, since the early years of the century, tended to drive religious thought back to subjectivism: to all these difficult questions

> the heart
> Stood up and answered "I have felt".

Coleridge had prophetically foreseen the necessity of something like this, and had pointed the way for this kind of apologetic: mainly through the influence of F. D. Maurice, it had found its way into current opinion among the young both at Oxford and Cambridge; and it found its poetical expression in *In Memoriam*. Naturally enough, without ecclesiastical or scriptural authority, what the heart felt tended less and less to resemble historic Christianity. It would also be misleading, however, to suggest that this movement, with its somewhat nebulous results, was due simply to confused thinking, or the use of a loose jargon. It is easy now to raise an eyebrow at the alarums and excursions, the panics and the strategic withdrawals of Victorian Broad Churchmen: but it is merely disingenuous to suggest that they had really nothing to worry about, or that they could have avoided their predicament by the use of more rigorous theological terminology. Orthodoxy to-day has various methods

135

of psychological accommodation which were not available in that more single-hearted age. Victorian agnostics and latitudinarians were constrained to a more naïve view of their position; they thought that on any reasonable interpretation of the evidence many things they had formerly believed quite simply were proved to be untrue.

There is no need to enlarge on the mental distress caused by these discoveries; it is a theme which Victorian fiction has treated very fully, in such novels as *Robert Elsmere*, *North and South*, and Winwood Reade's *The Outcast*. What is more significant is the resultant determination to preserve as much as possible of what still survived of the Christian tradition. Opinions about what survived are naturally varied: to some it was a vague theism; to some it was the figure of Christ as a purely human and historical example; to some it was the Bible as a repository of moral wisdom; but almost all were agreed on the maintenance of traditionally Christian standards of conduct. Robert Elsmere, for instance, after he is forced by his changing beliefs to leave the Church of England, goes on behaving in almost exactly the same way outside it; the pattern of his life is hardly changed. In a great variety of characters, and in many different forms, we find this constant desire to preserve certain moral habits and patterns of conduct, even when their historical and dogmatic sanctions are gone. It seems commonly to be assumed that there is something peculiarly perverse or wrong-headed about this. The objections vary from Chesterton's crude gibe at "those who do not have the Faith, and will not have the fun", to Mr. Eliot's more refined eyebrow-raising at Arnold's attempts to make a purely secular culture do the work of religion. It is surely the objections which are wrong-headed. It is not self-contradictory to say "This type of conduct is right, though the traditional sanctions for it are wrong". And if one holds this view it is perfectly reasonable to practise the conduct without any sanctions at all, or to attempt to find new and valid ones.

The purpose of Arnold's culture is precisely to do this. He hopes to find in the great undisputed classics of Europe a foundation for the European tradition of ethics and conduct, whose supposed supernatural foundations he believed to be gone. That is why there is so much that is moral, "truth and high seriousness", in his conception of the really classic: his famous doctrine of touchstones, the use of certain lines and passages as standards of the highest excellence, is a shoring of fragments against his ruins. Ethically Arnold is completely attached to the traditional moral scheme; emotionally he looks back with longing to the time when "the sea of Faith too was at the full". He intends to use the emotions associated with the greatest passages of the greatest literature as a perpetual monitor towards right action and right feeling; and he has not the slightest desire to alter the traditional conceptions of right action and right feeling. He wished in fact to go on behaving as if the beliefs of Dr. Arnold of Rugby were revealed truth, even when he had become convinced that they were not so. Nor is there anything disreputable about this; it is quite possible, without confusion of thought, to respect and try to perpetuate the moral practice of one's parents, without sharing their religious beliefs.

But what, one feels disposed to ask, is Pater doing in this company? For the whole emotional tone of his writing is strikingly different from Arnold's. If the road from Arnold to the nineties lies through Pater, it takes a remarkably sharp bend on the way. Pater has none of Arnold's nostalgia for the age of faith; on the contrary, he quite complacently identifies himself with modernity; he has none of Arnold's longing for certitude; instead, he shows considerable willingness to involve himself in the flux.

> Modern thought is distinguished from ancient by its cultivation of the "relative" spirit in place of the "absolute". . . . The relative spirit has invaded moral philosophy from the ground of the inductive sciences. There it has started a new analysis of the relations of body and mind, good and evil, freedom and necessity. Hard and abstract moralities are yielding to a more exact estimate of the subtlety and complexity of our life.[2]

We find here a quite contented recognition of the relative spirit of modern thought, and an obvious approval of the disintegration of accepted moral codes that has been its result.

Throughout his work we find the same tendency to hail the deliquescence of all rigid forms of belief. He likes to emphasise the informal, tentative and inquiring aspect of the Platonic method, and to minimise or depreciate Plato's realism.

> Sanguine about any form of absolute knowledge, of eternal, or indefectible or immutable truth, with our modern temperament as it is, we shall hardly become, even under the direction of Plato, and by the reading of the Platonic Dialogues. But if we are little likely to realise in his school the promise of "ontological" science, of a "doctrine of Being", or any increase in our consciousness of metaphysical security, we are likely, rather to acquire there that other sort of Platonism, a habit, namely, of tentative thinking and suspended judgment.[3]

The desire for metaphysical security, central in Arnold's life, is to Pater something a little unworthy; and the further we read in his work, the more evident it becomes that his kind of culture is not intended as a support for traditional certainties, but as a solvent. Pater's aim is not to defend a threatened set of moral values, but to release the sensibilities, to set them free to form new ones.

That Pater himself feared that his ethic might be a subversive one is evident from the fate of the conclusion to *The Renaissance*. This, which is probably the frankest and certainly the extremest version of his creed, was suppressed in the second edition, as it "might possibly mislead some of those young men into whose hands it might fall". This nervousness about presenting the findings of his own heart and his own conscience is characteristic of Pater; and it is probably responsible for the extremely compressed and elliptical form in which this short conclusion is presented. Whether Pater always realises how much he is saying is doubtful, but he is actually saying a great deal, and the wistful sigh of his sentences is apt to make us feel that they are more tenuous, more empty of content than they really are. When he worked and reworked these carefully moulded phrases, he was not concerned only with the minutiae of style, but with a prolonged and genuine development of feeling. In the case of this appendix to *The Renaissance*, we have to expand almost every paragraph by reference to pages in other essays and other books if we are to see what its real implications are; and Pater was perhaps not unwilling that his whole thought should only become apparent in this indirect and allusive way. Positivist assurance about the nature of things was deeply distasteful to him, almost as distasteful as controversy; he would rather suppress a passage than have to argue about it or defend it, and if there was one attitude he would have abhorred it was that of the overt revolutionary. He is therefore frequently guilty of that tiresome kind of reticence that consists in not following out the implications of what he says; or that even more tiresome kind that consists in giving reasons for what he says other than the fundamental ones. If therefore we want to find exactly how far he might have misled the young men, or in what direction, we must do a certain amount of piecing together of passages from different portions of his work.

When he prefaces the conclusion with a quotation from the *Cratylus*, λέγει που Ἡράκλειτος ὅτι πάντα χωρεῖ καῖ οὐδὲν μένει, and proceeds to discuss, in a brief couple of pages, the doctrine of the perpetual flux, we have to turn for further elucidation to the other place where he uses the same quotation, to the chapter in *Plato and Platonism* on the Doctrine of Motion. The Heraclitean πάντα ῥεῖ is fundamental to Pater's creed, and we find it appearing in one form or another throughout his writings. He does not, however, produce it as a piece of ancient wisdom; he regards the doctrine of Heraclitus as an early intuitive guess at a truth which modern philosophy and science have confirmed. He begins the conclusion to *The Renaissance* by saying "to regard all things and principles of things as inconstant modes or fashions has more and more become the tendency of modern thought". He means in the first place, it appears, scientific thought. The physical realities which we regard as actual are only the momentary combinations of forces that are perpetually at work and perpetually in motion in all nature and in all life. "That clear, perpetual outline of face and limb is but an image of ours, . . . a design in a web, the actual threads of which pass out beyond it." Pater seems quite happy about this. He shows no nostalgia for a more stable world-picture; and he is equally content to accept the complete continuity of man with nature. There is none of the Tennysonian discomfort about the scientific view of man's place in the natural world.

He then proceeds to reduce, in the manner of the eighteenth-century empiricists, material objects to sense-impressions; then to point out that the impressions are confined within "the narrow chamber of the individual mind"; and then to destroy the substantiality of the individual mind by suggesting that it reduces itself to the contents of consciousness, that these are only momentary impressions, the only continuity being given by "a relic, more or less fleeting, of such moments gone by". There is, of course, nothing particularly "modern" about this; we appear to have reached a radical scepticism like that of Hume, and as usual in such a situation, we begin to wonder where we go from here. But Pater does not really mean it. It is difficult to see where this atomised and solipsist epistemology is leading in the realm of conduct; probably nowhere. If the self is reduced in this way to a series of momentary impressions, each containing only a fleeting relic of such moments gone by, the elementary conditions for a philosophy of value disappear. And this is not what Pater intends at all. Like other sceptics before him, Pater is forced to rebuild with different materials the edifice he has just destroyed: like Hume he is destroying our supposed intellectual certainties in order to replace them by the authority of feeling.

In fact these introductory paragraphs of the conclusion to *The Renaissance* are little more than a pseudo-philosophical preamble; by painting a picture of dissolution and fluidity they set the emotional tone for what is to follow, but intellectually their connection with it is very slight. In the first chapter of *Plato and Platonism* Pater develops the idea of the Heraclitean flux in quite a different direction, and one which corresponds much more closely with his real intentions:

> πάντα χωρεῖ, πάντα ῥεῖ—it is the burden of Hegel on the one hand, to whom nature and art and polity, aye and religion too, each in its long historic series are but so many conscious movements in the secular process of the eternal mind; and on the other hand of Darwin and Darwinism, for which

"type" itself properly is not, but is only always becoming. The bold paradox of Heraclitus is, in effect, repeated on all sides, as the vital persuasion just now of a cautiously reasoned experience, and in illustration of the very law of change which it asserts, may itself presently be superseded as a commonplace.

Nay, the idea of development (that, too, a thing of growth, developed in the process of reflexion) is at last invading one by one, as the secret of their explanation, all the products of mind, the very mind itself, the abstract reason; our certainty, for instance, that two and two make four.[4]

What Pater wants to attack is not the existence of material objects apart from their being perceived, or causality, or the substantial existence of the self; or if he does want to attack these things, it is only as a mildly anti-dogmatic flourish. What he really wants to attack is the notion of an absolute and unchanging truth; and for this he wants to substitute a theory of development or emergence. He has in mind, vaguely enough, no doubt, some kind of evolutionism in ideas, an essentially historical way of thought which teaches "that nothing man has projected from himself is really intelligible except at its own date, and from its proper point of view in the 'secular process', the solidarity of the intellectual life with common or general history."[5] It is no use the young scholar asking himself whether Plato's opinions are or are not true in any absolute or final sense, he can only try to understand them in the setting of their own age; and as for the business of judging them, it is simply a matter of deciding what they mean to oneself in the setting of one's own age. The question of absolute truth is as irrelevant in philosophy as it is in literary criticism, where metaphysical questions are "as unprofitable as metaphysical questions elsewhere".

Braced by our bath in the eternal flux and lightened of the burden of metaphysics, we can now proceed to the next paragraph of the conclusion to *The Renaissance*. "The service of philosophy, of speculative culture, towards the human spirit, is to rouse, to startle it to a life of constant and eager observation." Philosophy cannot lead us to absolute truth, since there is no absolute truth; its pretensions in this respect are no more than moderately respectable delusions; but what it can do is to make us more aware of our immediate experience. It is not clear how philosophy does this; in the Winckelmann essay we are told that it is "by suggesting questions which help one to detect the passion, the strangeness and the dramatic contrasts of life". Pater does not elaborate the point; and in other places he frequently suggests that philosophy tends to lead us away from actual experience into a world of boojums, which are not real experience at all.

> Of course we are not naturally formed to love, or be interested in, or attracted towards, the abstract as such; to notions, we might think, carefully deprived of all the incident, the colour and variety, which fits things—this or that—to the constitution and natural habit of our minds, fits them for attachment to what we really are.[6]

The theme of the *Imaginary Portrait* Sebastian van Storck is precisely the conflict of experience and philosophy, the abandonment of what Pater regards as real experience, the winter landscape, the domestic comforts and pieties of an actual Holland, "in search of that true substance, the One, the Absolute, which to the majority of acute people is after all but zero, a mere algebraic symbol for nothingness".[7] But perhaps philosophy stimulates us to a life of constant and eager observation by contrast with its own colourless and impalpable abstractions: or perhaps Pater is aware of a mild professional predilection for philosophy, and wants to fit it into his scheme somewhere; and lulled by a soothing cadence is not disposed to inquire whether it really does stimulate us to the acute sensuous perception which he regards as the nearest thing to ultimate reality. The succeeding passage, describing the way of life, which should follow from these premises, is the crux of the essay.

> Every moment some form grows perfect in hand or face; some tone on the hills of the sea is choicer than the rest; some mood of passion or insight or intellectual excitement is irresistibly real and attractive to us,—for that moment only. Not the fruit of experience, but experience itself, is the end. A counted number of pulses only is given to us of a variegated dramatic life. How may we see in them all that is to be seen in them by the finest senses? How shall we pass most swiftly from point

to point, and be present always at the focus where the greatest
number of vital forces unite in their purest energy?

To burn always with this hard gemlike flame is success in life.[8]

All of which may well be true, though nothing that Pater
has said up to now really enforces its truth; the belief that time
like an ever-rolling stream bears all its sons away might have
led to a quite different conclusion, as the scepticism of Mon-
taigne is turned by Pascal to quite a different end. But the most
striking thing about this creed is the obscurity of its practical
consequences. The object of life is to be present always at the
focus where the greatest number of vital forces unite in their
purest energy; but obviously the focus is continually shifting,
and will be found in different regions by different people. There
is hardly any kind of conduct which could not be sanctioned by
this doctrine, including the conduct of the philosophic or
religious ascetic. The heroine of *Lady Chatterley's Lover* and
the Platonist in contemplation of the eternal verities equally
feel themselves to be at the focus where the greatest number
of vital forces unite in their purest energy. And this is precisely
what Pater intends. Though its expression is suppressed by
donnishness, timidity, and probably lack of physical vitality,
Pater has an immense appreciation of the variety and multi-
tudinousness of the world, and what is peculiar to his creed is
not its sensationalism, but its unwillingness to sacrifice any of
this variety.

It is not only that different men find their focus in different
places: each man finds it in different places at different times.
"What we have to do is to be for ever curiously testing new
opinions and courting new impressions." This does not imply
a search for the maximum intensity of experience. The man
who seeks intensity of experience does not commonly seek
variety as well: he finds that for him intense experience is only
possible within a fairly narrow range, and involves the renunci-
ation of many other experiences, desirable enough in their way.
But it is just this renunciation that Pater is unwilling to make.
"The theory or idea or system which requires of us the sacrifice
of any part of this experience, in consideration of some interest
into which we cannot enter, or some abstract theory we have

not identified with ourselves, or of what is only conventional, has no real claim upon us."[9] It is doubtful whether this is consistent with being always present at the focus of the greatest number of vital forces, a process which commonly involves much sacrifice for which we cannot see the reason, and renunciations which we cannot identify with ourselves, but which we soon find to be empirically necessary. And this reinforces the suspicion that for all Pater says about passion, eagerness and excitement, intensity of experience is not really what he is after; that whatever it may be to burn with a hard gemlike flame, it is something that takes place at a rather low temperature, and that the word passion has got into this essay not because it is particularly appropriate, but only because it is part of the pre-Raphaelite and aesthetic convention.

The Puritan or the ascetic is much more likely to have passionate experiences than the aesthetic liberal. It is the concentration of libido in a single channel, not the dissipation of it among a number of attractive diversions, that makes for intensity. There are natural monists and natural pluralists among the human race, and monism in any of its forms demands the renunciation of many lesser experiences in favour of one which is felt to be all-important. Pater always regrets such renunciations. But he does so in terms which may legitimately lead one to doubt how far he understands what is really involved. Plato, he says "is ready to sacrifice much of that graceful polytheism in which the Greeks anticipated the 'dulia' of saints and angels in the Roman Catholic Church. He does this to the advantage of a very abstract, and as it may seem disinterested, certainly an uninteresting notion of deity, which is in truth— well! one of the dry sticks of mere 'natural theology' as it is called."[10] It is not surprising that the man who can write this about Plato should show himself in writing of the age of the Antonines, as T. S. Eliot says, quite unconcerned with the intellectual activity which was then amalgamating Greek metaphysics with the tradition of Christ. "An uninteresting notion of deity." Pater hardly seems to be aware that he is thus casually dropping the whole tradition of Christian theology. However, the remark is true enough to his own feeling, if not to his historic sense; the metaphysical basis of monotheism is to Pater simply uninteresting, and is therefore abandoned. A new kind of pragmatism, not That is true which is useful, but That is true which is interesting.

Marius the Epicurean is the completest expression of Pater's religious attitude; though as usual it needs supplementing by reference to his other works, perhaps also to his practice in life. Aesthetically the book is an Imaginary Portrait enlarged, of the same genre as *Sebastian van Storck* and *A Prince of Court Painters*: its defect is that Pater found it difficult to fill the larger canvas, and had therefore to incorporate a good deal of translated and extraneous matter. But it has a more comprehensive purpose than the shorter portraits. It is the record of a religious development, and in its own day was widely taken as a contribution to the religious problems of the time. But fashions in religious development change, as in other matters; Pater's attitude is far outside the stream of current religious feeling, and it is now common to dismiss this aspect of the book as a mere aesthetic flirtation with the Church. It is as well, therefore, to recall at the start Pater's own statement of his purpose in writing *Marius*. In a letter to Vernon Lee, after speaking with some impatience of his wish to get the book finished, he says, "I regard this matter as a sort of duty. For you know I think that there is a . . . sort of religious phase possible for the modern mind, the condition of which phase it is the main object of my design to convey."[11] The importance of this is that, apart from any historical intention in the work, Pater is perfectly clear about its intended application to his own day. The religious development of a cultivated agnostic in the time of Marcus Aurelius is meant to indicate a possible development for a cultivated agnostic in the time of Queen Victoria.

It is perhaps worth while to consider for a moment Pater's personal religious practice. Externally he behaved very much as the normal devout High Churchman. As a boy he looked forward to taking Anglican Orders; and long after he had given up the idea himself, he was as a college tutor always particularly tender in his attitude to the ecclesiastical life, and anxious

145

to remove any doubts or difficulties from the path of those who aspired to it. He was an assiduous attendant at College chapel, where his attitude, especially during the Eucharist, was one of noticeably deep and solemn recollection. He was a steady advocate of compulsory attendance at Sunday services, on the grounds that many really wished to attend, but would be prevented by indolence if it were not made obligatory. In the years immediately preceding the writing of *Marius* he spent much time in the High Anglican community of St. Austin's, Walworth, and formed close friendships with some of its ministers.† On the other hand it was not uncommonly felt, especially in his early days, that his interest was mainly in ritual, ceremony, and ecclesiastical music. There is Jowett's famous remark, "Mr. Pater, you seem to think that religion is all idolatry". Under the influence of metaphysical reading he formed a transient idea (improbable though it may sound) of becoming a Unitarian minister; but later, presumably during the period of his early work and before the writing of *Marius*, he "used expressions which indicated an attitude of definite hostility to the Christian religion".[12] What are we to make of all this? Does it indicate a mere playing with the externals of religion, on a basis of real disbelief or indifference? It has become common to-day to assume that this was the state of the case; but judgments about the sincerity of other people's religious convictions are always dangerous; and I believe that this one does considerably less than justice to Pater. If we are to have an adequate account of his religious attitude his work must be read, if not with sympathy, at least with a good deal more attention than it commonly gets.

We must begin by considering his scepticism, which was not in its origins a religious, but a philosophical scepticism. It was not perhaps based on a very rigorous course of reasoning: but Pater read a good deal of philosophy, ancient and modern, and reached the conviction that "the relative spirit" was the only one possible to the modern mind. He came to feel that the

† There is much about this in T. Wright's life of Pater, chapter xxxi et seq. But the general tone of this biography does not inspire any great confidence in its interpretation of incident and character.

physical sciences, with their concentration on empirical knowledge, had rendered necessary the abandonment of all "high priori" doctrines in ethics and metaphysics also. As we have said, he was not at all disposed to regret this.

> What the moralist asks is, Shall we gain or lose by surrendering human life to the relative spirit? Experience answers that the dominant tendency of life is to turn ascertained truth into a dead letter, to make us all the phlegmatic servants of routine. The relative spirit, by its constant dwelling on the more fugitive conditions or circumstances of things, breaking through a thousand rough and brutal classifications, and giving elasticity to inflexible principles, begets an intellectual finesse of which the ethical result is a delicate and tender justice in the criticism of human life.[13]

With this attitude of mind there naturally goes a strong tendency to rely on immediate sensuous apprehension, and to be extremely suspicious of abstractions.

> Who would change the colour or curve of a rose-leaf for that . . . colourless, formless, intangible being Plato put so high? For the true illustration of the speculative temper is not the Hindoo mystic, lost to sense, understanding, individuality, but one such as Goethe, to whom every moment of life brought its contribution of experimental, individual knowledge; by whom no touch of the world of form, colour, and passion was disregarded.[14]

This aspect of his thought is indicated, too, in *The Child in the House*:

> In later years he came upon philosophies which occupied him much in the estimate of the proportion of the sensuous and the ideal elements in human knowledge, the relative parts they bear in it; and, in his intellectual scheme, was led to assign very little to the abstract thought, and much to its sensible vehicle or occasion.

It is natural, indeed inevitable, that with this temper of mind religion should appear as a matter of feeling, of sensible forms and practices, rather than a matter of abstract theological speculation. He describes such a religion in the first chapter of *Marius*—"A religion of usages and sentiment rather than of

facts and belief, and attached to very definite things and places".
This phase of religious experience is offensive to Protestant
tradition, and peculiarly offensive to the modern selfconscious
believer of any theological complexion; but it is of course what
religion has generally been to the great majority of the human
race. To the greater part of the faithful in all cultures, religion
has commonly meant customary ways of behaving, customary
ways of feeling, rather than formal theological belief. But in
the nature of things, such religion usually remains unanalysed
and unexpounded. What perhaps is found shocking and
repellent in Pater's position is that he attempts a sophisticated
defence of an attitude which would pass without comment in an
inarticulate peasant. To see what kind of religious sentiment
can grow from this modest root we have to follow the develop-
ment of *Marius*.

The first chapter, "The Religion of Numa", describes
beautifully the traditional "paganism" of the Roman country-
side, formal, serious, unspeculative, and rich in the pieties of
the home. Are we not meant to hear in it an echo of the decorous,
scrupulous Anglicanism of Pater's boyhood?

> A religion of usage and sentiment rather than of fact and
> belief, and attached to very definite things and places.
> A sense of conscious powers external to ourselves, pleased or
> displeased by the right or wrong conduct of every circumstance
> of daily life—that conscience, of which the old Roman religion
> was a formal habitual recognition, was become in him a powerful
> current of feeling and observance.[15]

> The persons about him, certainly, had never been challenged
> by those prayers and ceremonies to any ponderings on the
> divine nature: they conceived them rather to be the appointed
> means of setting such troublesome ponderings at rest. . . .
> But in the young Marius, the very absence from those venerable
> usages of all definite history and dogmatic interpretation had
> already awakened much speculative activity; and to-day, starting
> from the actual details of the divine service, some very lively
> surmises, though scarcely distinct enough to be thoughts, were
> moving backwards and forwards in his mind.[16]

> Then he thought of the sort of protection which that day's
> ceremonies assured. To procure an agreement with the Gods—
> *Pacem deorum exposcere*: that was the meaning of what they had

all day been busy upon. In a faith, sincere but half-suspicious, he would fain have those powers at least not against him. His own nearer household gods were all around his bed. The spell of his religion as a part of the very essence of home, its intimacy, its dignity and security, was forcible at that moment; only, it seemed to involve certain heavy demands upon him.[17]

I can find no "aesthetic" triviality here: only a singularly candid and sensitive account of the effect of a gracious inherited religion on an impressionable boy whose speculative faculties are just beginning to awaken. The stage to which this speculative activity conducted him is described in the chapter on the New Cyrenaicism, which corresponds closely enough to the doctrine of the conclusion to *The Renaissance*. Here the contemporary application is hardly disguised; one cannot be intended to miss the oblique reference to Matthew Arnold in the following:

> Pitched to a really high and serious key, the precept—Be perfect in regard to what is here and now: the precept of "culture" as it is called, or of a complete education—might at least save him from the vulgarity and heaviness of a generation, certainly of no general fineness of temper, though with a material well-being abundant enough.[18]

What follows is a fuller and less affected statement of the position already outlined in *The Renaissance*—the metaphysical scepticism leading to a determination to make the most of the here and now; and the belief that this can best be done by the cultivation of the arts. This statement of his ethical position is subject to the same limitations as the earlier one—that its practical consequences are extremely ill-defined, and that it is purely self-regarding. But the limitations are here seen pretty clearly. The Cyrenaicism of *Marius* therefore implies the possibility of development as the attitude of *The Renaissance* did not.

The development begins with the lecture on ethics delivered at court by Cornelius Fronto (chapter xv). The Stoic professor is drawn with little attempt at naturalism or historic probability. He is only a thin disguise for his author's own sentiments, so it is not surprising that he puts his finger at once on the weakness of Pater's position up to now. He puts the case of a Cyrenaic or Epicurean who feels after all the lack of a central principle of conduct, something to give unity of motive to behaviour which, if it has been conventionally moral, has hitherto been so for no particular reason. He finds it in the idea of a commonwealth of humanity, in which the highest ethical apprehensions of men would be as the laws of a single city. He quotes the words of Marcus Aurelius himself, and says that righteousness would be but a "following of the reasonable will of the oldest, the most venerable of cities, or politics—of the royal, the law-giving element therein—forasmuch as we are citizens also in that supreme city on high, of which all other cities besides are but single habitations". But as Marius listens to this discourse on the purely ideal City of God, his own thoughts take a different turn, "not in the direction of any clearer theoretic or abstract definition of that ideal Commonwealth, but rather in search of its visible locality and abiding place, the walls and towers of which, so to speak, he might really trace and tell, according to his own old natural habit of mind. . . . At moments, Marius even asked himself with surprise, whether it might be some vast secret society the speaker had in view: that august community, to be an outlaw from which, to be foreign to the manners of which, was a loss so much greater than to be excluded, into the ends of the earth, from the sovereign Roman commonwealth."[19]

The intention of this is hardly ambiguous. Does it not mean that Pater, as a result perhaps of his reading in moral philosophy, is becoming dissatisfied with the position of the isolated Epicurean, alone with his own sensations; that he feels the need of belonging to a society; that the need is not met by existing political societies, or by the notion of a purely ideal commonwealth, and that he is beginning to consider the claims of the historic Church?

But the Church after all is a society founded upon a belief: it is not a society formed for the purpose of being sociable, and one cannot properly belong to it merely because of the need to belong to something. Pater sometimes seems to be perilously near to that attitude. It is easy to laugh at those who admire the Church but unfortunately do not believe in God: but it is an unintelligent failure of the historical imagination not to see how real the dilemma was to many in Pater's age. Marius of course can hardly be represented as experiencing the conflict in quite this form: but we have a hint of it in the ride among the Sabine hills, when he reflects on the notion he has learnt from the lips of Marcus Aurelius: "'Tis in thy power to think as thou wilt." He wonders whether he can, by such an exercise of the will, adopt "the hypothesis of an eternal friend to man, just hidden behind the veil of a mechanical and material order, but only just behind it, ready perhaps even now to break through". Later, the Platonic discourse of Apuleius gives him the notion of a possible intermediary, "a celestial ladder, a ladder from heaven to earth". But the idea is too fantastic, too completely untested to command his assent. "For himself, it was clear, he must still hold by what his eyes really saw."

However, at the house of the Christian Cecilia his eyes do really see: and that is the importance of the episode. For Marius–Pater religious conviction could never come in the form of abstract theological doctrine; his scepticism is too radical: nor in the form of some supernatural fantasy: he is too determined to rely on the testimony of sense. It must come as an actual experience, the experience of a society which he can see, whose atmosphere he can feel, in which he has some hope of participating. So that the effect of Marius's first experience of a Christian society is felt as a series of impressions—impressions of sense, or feelings very closely connected with impressions of sense. He hears the singing in the church:

> It was the expression not altogether of mirth, yet of some wonderful sort of happiness—the blithe self-expansion of a joyful soul in people upon whom some all-subduing experience had wrought heroically, and who still remembered, on this bland afternoon, the hour of a great deliverance.[20]

As he goes through the house he receives a dominant impression "of all the various affections of family life under its most natural conditions, yet developed, as if in devout imitation of some sublime new type of it, into large controlling passions". He observes the funeral ornament in the catacomb.

Yet these imageries after all, it must be confessed, formed but a slight contribution to the dominant effect of tranquil hope there—a kind of heroic cheerfulness and grateful expansion of heart, as with the sense, again, of some real deliverance, which seemed to deepen the longer one lingered through these strange and awful passages.[21]

Nor is Pater in any doubt about the nature of these physical impressions, and their relation to a possible moral or spiritual world.

It was still, indeed, according to the unchanging law of his temperament, to the eye, to the visual faculty of mind, that those experiences appealed—the peaceful light and shade, the boys whose very faces seemed to sing, the virginal beauty of the mother and her children. But, in his case, what was thus visible constituted a moral or spiritual influence, of a somewhat exigent and controlling character, added anew to life, a new element therein, with which, consistently with his own chosen maxim, he must make terms.

Might this new vision, like the malignant beauty of pagan Medusa, be exclusive of any admiring gaze upon anything but itself? At least he suspected that, after the beholding of it, he could never again be altogether as he had been before.[22]

Marius, like T. S. Eliot's Magi, returns to his place,

But no longer at ease here, in the old dispensation,
With an alien people clutching their gods.

Later, he attends the mass at Cecilia's house.

And last of all came a narrative which, with a thousand tender memories, everyone appeared to know by heart, displaying, in all the vividness of a picture for the eye, the mournful figure of him towards whom this whole act of worship still consistently turned—a figure which seemed to have absorbed, like some rich tincture in his garment, all that was deeply felt and impassioned in the experience of the past.[23]

He hears the cry *Adoremus te Christe, quia per crucem tuam redemisti mundum*: and it seems to him at moments as if the very object of the cry was actually drawing near. We need probably look no further for the evident devotion of the sceptic Pater at celebrations in Brasenose chapel.

Later we have extracts from Marius's diary, mostly describing incidents which touch the sense of pity—the appreciation by the roughest labouring people of the beauty of their children; the sight of a girl who thinks her life a perfectly good thing spent in the service of a crippled brother. The aim is to show a development of feeling in Marius that is outside the range of Cyrenaicism, or the Stoicism of the Imperial court. But the experience of the Eucharist at Cecilia's house is the farthest limit of Marius's approach to Christianity. He dies uncertain, in the company of Christians, and comforted by their rites, but with no formal admission to their society, and no inward assurance of the truth of their beliefs.

A. C. Benson has written, in a passage which has been commended by T. S. Eliot:

> But the weakness of the case is, that instead of emphasising the power of sympathy, the Christian conception of love, which differentiates Christianity from all other religious systems, Marius is after all converted, or brought near the threshold of the faith, more by its sensuous appeal, its liturgical solemnities; the element, that is to say, which Christianity has in common with all religions, and which is essentially human in character. And more than that, even the very peace which Marius discerns in Christianity is the old philosophical peace over again.[24]

What Benson wrote and Eliot approved of course demands reverent consideration: but is this really true? It has become the fashion for some reason vastly to exaggerate the extent of Pater's liturgical preoccupations. It is perhaps inevitable, since the turn of the century, that Pater should be looked at through the distorting medium of the nineties, and the result is a composite picture of the ecclesiastically minded aesthete: we remember how "Johnson [Lionel] died by falling from a high stool in a pub"; and perhaps the final comic vulgarisation of the type in the Carling of Mr. Huxley's *Point Counter Point*. Eliot credits Pater with a few "conversions" in the generation after his own, and with the responsibility for a few untidy lives. These may indeed be accidental consequences of some of Pater's attitudes, but they have not a great deal to do with Pater himself, and they should not be allowed to get in the way of fair consideration of what Pater really said. I have tried to show that Marius, far from being drawn to Christianity by ceremony (he had found that as a boy in the religion of Numa) was drawn to it precisely by the sense of a community bound together in charity. It was the need for this that took him beyond his early Cyrenaicism; and it was in the society of Cecilia's house that he found the possibility of satisfying the need. Experience of a Christian society is not a disreputable motive for being attracted to Christianity; and if the peace Marius finds there appears only as the philosophical peace over again, how could it have done otherwise, since he never makes the final submission to Christian supernaturalism?

We may safely conclude, I suppose, that the final position of Marius was also that of his creator. And here an irritated orthodoxy will demand: But what, after all did Pater really believe? The sentiments, the intimations, the delicate longings for a spiritual revelation that is always just round the corner —what kind of intellectual conviction do they really cover? Part of the answer is likely only to irritate the orthodox even more; it is, as we have said, and as Pater himself is constantly saying, that he attaches very little importance to formal intellectual beliefs and inclines to test all these matters by their visible and sensible expression. Benson has suggested, however, that if there is a place where Pater's own intellectual position is indicated, it is probably in his review of *Robert Elsmere*.

> Robert Elsmere was a type of a large class of minds which cannot be sure that the sacred story is true. It is philosophical, doubtless, and a duty to the intellect to recognise our doubts, to locate them, perhaps to give them practical effect. It may also be a moral duty to do this. But then there is also a large class of minds which cannot be sure it is false—minds of very various degrees of consciousness and intellectual power, up to the highest. They will think those who are quite sure it is false unphilosophical through lack of doubt. For their part, they make allowance in their scheme of life for a great possibility, and with some of them that bare concession of possibility (the subject of it being what it is) becomes the most important fact in the world. The recognition of it straightway opens wide the door to hope and love; and such persons are, as we fancy they always will be, the nucleus of a Church. Their particular phase of

doubt, of philosophic uncertainty, has been the secret of millions
of good Christians, multitudes of worthy priests.[25]

It would indeed be tempting, with the evidence of *Marius*
before us, to take this as Benson does, as a characteristically
oblique revelation of the inner attitude of Pater's mind. Mrs.
Humphry Ward's famous latitudinarian romance would then
serve as a commentary on Pater himself, and he would appear
as a sort of Broad Churchman, a Broad Churchman who had
been to Italy. What would then distinguish him from other
latitudinarians of his time would be his superior sensitivity.
The element of unspiritual dullness in the Robert Elsmeres of
the age is that their persistence in something like their old
religious practices after the disappearance of their faith has so
much in it of mere habit: while Pater's outward conformity at
least springs from a fresh and vivid apprehension of the beauty
of holiness. Nor is this view of the matter altogether untrue:
it is a close enough picture of one side of Pater's mind.

However, we began by saying that Pater's ethos was
genuinely subversive, and it is now time to substantiate it,
in spite of this long discussion of his velleities towards the
Christian tradition. This can be done quite easily by con-
tinuing the quotation from the *Robert Elsmere* review. Stopping
at the point where Benson does we get the impression that this
is Pater's last word, that he is associating himself with those
who in spite of an obstinate scepticism are in some degree
believers, that the only question for him is how much or how
finally one is to believe. Pater goes on to say, however, that
the differences between believers of different kinds are not
unconquerable, and that it is not there that the really vital
question of the day will be found to lie. The real opposition
—he quotes the formulation of it from the book he is reviewing
—is between "Two estimates of life—the estimate which is the
offspring of the scientific spirit, and which is for ever making
the visible world fairer and more desirable in mortal eyes; and
the estimate of Saint Augustine". Between these two estimates,
he seems to imply, there is no possibility of reconciliation, there
is only the necessity of choice. And he thus reopens the whole
question, for it is this choice which Marius never made. Marius

realises dimly that the new vision of the Christian life "might be exclusive of any admiring gaze upon anything but itself". But he never accepts the full implication of this; and that is why he does not die a Christian.

This is also why we cannot fit Pater into the pattern of even the broadest of Broad Churchmanship. The Augustinian element is not the whole of Christianity, but there is no Christianity without it.

> The soul hath, through the same senses of the body, a certain vain and curious desire, veiled under the title of knowledge and learning, not of delighting in the flesh. The seat whereof being in the appetite of knowledge, and sight being the sense chiefly used for attaining knowledge, it is in Divine language called, The lust of the eyes.
>
> Thou art the Truth who presidest over all, but I through my covetousness, would not indeed forgo thee, but would with thee possess a lie. . . . So then I lost thee, because Thou vouchsafest not to be possessed with a lie.[26]

A renunciation is required, and to this Pater never commits himself; the whole development described in *Marius* after all takes place within the framework of the ethic of the Renaissance.

> While all melts under our feet, we may well grasp at any exquisite passion, or any contribution to knowledge that seems by a lifted horizon to set the spirit free for a moment.[27]

The Christian ethos is one of these exquisite passions, and one on which Pater's mind happens to have dwelt for long: but it has as its possible rivals "any stirring of the senses, strange dyes, strange colours, and curious odours, or work of the artist's hand, or the face of one's friend". Pater feels so exquisitely for a time the beauty of a Christian society that one almost fancies he is on his way to becoming a believer. But you have only to confront him for a moment with a real believer to see where his destination lies. Dante would have placed him unhesitatingly, just inside the gates of Hell, among the trimmers; and he has delivered his verdict on such; *Non ragioniam di lor, ma guarda e passa*; a verdict in which Mr. Eliot seems to concur, as he passes on his way from Arnold to the nineties.

PATER

However, let us turn this scandal to the ends of edification if we may. As much as many more decisive characters, the trimmer has a contribution to make to our culture; he is one who is genuinely in suspense, and he serves to remind us that suspense is a not dishonourable attitude. However undramatic a figure he may be himself, he exhibits in a peculiarly dramatic form the tension of a conflict between two powerful and equally balanced forces. The position is an exhausting one; and the weariness of Pater's style is not wholly constitutional; it is partly due to the continued presence of this conflict. His writing represents the slight and hardly won successes, now of one side and now of the other, in a contest which, however little we like to be reminded of it, is no nearer decision now than it was in Pater's day.

II. IMPRESSIONIST CRITICISM

It may seem that in thus tracing the development of Pater's ethical and religious experience we are deserting what was after all his major work; for if Pater was anything in particular he was a critic, and it was ostensibly as a critic of literature and painting that he exerted most of his influence. Yet if we try to recall the places in Pater to which we really go for critical enlightenment, from which we really seek information or exposition, very few come to the mind; the essay on Coleridge, possibly parts of *Plato and Platonism*. His critical writing has the same tentative and undogmatic quality as his dealing with philosophy and religion. He never makes pretence at objective judgment, and rarely at formal analysis. The body of his critical writing is not negligible, but much of it is propaganda for the arts, the outlining of a suitable attitude towards them; and much more is the recording of impressions which are only accidentally impressions of works of art at all; his sensitive vignettes of landscape or of character are done in exactly the same spirit. His position was the extreme subjective one, as he himself was well aware. He quotes Arnold's "To see the object as in itself it really is", but hurries on to say that the necessary preliminary is to know one's own impression as it really is.

157

What is this song or picture, this engaging personality presented in life or in a book, to me? What effect does it really produce on me? Does it give me pleasure? And if so, what sort or degree of pleasure? How is my nature modified by its presence and under its influence?[28]

And he goes on to exhibit his customary impatience of the science of abstract definition:

What is important, then, is not that the critic should possess a correct abstract definition of beauty for the intellect, but a certain kind of temperament, the power of being deeply moved by the presence of beautiful objects.[29]

It is noticeable that he makes no distinction between beautiful objects themselves and their representation in art; between "this engaging personality presented in life or in a book"; and his impatience with theory and abstraction leads him at times into curiously unsophisticated expressions about representation in art. Here, however, his main point is to insist on the direct contact of the critic's sensibility with its object, to get as close as possible to the original experience. "To define beauty, not in the most abstract, but in the most concrete terms possible, to find, not its universal formula, but the formula which expresses most adequately this or that special manifestation of it, is the aim of the true student of aesthetics."[30] He likes to point out that critical attempts to set *a priori* limits to the capacity of different artistic materials are always liable to be discredited by the event; and it is noticeable that he is attracted not so much to the main streams of tradition, but to works with a markedly individual or eccentric flavour of their own.

Of course the question, What is this song or picture to me? could become the overture to the grossest Philistinism—I don't know much about art but I know what I like; and it must almost inevitably do so unless some other questions are asked as well. What did it mean to the man who made it? What does it mean to the cultivated common reader? are both relevant questions; and actually Pater is not wholly unconcerned with them. He takes the common cultured background of his time for granted, without much attempt at revaluations and rehabilitations; and he is quite consciously concerned with historical interpretation. Arnold had contrasted the personal and the historic estimates with the real estimate of art. Pater is doubtful whether a "real" estimate is possible; if so it is a summation of the personal and the historic ones. He himself distinguishes between dogmatic, eclectic and historic criticism, and believes that the historic method is especially that of modern times. It bids us to believe that "nothing man has projected from himself is really intelligible except at its own date, and from its proper point of view in the never-resting 'secular process'".[31] This is meant mainly as a counsel of detachment, a warning against any contemporary *parti pris*, theological, philosophical or otherwise. It is the business of the student "to follow intelligently, but with strict indifference, the mental processes" of his author, not to use them as weapons in his private ideological conflicts. Then, having seen the object as clearly as possible in its historic setting, the student or critic must go on to the consideration of individual genius. "If in reading Plato, for instance, the philosophic student has to reconstruct for himself, as far as possible, the general character of an age, he must also, so far as he may, reproduce the portrait of a *person*."[32]

One may as well admit that Pater interprets this imposing programme in a highly personal way. Both his historical sketches and his portraits of persons are very considerably modified by the Paterian atmosphere. For one who puts the historic method so high he takes very little notice of literary history, or questions of attribution in painting. He has clearly no desire to appear as the expert on anything in particular: facts and dates, when they arrive at all, are slipped in shyly as though apologising for their presence; and some of Pater's work would be better for a rather more robust attitude to this prosaic apparatus. However, one is not disposed to complain that the seemly pages of the library edition are undefaced by footnotes; and indeed the very form of Pater's writing forbids anything of the sort. For Pater remains always attached to the essay, "that characteristic literary type of our own time" as he calls it;

a time so rich and various in special apprehensions of truth, so tentative and dubious in its sense of their ensemble and issues. Strictly appropriate form of our modern philosophical literature, the essay came into use at what was really the invention of the relative, or "modern" spirit, in the Renaissance of the sixteenth century.[33]

He contrasts it with the treatise, which "with its ambitious array of premises and conclusion, is the natural art-form of scholastic all-sufficiency". Part of the attraction he felt in the essay was the tentative and informal quality; but part of it was the possibility of embodying criticism in a literary form attractive in itself. Pater was always willing to sacrifice scholarly completeness for a pleasing unity of impression—even in *Plato and Platonism*, which aims more or less at utility, he quite visibly alters the emphasis of Plato's doctrines for the sake of his own chosen picture of Plato's character. Pater's critical writing then must be regarded mainly as a series of impressions; and if we were to call it impressionist criticism the suggested parallel with impressionist painting would not be wholy inapt. In both there is the formal allegiance to science, but behind it an essentially lyrical mood; the same neglect of structure and definition in pursuit of delicate evanescent effects that are felt to be more real and more important, because more immediate.

However, even impressionist criticism has its canons, and in dissolving glimpses scattered through Pater's work we can get some notion of what they were. The first, as we have suggested, is the denial of all dogmatism, the abandonment of all Johnsonian claims to be a judge of art and letters. In the *Guardian* essays, mostly on the works of living writers, this reluctance to judge is sometimes painfully evident. Pater clearly wants to condemn, for instance, the harshness and muddle of Browning's later work; but after much wrestling with the spirit he gets no nearer to it than this:

> After all, we have to conjure up ideal poets for ourselves out of those who stand in or behind the range of volumes on our bookshelves; and our ideal Browning would have for his entire structural type those two volumes of Men and Women with Pippa Passes.[34]

And this is all part of Pater's self-imposed scheme; he permits himself to express wishes, leanings, preferences; but not judgments.

A more important principle concerns the relation between art and morals; here the situation becomes more confused. Pater is generally regarded as the original apostle of art for art's sake, whatever that may mean; and he does in fact use the phrase and discuss it in several places. But he is equally insistent on the close connection between ethics and aesthetics; and his various pronouncements on the matter are hardly consistent with each other. Or more accurately, it is hard to discover what Pater's pronouncements really are, since he has the habit of putting his own ideas, often inappropriately enough, into other people's mouths. Sometimes when he praises a writer for his devotion to "art for its own sake" he merely means that he was a painstaking craftsman, as he does about Lamb in *Appreciations*. But the doctrine of art for art's sake can mean that art is a sufficient end in itself, not a contribution to life but the purpose of it, to the exclusion as far as possible of everything else. Sometimes Pater seems to commend this view, at any rate where the artist himself is concerned; as he does in the passage on Flaubert in the essay on Style. More often, however, he does not; and his customary tone does not imply approval of this kind of artistic asceticism. Far more typical of him is the attempt to treat life and art in the same spirit: a character in life and a character in a book are apparently to be appreciated in the same way: and in the conclusion to *The Renaissance* "any exquisite passion", "work of the artist's hand", and "the face of one's friend" are equally final, equally ends in themselves. Most likely we are meant to find his own view in his exposition of the Platonic one: that "art as such has no end but its own perfection", that it is in itself morally irresponsible, but that it has nevertheless the most powerful moral effects; that there is "some close connection between what may be called the aesthetic qualities of the world about us and the formation of moral character".

Wherever people have been inclined to lay stress on the colouring, for instance, cheerful or otherwise, of the walls of the room where children learn to read, as though that had something to do with the colouring of their minds; on the possible moral effect of the beautiful ancient buildings of some of our own schools and colleges; on the building of character, in any way, through the eye and ear; there the spirit of Plato has been understood to be.[35]

And there stands the spirit of Pater also. But this is not the whole story; Pater characteristically under-emphasises both Plato's puritanism and his own dissent from it. To say that ethics and aesthetics are connected is not to say much, unless we know also how they are connected, and what are their relative positions in the hierarchy. Plato ends by expelling the poets for moral irresponsibility; the aesthetic forces are so powerful that they must be firmly subordinated to morality. Pater is moving in quite another direction—towards some sort of inclusion of ethics in aesthetics. This is never fully stated, even in the conclusion to *The Renaissance*, but the deduction the later aesthetes made from his work is not illegitimate. His approval of ethical relativism and for more flexible codes of morality, his emphasis on the equal value of varied kinds of experience, are all tending this way. The whole tone of *Marius*, as well as that of the *Imaginary Portraits* and many passages in the critical essays suggests that moral goodness is a kind of beauty, one kind among many, and worthy of appreciation equally with the rest. Here of course the door is wide open to the ethical eccentricities of the *fin-de-siècle*: which it would nevertheless be a mistake to attribute to Pater himself. Here we step into a cloudy no-man's-land where the Idea of the Good and the Idea of the Beautiful approach and mingle in the sensitive mind; as at the highest level, I suppose, they really do mingle; where any formal statement of their relations does injustice either to the actual distinction between the two, or to their essential community. To confuse them too easily is perhaps a more venial error than to separate them too widely: and one who has never felt the beauty of holiness is not likely to know very much, in the end, about either holiness or beauty.

The question is closely allied with another which occupied much of Pater's attention.

Spirit and matter, indeed, have been for the most part opposed, with a false contrast or antagonism by schoolmen, whose artificial creation those abstractions really are. In our actual concrete experience, the two trains of phenomena which the words *matter* and *spirit* do but roughly distinguish, play inextricably into each other.[36]

And this itself is closely allied with one of Pater's major critical preoccupations—the relation of form to matter in art. Here, as always, his tendency is towards fusion, towards unity: and it is not always easy to see whether he is merely blurring outlines, or really transcending dualities in a higher synthesis. His ideal is the kind of art where thought and its sensible embodiment are completely fused. He gives various types of it —one he finds in the plastic art of Greece, and he discusses this in the essay on Winckelmann: "The mind begins and ends with the first image, yet loses no part of the spiritual motive. That motive is not lightly and loosely attached to the sensuous form, as its meaning to an allegory, but saturates and is identical with it." In poetry he finds the ideal type in the lyric "precisely because in it we are least able to detach the matter from the form". In music the matter and the form are still less separable; music therefore is the ideal type of all the arts. "All art aspires towards the condition of music."[37] The idea first appears in *The School of Giorgione*, and Pater finds it sufficiently fruitful to repeat it in the essay on Style. The thesis of this important passage in the Giorgione essay is that though each art has its specific sphere, they tend to transcend their own special limitations, and begin to approach or pass into each other. We have seen a similar attempt to reduce the several excellences of all the arts to a common scale of values in the theory of Ruskin and the practice of Morris and Rossetti.

It is Pater's distinction, however, that he approaches this reunion between the arts without the muddle and the pietistic flummery that so often obscure Ruskin's real intentions. The same essay on Giorgione includes a protest against the merely technical or the merely literary criticism of painting which stands out among the utterances both of its own age and of ours as a just and balanced statement of the case. He admits that each art has its own peculiar sensuous expressions, and its own special responsibilities. It is one of the functions of aesthetic criticism to define these limitations, "to estimate the degree in which a given work of art fulfils its responsibilities to its special material". This can only be done in the light of what he calls "a whole system of art casuistry"; using the word casuistry, of course, in its proper sense—the application of general principles to special cases. The special case which most needs that kind of consideration is that of painting, for "it is in popular judgments on pictures that the false generalisation of all art into forms of poetry is most prevalent". By forms of poetry he means, I suspect, forms of sentiment, and would include other kinds of confusion too; that, for instance which led Thackeray to turn a picture into "A sweet and touching hymn-tune, with rude notes of cheerful voices, and peal of soft melodious organ". And his statement is equally a protest against the other heresy, that the only excellence of painting is a purely technical one.

> To suppose that all is mere technical acquirement in delineation or touch, working through and addressing itself to the intelligence, on the one side, or a merely poetical, or what may be called literary interest, addressed also to the pure intelligence, on the other;—this is the way of most spectators, and of many critics, who have never caught sight all the time of that true pictorial quality which lies between, unique pledge, as it is, of the possession of the pictorial gift, that inventive or creative handling of pure line and colour, which . . . is quite independent of anything definitely poetical in the subject it accompanies.[38]

But there, of course, lies the difficulty. "That true pictorial quality that lies between" is precisely that which so constantly defeats verbal analysis; just as in the other arts it is when form and matter are so fused as to be inseparable, even by an effort of intellectual abstraction, that there seems least to say, least possibility of explaining how the effect is attained.

Pater's critical theory, then, sketchy and allusive though it is, is generally admirable. It provides a continual directive towards sincerity and against irrelevance. But it must be confessed that by no means all of these admirable intentions are fulfilled in practice; the general impression is inconclusive, even more inconclusive than Pater would have desired. The essays on Pascal and Winckelmann do succeed in their aim of defining both a moment in cultural history, and a man within it. The one on Coleridge, probably Pater's finest critical work, gives a lucid untechnical account of Coleridge's philosophical position and its relation to his poetry. But the essays on Lamb and Browne in *Appreciations* leave curiously little mark on the mind; and those on contemporary writers commonly add little to our understanding of them. More successful are the literary studies in *The Renaissance*—those on the two French romances and Joachim du Bellay. But they are hardly criticism in any substantial sense; they convey an atmosphere, and help us to perceive some subtle overtones that we should hardly have noticed for ourselves.

> A sudden light transfigures some trivial thing, a weather vane, a windmill, a winnowing fan, the dust in the barn door. A moment—and the thing has vanished, because it was pure effect; but it leaves a relish behind it, a longing that the accident may happen again.[39]

This, besides being charming, might well serve as a description of much of Pater's critical writing itself. And his criticisms of art belong almost wholly to this mode. They certainly do little to define that true pictorial quality that lies between the technical and the literary appeal. They are reveries, fantasies on pictorial themes; their value is in themselves rather than in any light they throw on their subjects. They include too much of mere capricious personal association to come within the critical field; and the essays on Leonardo, for instance, and on Botticelli, tend to split up in the mind of the reader into a few famous purple patches.

This is perhaps less than just to Pater; but it is just to say that the most vigorous and decisive criticism, in any of the arts, has been done either in the service of recognised tradition, like that of Johnson or Sir Joshua Reynolds; or as jungle-clearing for contemporary creative work, like that of Dryden, Coleridge, or, in our own day, T. S. Eliot and Roger Fry. Pater substitutes for these aims the spectator's pleasure, the spectator's interests; the reveries of an imaginative visitor to a picture gallery; the reflections of a sensitive reader on works and personalities that have fortuitously touched him. This gives us something very different from the sense of purpose in the critic who is upholding what he believes to be the true principles of his art, or attempting to shape the course of the art of his own day. Pater's triumph, and he had his years of triumph, between the late seventies and the turn of the century, is the triumph not of a purpose but of a temperament. His work, for all its lack of definition, leaves its own specific flavour in the mouth; and it is perhaps this which is his special contribution to letters. It would be unfair to leave him without trying to indicate in what that peculiar flavour consists.

III. THE PATERIAN TEMPERAMENT

As it happens, he makes precisely this attempt himself, in *The Child in the House*,[40] which has as its intention "the noting, namely, of some things in the story of his spirit, in that process of brain-building, by which we are, each one of us, what we are". There is no clearer guide to the elements that go to compose Pater's temperament. The note which is first struck is one which we do not usually associate with Pater—the note of domesticity and homeliness. He was later very uncommunicative about the circumstances of his own life, but what the first few pages of *The Child in the House*, with an almost Jamesian circumlocution, contrive to say, is that he was brought up in a suburb and loved it; and that ever after, this delightful, English and typically bourgeois sense of home remained quite fundamental to him.

> With Florian then the sense of home became singularly intense, his good fortune being that the special character of his home was in itself so essentially home-like. As after many wanderings I have come to fancy that some parts of Surrey and Kent are, for Englishmen, the true landscape, true home-counties, by right, partly, or a certain earthy warmth in the yellow of the sand below their gorse-bushes, and of a certain grey-blue mist after rain, in the hollows of the hills there, welcome to fatigued eyes, and never seen farther south; so I think that the sort of house I have described, with precisely those

proportions of red-brick and green, and with a just perceptible monotony in the subdued order of it, for its distinguishing note, is for Englishmen at least typically home-life.

This is true enough, and delicately observed; but not, one would have said, the appropriate *ambiente* for burning with a hard gemlike flame. On further reflection one realises that the passages in Pater which are done with most affection are often descriptions of homely and unexotic scenes; and that a tension between the familiar pieties and later ways of feeling that appear to contradict them plays a considerable part in the Paterian ethics.

> The wistful yearning towards home, in absence from it, as the shadows of evening deepened, and he followed in thought what was doing there from hour to hour, interpreted to him much of a yearning and regret he experienced afterwards, towards he knew not what, out of strange ways of feeling and thought in which, from time to time, his spirit found itself alone.

His longing for emotional security characteristically finds its satisfaction in the physical image of a familiar childhood spot, "a place 'inclosed' and 'sealed'", as he calls it with pre-Freudian simplicity, from which it is yet possible to look out upon other fields and other ranges of experience: "a womb with a view", in the crisper idiom of Palinurus.

From the outside world two streams of impressions flow in upon him, impressions of beauty and impressions of pain.

> From this point he could trace two predominant processes of mental change in him—the growth of an almost diseased sensibility to the spectacle of suffering, and, parallel with this, the rapid growth of a certain capacity of fascination by bright colour and choice form— . . . marking early the activity in him of a more than customary sensuousness, "the lust of the eye", as the Preacher says, which might lead him, one day, how far! Could he have foreseen the weariness of the way! In some music sometimes the two sorts of impressions came together, and he would weep, to the surprise of older people.

The lust of the eye brings with it a sort of weariness: later he speaks of "the tyranny of the senses", "a passionateness in his relation to fair outward objects, an inexplicable excitement in their presence, which disturbed him, and from which he half-longed to be free". In music (all art aspires to the condition of music) impressions of pain and impressions of beauty are both present; "a touch of regret or desire" mingles with his memory of beautiful objects, and "the longing for some undivided, entire possession of them". To the reader of Pater these sentiments are all familiar enough; what is important here is the effort at introspective research, the attempt to trace attitudes which, when they appear in his writing, are often put down to pose or fashion, to their real origins in childhood. One need not regret the absence of a later psychological sophistication, which if it might have taught him to push the investigation further, would also probably have made the confession impossible.

He likes to find some sanction for his sensuous preoccupations, "the necessity he was under of associating all thoughts to touch and sight", in Christianity, which, almost as much as ancient Greek religion, contrives to translate a great part of its spiritual truth into visible forms: and this absorption of Christianity into his private myth, or of his private myth into Christianity, is made easier by the dominance in him of the sense of pity (is there not some proverb about pity being akin to love?), the fusion of the sense of beauty and the sense of pain. For in Pater pity takes a sensuously appreciable form, "fastening those who suffered in anywise to his affections by a kind of sensible attachment".

We see the development of this in *Marius*, where it is in part the sense of pity, or to put it more noncommittally, some consequence of the feeling for suffering—the sight of the girl and her crippled brother, of the workman's boy injured by a fall of brickwork—that takes him beyond his earlier Epicureanism. And a similar complex of feeling seems to lie behind Pater's favourite cultural myth—the outcrop of pagan culture in the Christian world. Pater refers often to Heine's notion of the gods in exile taking modest employment under the new dispensation, and the two fantasies *Denys l'Auxerrois* and *Apollo in Picardy* deal with this theme. If they are not particularly successful this is probably because Pater is not altogether

168

clear about what he is trying to do. Denys-Dionysus has "a fondness for oddly-grown or even misshapen but potentially happy children; for odd animals also: he sympathised with them all, was skilful in healing their maladies, saved the hare in the chase, and sold his mantle to redeem a lamb from the butcher".[41] Yet he is later suspected of a brutal murder committed with a great vine-axe. Apollyon-Apollo "seemed able to draw the wild animals too, to share their sport, yet not altogether kindly. Tired, surfeited, he destroys them when his game with them is at an end: breaks the toy; deftly snaps asunder the fragile back. . . . The small furry thing he pierced with his arrow fled to him nevertheless caressingly, with broken limb, to die palpitating in his hand."[42] Denys and Brother Apollyon both apparently symbolise the same thing, "the power of untutored natural impulse, of natural inspiration". Is not Pater trying to suggest some obscure alliance in the natural world between love and pain, something beyond the pleasure principle which moves "the springs and handles of that great machine in things, constructed so ingeniously to play pain-fugues on the delicate nerve-work of living creatures"; a something which even Christian feeling finds it hard to assimilate?

The child in the house goes on to experience the fear of death —"the fear of death intensified by the desire of beauty"; and this fear is not, as often happens, suggested to his mind by religious books, but arises spontaneously; and religious sentiment first occurs to him as something that might light up and dignify these sombre imaginings. Hence comes a preoccupation with at least the externals of the religious life.

> He began to love, for their own sakes, church lights, holy days, all that belonged to the comely order of the sanctuary, the secrets of its white linen, and holy vessels, and fonts of pure water; and its hieratic purity and simplicity became the type of something he desired always to have about him in actual life.

But it is not wholly a matter of externals; the hieratic solemnities, originally appreciated as a means of tempering his own glooms and terrors, became symbolical of daily life at the most ideally perfect level.

Thus a constant substitution of the typical for the actual took place in his thoughts. Angels might be met by the way, under English elm or beech-tree; mere messengers seemed like angels, bound on celestial errands; a deep mysticity brooded over real meetings and partings; . . . All the acts and accidents of daily life borrowed a sacred colour and significance.

Sensibility—the desire of physical beauty—a strange biblical awe, which made any reference to the unseen act on him like solemn music, these qualities the child took away with him, when, at about the age of twelve years, he left the old house, and was taken to live in another place.

The essay ends with a recurrence to the note of its beginning, the sentiment of home. The child has been looking forward to the change from the old house, but at the end, a clinging back to the old surroundings comes over him, "so intense that he knew it would last long, and spoiling all his pleasure in a thing so eagerly anticipated".

It would not be hard to relate most of the later developments of Pater's nature to this piece of *recherche du temps perdu*. (It is not unlike Proust, with more primness and reticence, and none of the self-critical wit.) Through all the careful delicacy of the writing the flavour of what has often been called Pater's morbidity is still apparent. Morbid is often a question-begging term; but what is really meant by it here is I suppose the suggestion in Pater's writing of some half-developed sexual deviation, of which we catch hints in the alliance between love and pain, the half-fear of sensuous impressions, the resultant languor. And this raises the question of a prevalent sexual unbalance in much of the work of the aesthetic school: the dominance of erotic reverie in Rossetti; the incapacity or refusal of normal sexual experience in Ruskin and Pater; the more obvious manifestations of both in the nineties; all so generally felt that in popular speech the word "aesthetic" not uncommonly carries with it something of this connotation. Remembering too the continual evidences of homosexual feeling in Pater's life and writing, one almost inevitably begins to form a composite picture of a kind of temperament in which more or less suppressed erotic fantasy, combined perhaps with the frustration or diversion of normal sexuality; a preoccupation

170

with the periphery of religious experience; a tremulous sensitiveness to aesthetic impressions; a conscious pursuit of beauty; and the conscious cultivation of a precious or elaborate style, all play a major part; and the more usual kinds of adjustment and efficiency become unimportant. The type reached its climax of development in the *poètes maudits*, mostly of a slightly later generation, in England and in France; for they translated their sensibilities into terms of actual life; in Pater's more sheltered and more cautious career the characteristics are less obvious. It is I suppose sufficiently plain that the origins of this kind of attitude, if not congenital, at any rate go very far back in Pater's life, and owe very little to the social circumstances in which he found himself; though it is no doubt true that the influence of the Paterian ethos on a later literary generation is in part time's revenge on Victorian convention—the convention that the only possible type of sexual behaviour is tender romantic love consummated by perpetual monogamy. There is little danger now of that particular convention exercising a stifling effect on letters; but there is a new kind of Puritanism, a sort of self-conscious post-analytical rectitude, a knowing superiority over non-Freudian self-deceivers, which results in a tacit disapproval of the Paterian temperament, without much effort to do what is alone critically relevant, to find the effect of this temperament on the quality of his writing. This task is not made any easier by the fact that so many of what profess to be judgments on his work are really judgments on his psycho-physical constitution.

Yeats began the *Oxford Book of Modern Verse* with the Gioconda passage from *The Renaissance*. To a later generation for whom modern verse meant something that began to happen in the twenties, the point of this was not immediately obvious. Yeats's compilation, as well as a great deal of his own prose writing, served to remind them of the considerable influence of Pater's manner on the early part of this century. Its real character has perhaps not been wholly understood. For all that Pater says about the tyranny of the senses, his writing is not really marked by any particular acuteness of sense-perception. It is in fact mainly concerned with the moral and emotional overtones of sensuous experience, the feelings that arise posthumously from experiences of sound, form and colour, and the thoughts that are the products of those feelings. Much of Pater's work, in the *Imaginary Portraits*, for instance, consists of attempts to relate a philosophical attitude, such as that of Sebastian van Storck, to a temperament, to a culture, and beyond that, to a landscape and a physical environment. A thing which is worth doing; for the most rigorously logical system is after all the residual deposit of a thousand impressions that have gone perhaps unheeded, the ghosts of people, of places, of forgotten childhood impressions; which ultimately, however, fall into an ordered scheme under the power of a formalising intellect. He does indeed describe physical things, but tends at once to translate them from sensations into sentiments. Often his own ruling sentiments take charge, and he justifies this by choosing for his most elaborate set-pieces subjects which have some coincidence with his own dominant moods —Mona Lisa, and Botticelli's Venus. But even the marbles of Aegina, which might seem to offer little room for Pater's obsessions, become the occasion of a passage on the combination of tenderness and cruelty: and the red hawthorn, the first experience of beauty in *The Child in the House*, instigates a reflection on regret and longing, and its connection with the tyranny of the senses. This perpetual dominance of a certain emotional mood leads to some monotony in the writing, and to a languor in its rhythms. It is not only Mona Lisa's eyelids that are a little weary; Pater's generally seem to be so too. As a purely literary quality this languor was to be deliberately sought after by Pater's disciples, as we can see in Yeats's early essays; but in Pater himself it is the consequence of emotional obsession; and of conflict also, conflict going on quietly, and far underground, but still perpetual. There is a sense of constraint, too, in the more highly wrought passages, as of a man determined on sincerity, yet afraid of saying too much. And this constraint is closely connected with one of Pater's major virtues, a scrupulousness, a resolve, if not to say everything, at least not to under- or overstate what is said. This gives Pater's virtuosity a quite different accent from that of other practitioners of decorative prose, Ruskin, for instance, or de Quincey. Decorative prose of any kind, however, arouses little enthusiasm in our day; and perhaps no one but Yeats could in 1936 have boldly transcribed the Gioconda passage as poetry. Yet that is probably what it was—the only kind of poetry possible to a man like Pater, without the energy of self-dramatisation necessary for full creative work. Pater's practice of the genre is distinguished by a sense of order and control that is rare in prose poetry.

He is open to the charge of preciosity and affectation, and his deliberate obliviousness of most of the interests of mankind will always be viewed with impatience by those who demand a more obvious kind of effectiveness. We have shown, I suppose, that it was psychologically inevitable, a part of Pater's basic longing for home as a place enclosed and sealed against the turbulence of the outside world. Historically, the important thing to say is that this withdrawal was necessary. There were more than enough influences at work in late Victorian life to drag the arts into the commonplace of day-to-day existence. In an age that was boiling up for the Boer War and the windy degradation of the daily press it was necessary that a small group of hierophants should keep the sacred flame burning in some still retreat. It was not perhaps particularly good for their own health; the atmosphere of shrines is notoriously insalubrious. But it is not a very profitable exercise to estimate the value of an attitude like Pater's apart from its effect; its justification is that in a world not inclined to be sympathetic to such delicate plants, it has continued to exist; and continues to represent a certain phase of our culture. And it would be a mistake to suppose that Pater's preoccupations were altogether apart from the main stream of cultural development. One might reply to objections against Pater's achievement in the words he himself uses about criticism:

> In truth the legitimate contention is, not of one age or school of literary art against another, but of all successive schools alike, against the stupidity which is dead to the substance, and the vulgarity which is dead to form. [43]

It is in this after all quite fundamental conflict that retired and highly specialised natures like Pater's are capable of producing lasting effects: and it has been the purpose of this chapter to suggest that Pater's part in the struggle was a not dishonourable one.

Chapter V

FIN-DE-SIÈCLE

I. WHISTLER

THE loosening of the bonds between the artist and society is one of the most obvious developments of the *fin-de-siècle*. Many influences contributed to this, not the least important being the personal impact of Whistler. We left pre-Raphaelitism in the late fifties, already almost respectable. Indeed, for the most part official pre-Raphaelitism was naturally *bien-pensant*: Holman Hunt's Broad Church piety, Burne-Jones's gentle idealism, merged easily with the social purposes of Morris, and the revolutionary side of Morris's Socialism was surprisingly little felt. The arts and crafts absolved the Communism, and both were classed with the more or less accepted social doctrine of Ruskin, under whose influence it had come to seem right and natural for the artists to be concerned with the social order and the condition of England. Since the dominant influence was that of Ruskin, and since Ruskin was a critic, not a practising artist, it also seemed natural for artists to recognise the authority of criticism; and, for the creative artist, criticism represents society in general, the non-artist public. Rossetti was to some extent a renegade; his attitude to society was exceedingly simple; he divided it into two classes—those who painted pictures, and the others whose duty was to buy them. Tacitly he assumed that the painters should not be subject to any external claims, and to avoid them, after his earliest years, he refused to exhibit in public. But he was very little of a theorist, and he made no open claim for the absolute autonomy of art, or its inherent superiority to all critical and social considerations. In fact he hated and distrusted criticism,

175

especially in the darkened and suspicious years of his later life; and he became estranged from Ruskin mainly because Ruskin insisted on assuming towards him the role of mentor. But Ruskin's attitude to Rossetti was, for him, relatively humble: and Rossetti himself was pathetically distressed at overt social and ethical disapproval, as his reaction to Buchanan's "Fleshly School of Poetry" showed.

It was left to Whistler to develop an attitude, the germs of which had always perhaps been implicit in pre-Raphaelitism, but which had never actually developed among the pre-Raphaelites themselves—a belief in the superiority of the artist, merely because he is an artist, to anything that the non-creative critic could say about him, and his utter independence of all moral and social considerations. Whistler is, among other things, such a mountebank that it is easy to underrate the importance of what he was doing. In fact he is turning the whole aesthetic tradition derived from Ruskin into a different channel. He himself derived little or nothing from Ruskin: he did not read books, and his associations were French rather than English. His notion of the arts and their position was picked up from café conversation in Paris, not from sober speculation on Denmark Hill. But if it had not been for the energies that Ruskin had released, Whistler's success could never have been achieved. The generation that had been taught by Ruskin to attach a new importance to the visual arts, that was further learning from Pater to regard the arts as at least a semi-autonomous realm with laws of its own, was ready enough in the seventies to receive a new aesthetic doctrine, put over with incomparable wit and impudence and an agreeable Parisian chic. The effect on many minds was a curious fusion of Ruskinian ideas with the wholly incompatible ones of Whistler, which can be seen, in all its patchwork muddle, in the essays and lectures of Wilde. Whistler liked to pose as an aesthetic David alone in a Philistine world; actually he found a flourishing and receptive artistic public already half disposed to accept his own estimate of the importance of his function.

Whistler of course was far from appreciating this. He and Ruskin were predestined to come to blows, for Ruskin in the seventies was no longer the champion of innovation. The notorious climax was reached in 1877, when Ruskin wrote in *Fors Clavigera*:

> For Mr. Whistler's own sake, no less than for the protection of the purchaser, Sir Coutts Lindsay ought not to have admitted works into the gallery in which the ill-educated conceit of the artist so nearly approached the aspect of wilful imposture. I have seen, and heard, much of cockney impudence before now; but never expected to hear a coxcomb ask two hundred guineas for flinging a pot of paint in the public's face.[1]

Whistler sued him for libel, conducted his case with consummate wit and spirit, and was awarded a farthing damages. The costs left Whistler bankrupt: Ruskin's share of them was paid by public subscription. Our sympathies are inevitably with Whistler (unless indeed they are still more with the unhappy Burne-Jones, forced by friendship for Ruskin to engage in a distasteful persecution of another artist): but what is necessary to complete the account of the whole undignified business is that without the work of Ruskin and the pre-Raphaelites Whistler would never have been in a position to raise his voice against the established orthodoxies at all.

As it is, it was he more than anyone else who turned the aesthetes of the *fin-de-siècle* into a *côterie*, a closed corporation, contemptuous of outside values and jealously isolating themselves from outside influence. When Whistler ultimately quarrelled with Swinburne, he concluded the exchange with "Thank you, my dear! I have lost a confrère, but then I have gained an acquaintance—one Algernon Swinburne, 'Outsider', Putney." The implication is sufficiently obvious. The confraternity of artists is not only in honour bound to hang together, it is bound to enlist under Whistler's banner; and recusants are to be driven out to become outsiders in Putney, essentially no different from all the other outsiders who live in Putney. Soon indeed he had a great measure of success: not to accept a great part of Whistler's doctrine, even if one could not stomach Whistler, was virtually to write oneself down an Academician, a Philistine, or a newspaper hack.

The controversy with Swinburne outlines particularly neatly

the change in the aesthetic front. Before returning to it let us take a glance at Whistler's antecedents.[2] His notion of the artist's life had been largely formed by reading Murger's *Vie de Bohème*, while he was still in Babylonish captivity to the coastal survey at Washington. In 1855 he left America for good and came to Paris, where he found his hotel inhabited by Lamont, "the Laird" of du Maurier's *Trilby*, and by du Maurier himself. But he was by no means anxious to spend too much time in English company, and plunged enthusiastically into the life of the Latin Quarter, then in its Second Empire glory. The artists of Paris, unlike Ruskin and the P.R.B., were without the ambition of converting the bourgeois world, or of finding a position within it. Whistler became deeply imbued with the notion of artists as a class set apart, whose standards and aspirations were outside the comprehension of the vulgar. Such systematic training in painting as he had, and it was not much, was derived from Courbet and Fantin-Latour, the apostles of Realism. His first essays in painting were as a member of this school, and Courbet regarded him as a pupil. We may omit discussion of how many different meanings can be attached to "realism": the most relevant sense here is Courbet's abandonment of literary and historical themes, his frank acceptance of the life of everyday. Whistler followed his master in this; in any case his own tastes inclined him in the same direction. His early etchings—the series done in Germany, for instance—are candid sketches of the life around him, and when he came to England he devoted himself first to etchings of the lower Thames. So Whistler's development proceeded without benefit of botany, evangelical religion, or the reverent study of the pure Italian masters.

He left Paris and came to England in 1859. Here he met Rossetti and the men soon became friends. But their contacts were social and personal: their artistic theory and practice were too different for much real influence either way. He later referred to Rossetti as "no painter, you know, but a poet and a gentleman"; and when Rossetti showed him a sonnet he had written for a picture, Whistler said "Why trouble to paint the picture at all? Why not simply frame the sonnet?" Of course

the Ruskinian–pre-Raphaelite reform could have been des-
cribed as a kind of realism in intention, or at any rate natural-
ism. But the P.R.B. had interpreted their realism in a highly
Pickwickian sense. They meant patient study of detail and
minute accuracy of local colour; and if there had been some
notion of using contemporary subjects, few pictures of this
kind were actually painted, and their appeal was usually
anecdotal. To the casual observer, what makes the obvious
difference between pre-Raphaelite and Whistlerian pictures is
the deliberate archaism of the P.R.B., and its perpetual outside
reference to literature and history, contrasted with Whistler's
reliance on the purely visual appeal of modern themes.

Soon after Whistler arrived in England his painting under-
went a development that removed it still further from the pre-
Raphaelite ideal. The contemporary realist and the archaist
are at least both interested in their subjects as such. The
development which began with Whistler's *White Girl* in 1861
was to end in his calling his pictures Symphonies, Arrangements,
Harmonies in Grey and Gold and so forth. The musical ter-
minology is a more or less accidental affectation: Gautier was in
the air in Whistler's Paris days, and Whistler must have known
of his habit of giving his poems titles derived from the other
arts, among them the *Symphonie en Blanc Majeur*. But the
point is serious enough. Whistler is diverting attention from
the subject of his picture, the picture as *mimesis*, to its existence
in itself as a harmoniously constructed object.

> Why should not I call my works "symphonies", "arrange-
> ments", "harmonies" and "nocturnes"? . . . The vast majority
> of English folk cannot and will not consider a picture as a picture,
> apart from any story which it may be supposed to tell.
>
> My picture of a *Harmony in Grey and Gold* is an illustration
> of my meaning—a snow scene with a single black figure and a
> lighted tavern. I care nothing for the past, present or future
> of the black figure, placed there because the black was wanted
> at that spot. All I know is that my combination of grey and
> gold is the basis of the picture.
>
> Art should be independent of all clap-trap, should stand alone,
> and appeal to the artistic sense of eye or ear, without confounding
> this with emotions entirely foreign to it, as devotion, pity, love,
> patriotism, and the like. All these have no kind of concern with

it and that is why I insist on calling my works "arrangements" and "harmonies".

Take the picture of my mother, exhibited at the Royal Academy as an *Arrangement in Grey and Black*. Now that is what it is. To me it is interesting as a picture of my mother; but what can or ought the public to care about the identity of the portrait?[3]

We are already within hailing distance of significant form and the pure aesthetic emotion; and the next thirty years were to see Roger Fry's struggles with the same recalcitrant problem.† As a protest against Victorian anecdotalism it is all clearly justified; but when we ask ourselves how much of it Whistler really meant, or what he really meant, the answer is less certain. To say that art should stand alone "and appeal to the artistic sense of eye or ear, without confounding this with emotions entirely foreign to it", may be true enough to Whistler's own personal intentions, but it is quite inadequate as a statement about painting in general. It is true to say that the ostensible subject of a painting has often served merely as the occasion for a "harmony" or an "arrangement": but it is equally true that the subject has often signified exactly what it appears to do, and that the desire to do it justice formed a large part of the artist's motive. To give an account of Giotto or Fra Angelico without considering their devotional purpose would be manifestly absurd. And some of Whistler's admirers have pointed out that even his own pictures cannot be fully accounted for in his own terms. Swinburne protests:

It is true again, that Mr. Whistler's own merest "arrangements" in colour are lovely and effective; but his portraits, to speak of these alone, are liable to the damning and intolerable imputation of possessing not merely other qualities than these, but qualities which actually appeal—I blush to remember and I shudder to record it—which actually appeal to the intelligence and the emotions, to the mind and heart of the spectator. It would be quite useless for Mr. Whistler to protest—if haply he should be so disposed—that he never meant to put study of character and revelation of intellect into his portrait of Mr. Carlyle, or intense pathos of significance and tender depth of

† I have discussed it at greater length in "Ruskin and Roger Fry: Two Aesthetic Theories". *Cambridge Journal*, October 1947.

expression into the portrait of his own venerable mother. The scandalous fact remains that he has done so; and in so doing has explicitly violated and implicitly abjured the creed and the canons, the counsels and the catechism of Japan. . . .[4]

Swinburne could if he had wished have confuted his antagonist out of his own mouth. Whistler's passage about the portrait of his mother goes on as follows:

> The imitator is a poor kind of creature. If the man who paints only the tree, or flower, or other surface he sees before him were an artist, the king of artists would be the photographer. It is for the artist to do something beyond this, in portrait painting to put on canvas something more than the face the model wears for that one day; to paint the man, in short, as well as his features. . . .[5]

The revealing phrase is the last: it is hard to see how the artist is "to paint the man", in this sense, without the slightest interest in his past, present or future, regarding him simply as an appropriately coloured spot: and, as Swinburne rightly points out, Whistler himself did not do so. There is a great deal of muddle going on, as we might expect. One would not look to Whistler's impromptu fireworks for a considered statement of aesthetic doctrine; or to Swinburne's brilliant critical endowment for the particular gift of exact analysis. Swinburne is in effect defending the Ruskinian thesis that the work of art must be inextricably involved with the whole emotional life and the whole ethos of the artist. Whistler wishes to deny this, to say that the work of art is *sui generis*, giving a pleasure of its own, unconnected with anything else. He does not, as I do not think anybody can, really succeed in doing this. What he can do is to show that the work of visual art is involved with the rest of experience in a special way—that if it is to involve the other emotional experiences of the artist and the spectator, it must do so by formal means, not merely by calling up reminiscences of sentiments previously experienced on non-aesthetic occasions. But the cruder statement is what Whistler commits himself to, and it is this that exercised such a compelling effect on the sensibilities of the *fin-de-siècle*. It marks a sharp break with the aesthetic tradition derived from Ruskin, which from being a puzzling novelty in the forties had now become the accepted orthodoxy.

The famous Ten o'Clock Lecture[6] is the place to find the least fragmentary exposition of Whistler's ideas' Its delivery was not entirely inspired by proselytising fervour. The desire to make a personal appearance (not unknown to film actors and others whose manifestations before the public are normally at second hand) played a great part in it. For Whistler the desire to make a personal appearance was, unlike the film star's, not only the need for adulation and publicity, but also the desire to startle, to astonish and to shock. The point is not wholly trivial. The gentle penetration of truth and patient merit formed no part of Whistler's programme. Ruskin's sneer about flinging a pot of paint in the public's face, however stupid as a description of his painting, is a not unfair description of his method of approach to the outside world. Ruskin gently introduced his middle-class public to art by approaching it along the ethical route with which they were already more or less familiar. His patient analyses of the delicacies of nature and the detail of Gothic art furnished a gradual initiation into the mysteries; and the thoroughness, from its own point of view, of the visual education that he provided, soon created a large "artistic" public, most of whom had probably never touched a brush, or ever intended to practise any of the arts, but were yet convinced that they knew all about them. Whistler opens a brisk attack on this artistic public (although they had been the medium of his success) by insisting that their pretensions are humbug, and that only the practising artist knows anything about art.

> Art is upon the town!—to be chucked under the chin by the passing gallant—to be enticed within the gates of the householder—to be coaxed into company, as a proof of culture and refinement.
> The people have been harassed with art in every guise, and vexed with many methods as to its endurance. Their homes have been invaded, their walls covered with paper, their very dress taken to task. . . .
> Alas! ladies and gentlemen, Art has been maligned. She has naught in common with such practices. She is a goddess of

dainty thought—reticent of habit, abjuring all obtrusiveness, purposing in no way to better others. . . . She is, withal, selfishly occupied with her own perfection only. . . . [7]

For Ruskin it was the business of art "to summon the moral energies of the nation to a forgotten duty". The artist for Whistler is a social misfit, absorbed in private preoccupations of his own. He carves gourds, makes vases, builds palaces, because it pleases him to do so, and because he prefers it to battle or the chase. In earlier times he was the only craftsman, but he owes no obligation to society, nor society to him; "the people lived in marvels of art—and ate and drank out of masterpieces—for there was nothing else to eat and drink out of, and no bad building to live in". Above all—and this is the important point for Whistler—"The people questioned not, *and had nothing to say in the matter.* . . . And the Amateur was unknown—and the Dilettante undreamed of!" This is the ideal state of affairs—the artist works to satisfy himself; the people accept his products and are thankful—or not, as the case may be, it does not really matter: and the critic does not exist. This desirable condition Whistler regards it as his mission to restore. It is not his business to load a bewildered public with the burden of art. "No! I would save them from further fatigue. I would come to their relief, and would lift from their shoulders this incubus of Art." Art has been foolishly confounded with the sort of general culture in which all should be qualified. Nothing could be more absurd: it is no reproach to the scholar or the gentleman that he knows nothing about art—all that is required of him is to admit his ignorance. Art is not the common possession of the whole human race—the only inheritance common to all humanity is vulgarity; and those who claim a share in art for everyone only show themselves to be ignorant of its true nature, and condemn themselves to remain for ever outside with the vulgar.

Still worse is the middleman, the literary art-student, who deals with a picture as with an anecdote, and looks to it for elevating and touching suggestions. The painter's real motives are lost on him, but he revels in the emotional suggestions offered by the painter's subject. "So that a painting with a mountain, a lake, and an ocean—however poor in paint—is inevitably 'lofty', 'vast', 'infinite', 'glorious'—on paper." This mere parody of Ruskin's doctrines is accompanied by a more serious attack on naturalist principles.

> Nature contains the elements, in colour and form, of all pictures, as the keyboard contains the notes of all music. But the artist is born to pick, and choose, and group with science, these elements, that the result may be beautiful. . . .
>
> To say to the painter, that Nature is to be taken as she is, is to say to the player, that he may sit on the piano.[8]

It is not the business of the artist to copy leaves or blades of grass; but he may learn from the form of the leaf and the blade of grass "how grace is wedded to dignity, how strength enhances sweetness, that elegance shall be the result". Nature is the artist's raw material. He should not copy the formal harmonies of nature: he finds suggestion in them, and from them he composes his own harmonies. Such is Whistler's account of the business; and surely, as far as it goes, it is a much more adequate one than that of crude pre-Raphaelitism. Pre-Raphaelite theory, and often enough its practice also, had sacrificed design to the mere "following Nature", scorning nothing and rejecting nothing. It had sacrificed harmony of colour to fidelity of local colour, and that was the element of truth in the early criticisms of the garishness of pre-Raphaelite colouring. Whistler's preference for low tones and twilight effects was not merely a temporary fashion for the misty; it sprang from the need to see the picture as a harmony in its own right, not a series of separately noted local hues. An obscured atmosphere, a subdued and restricted palette are the easiest ways of securing this; perhaps indeed the only ones open to Whistler, for his technical range was never very wide. Of his painting, as well as his theory, one might say that it is excellent as far as it goes.

The further question of why the artist's harmonies and arrangements should delight us, and to what faculties they appeal, Whistler does not touch at all. For him this was all part of the meaningless jargon of critics and amateurs. The importance of his theory was not that it said very much, but that it was a starting-point, and that it said nothing that was wrong. It was a starting-point from which all sorts of divergent courses were possible. It could lead to the abstract art of the twentieth century; for what is it to abstract, but to pick and choose and group with science, the elements that have been found in nature? The analytical still-lifes of Picasso and Braque are clearly doing nothing else: and the most resolutely non-representational painting is only carrying the same process a stage further. On the other hand, Whistler's doctrine is still quite consistent with a kind of naturalism—Whistler's own kind of naturalism, in which he relied on mist or a low illumination to do his selecting and reconciling for him. For all his insistence on the freedom of the artist to make his own "harmonies", Whistler in fact always gives his own harmonies this kind of naturalistic support. It is possibly here that the split really comes between the abstractionist and the representational painter. Both obviously re-arrange nature to suit their own ends. But the first does it frankly, with no concealment of what he is up to, while the second, if he wishes to omit some detail, or to stress some element for purely formal reasons, feels bound to select an accident of light or viewpoint by which the subject could actually have been thus seen in nature. On Whistler's theory both processes are equally legitimate; on Ruskin's only the second. And surely Whistler is right.

His purely technical preference for low tones and absence of definition has really very little in common with symbolist and decadent admiration for obscurity and dream-like vagueness; there is very little of the greenery-yallery about Whistler, and his brisk pugnacity is very unlike the fashionable artistic temper of his day. But his twilight scenes on the Thames produced in him a kind of secondary infection of aestheticism which had probably little to do with his real inspiration.

And when the evening mist clothes the riverside with poetry, as with a veil, and the poor buildings lose themselves in the dim sky, and the tall chimneys become campanili, and the warehouses are palaces in the night, and the whole city hangs in the heavens, and fairy-land is before us—then the wayfarer hastens home; the working man and the cultured one, the wise man and the one of pleasure, cease to understand as they have ceased to see, and

Nature, who for once has sung in tune, sings her exquisite song to the artist alone, her son and her master—her son in that he loves her, her master in that he knows her.[9]

What rubbish! Whistler, the apostle of the contemporary, of form and colour for their own sakes, can only enjoy the warehouses and chimneys because in the dark they look like palaces and campanili; and supposes that only the artist can see the resemblance, as if every commonplace romantic writer had not said the same sort of thing; and feels at liberty, on that score, to patronise nature and the rest of humanity. It is hardly worthy of him—surely he is writing like the amateurs and dilettanti whom he most despised.

He was duly hoist with his own petard, for of course they set about admiring him for what he would have certainly have considered all the wrong reasons. When he returned to France in 1892 he became the idol, not of the artists, who indeed had almost forgotten about him, but of the literary symbolists. Mallarmé translated the Ten o'Clock Lecture into French; but one may be permitted to doubt how much of what Mallarmé read into it Whistler can ever have understood. One can imagine few persons less sympathetic to Whistler than the members of the Rhymers' Club, and few suggestions less likely to please him than that of Yeats, that the non-artist public could "make their souls" by contemplating his pictures. True to his principles, Whistler despised the prevalent aestheticism, the vociferous pursuit of art by those who are not artists. He derided "aesthetic" garments and the pursuit of the past, preferring a purely mondain smartness.

Shall this gaunt, ill-at-ease, distressed, abashed mixture of mauvaise honte and desperate assertion call itself artistic, and claim cousinship with the artist—who delights in the dainty, the sharp, bright gaiety of beauty?

No!—a thousand times no! Here are no connections of ours.

Know, then, all beautiful women, that we are with you. Pay no heed, we pray you, to this outcry of the unbecoming—this last plea for the plain.

Your own instinct is nearer the truth—your own wit far surer guide than the untaught ventures of thick-heeled Apollos.

Why this lifting of the brow in deprecation of the present—this pathos in reference to the past?[10]

The only place where Whistler's path ran parallel with that of the thick-heeled Apollos, the Ruskinians, the Morrisites, the followers of arts and crafts, was in a taste for interior decoration. And here the taste was of a very different kind. Morris's passion for simplicity had produced something very far from simple—walls hung with figured tapestries, or diapered with the luxuriant flowers and fruit of the Morris wallpapers; cabinets painted with panels by Burne-Jones; beds, chairs and couches carved, embroidered and inscribed. All conscientious craftsmanship, and expressing the joy of the workman in his work, but a standing contradiction to all the actualities of nineteenth-century life. With all this Whistler was totally out of sympathy, and it is to his credit that he realised how hopelessly incongruous it was. Without any of Morris's social interests, without any troubled brooding on the degradation of an industrial age, he devised a type of decoration that was simple, cheap and unobtrusive, that could provide an agreeable background to domestic life, of a kind available to all. Though the impulse to think at all about the decoration of our houses, the stimulus to change, came from Morris, the taste that actually prevailed came from Whistler. His ideal of interior decoration has been described by Mr. James Laver as a plain wall, with two pictures, both of them by Whistler; and he not infrequently saw it realised. In a more general way, the use of plain walls, clear light colours, few pictures and limited ornament is pretty exactly that which was first practised by Whistler at the White House in Chelsea. It is ironical that the concerted labours of the artist-sociologists should have left so little result, while the private fancy of Whistler, who cared less than nothing for the place of art in society, should have established the fashion that is now almost universal.

II. FRENCH INFLUENCES. THE NEW AESTHETICISM. THE RHYMERS' CLUB

It has been said that "the nineties" are not a period, but a state of mind—that is, that there are many writers who chronologically speaking were most productive in that decade, yet had nothing in common with what is supposed to be its spirit. There would indeed not be much sense in a grouping that tried to include both Kipling and Dowson. Taking the nineties then, in this way, we must say at once that they were a state of mind that originated in France. Anyone who is interested in the decadents as a psychological phenomenon will hardly find the answer to his questions in the published English documents. He will have to go to French literature to observe the genesis of the various eccentricities and obsessions that haunt so many of the imaginative minds of the time, and even for the literary models that showed the English writers how to give them expression. It is possibly for this reason that English "decadent" and "aesthetic" writers (to use the words without prejudice, merely as labels) are such small beer compared with their French counterparts. For the most part they are translators and adaptors of ideas not their own. Even if they have an obvious community of sympathy with their French predecessors, their sensibilities remain more or less literary and factitious, and have rather the air of being decked out for public exhibition in ready-made suits.

The exotic growths from across the Channel, on arrival in England, were of course grafted on to existing English stock. There is the muddled aesthetic doctrine contrived out of a mixture of Whistler and Ruskin: still odder is the fusion of Ruskinian and pre-Raphaelite ideas with others whose natural habitat is the pages of Gautier or Huysmans. French romanticism had had its perverse and horrifying aspects, sometimes displayed compulsively, sometimes *pour épater*, from relatively early days. It had early exalted art into a kind of religion, supposedly destined to supersede all other faiths. English mid-Victorian literature had already absorbed a certain amount of this influence, almost without realising it, certainly without the connivance of the general public. Pater's aesthetic gospel could not have been preached if Gautier, in the earlier romantic generation, had not initiated the doctrine of *"l'art pour l'art"* —the phase which Pater himself translates as "art for art's sake"—a sufficiently meaningless tag, but destined to become the slogan of the *fin-de-siècle*. Gautier meant by it chiefly two things—first the independence of art from political and social considerations; secondly the superiority of the formal perfection of art to any other kind of value. The first he expresses in the Preface to *Emaux et Camées*, a collection begun in 1848, amid the stormy opening of the Second Empire:

> Pendant les guerres de l'empire,
> Goethe, au bruit du canon brutal,
> Fit le Divan occidental,
> Fraîche oasis oû l'art respire.

> Comme Goethe sur son divan
> A Weimar s'isolait des choses
> Et d'Hafiz effeuillait les roses,
> Sans prendre garde a l'ouragan
> Qui fouettait mes vitres fermées,
> Moi, j'ai fait Emaux et Camées.

The second is affirmed in the famous closing stanzas of the same volume:

> Tout passe.—L'Art robuste
> Seule a l'éternité,
> Le buste
> Survit à la cité.

> Les dieux eux-memes meurent,
> Mais les vers souverains
> Demeurent
> Plus forts que les airains.

Still more was the influence of Gautier felt by Swinburne. He did not adopt Gautier's ideals of poetic form:

> Point de contraintes fausses!
> Mais que pour marcher droit
> Tu chausses,
> Muse, un cothurne étroit.

No false constraints, indeed; but no one could accuse Swinburne's muse of wearing tight boots. Nor was he ever a devotee of art for art's sake. It was in choice of subjects and general ethos that Swinburne felt Gautier's influence most. *Mademoiselle de Maupin*, with its ambiguous sensual themes, was an obvious source-book for romantics like Swinburne whose artistic production was largely founded on sexual disequilibrium. He describes it in his *Memorial Verses* on Gautier's death:

> Veiled loves that shifted shapes and shafts, and gave
> Laughing, strange gifts to hands that durst not crave,
> Flowers double-blossomed, fruits of scent and hue
> Sweet as the bride-bed, stranger than the grave.

There are continual parallels with Gautier's poetry; Swinburne would hardly have written *Hermaphroditus* and *Fragoletta* if Gautier had not already written *Contralto*; the spirit of the *Hymn to Proserpine* is precisely that of *Bûchers et Tombeaux*.

> Des dieux que l'art toujours révère
> Trônaient au ciel marmoréen;
> Mais l'Olympe cède au Calvaire,
> Jupiter au Nazaréen;
>
> Une voix dit: Pan est mort!—L'ombre
> S'étend.

This is Gautier, and here is the Swinburne echo:

> O Gods dethroned and deceased, cast forth, wiped out in a day!
> From your wrath is the world released, redeemed from your chains, men say.
>
> Thou hast conquered, O pale Galilean; the world has grown grey from thy breath;
> We have drunken of things Lethean, and fed on the fulness of death.

And Swinburne's general conception of pagan antiquity as something nude, splendid, joyous and cruel (we have already seen something like it in Pater's Apollo and Dionysus sketches) was certainly not picked up from Jowett at Balliol, but at the feet of Gautier. In particular, *L'âcre Venus du gouffre amer*, a Venus who is also a goddess of pain and cruelty, is one of the personages that Swinburne takes over from his master.

Of course Gautier, and the later French writers who similarly served as models for the English, were not introducing anything absolutely new to England. They were merely providing literary examples for the expression of certain kinds of sensi-

bility. French literature, formally more constrained, has always
been psychologically more experimental than English, and
what the English writers of the eighties and nineties found in
France was not so much new modes of experience as precedents
for talking about them. A fair amount of perverse nonsense
was produced in France, and imitated in England, in the hope
of a scandalous success, or as a protest against prevailing
bourgeois hypocrisy. The derivative English examples would
include some of the work of Wilde and Beardsley's *Under the
Hill*. But often enough, French writing was really revealing
the English writers to themselves, making genuine aspects of
their sensibility articulate for the first time. Swinburne's
algolagnia would have been the same if no other literature had
ever existed; but without Gautier and Baudelaire he would
have had considerable difficulty in finding means to express his
abnormalities. Any full treatment of the culture of the period
would have to explain the lavish and eccentric display of erotic
symbolism that made its appearance on both sides of the
Channel after the middle of the century—the obsession with
various illicit alliances between love, pain and death; the
femme fatale or the vampire; homosexuality, male and female;
hermaphroditism, and all the rest of it. No doubt some of the
mythological embodiments of these states of mind, notably the
conception of woman as some sort of mysterious fatality, were
what Jung would call archetypes, personifications of forces and
ideas buried very deep in the human psyche, which social and
literary decorum had formerly prevented from finding expres-
sion. But others were the result of purely private aberrations
of the erotic sensibility. No doubt the later nineteenth century,
in England as in France, was a period when the most sensitive
minds were liable to be driven into abnormality. No adequate
account of the English decadent literature could be given
without a pretty exhaustive study of reciprocal French-English
influences, and though there have been many isolated pieces
of source-hunting, as a whole this has not yet been done.
Most English studies of the *fin-de-siècle* tend to hover in fascin-
ated speechlessness round the strange divagations of the age,
and end by saying almost nothing at all. The whole field,

French and English, has been treated with exemplary fullness, from a specialised point of view, by Dr. Mario Praz in *The Romantic Agony*, and without further extensive explorations into literary history and psychological interpretation, nothing could be added from the English side to what is contained in that very thoroughly documented work.

We may indicate, however, a few parallels and a few lines of divergence. Gautier belongs to an earlier generation, and must be considered an influential forerunner. And Gautier gave rise to Baudelaire. Swinburne should be the Baudelaire of the English movement; he was probably considered so both by himself and others. He hails Baudelaire as brother in *Ave atque Vale*, and Taine described his verse as "dans le genre de Baudelaire". But it is here that we come to what is probably the weightiest difference between French and English literary development at this time. England has no Baudelaire. The parallel between him and Swinburne is superficial; Swinburne is an altogether smaller phenomenon. Swinburne has probably not lost much in general estimation since the end of the last century, but neither has he gained. He is read, and I suppose will continue to be read, as a virtuoso on the English metrical keyboard, much of whose significance lies in his versification for its own sake. The dash and vitality of his best verse is at the service of a rather monotonous range of ideas, and his best effects are as a rule merely verbal. To say this is not merely to depreciate his work; poetry is made with words; but it is to warn us against looking in him for kinds of significance that are not there. The Victorian *enfant terrible* retains a certain lasting charm; his subjects had an exotic appeal to English readers, and add an unusual and individual note to English verse; but their relevance remains a private one. Swinburne hardly ever succeeds in tying up his eccentric emotional patterns with the general experience of mankind, and his hymns to pain, passion, death and the gods remain the expression of a sensibility that is more or less *détraqué*, not comments on the human situation. However little this tells us about Swinburne as a person, it is perhaps a fair enough summary of the position he has occupied in English poetry for the last fifty years.

By contrast, we have seen the importance of Baudelaire to the modern world steadily increasing. Official opinion at the end of the last century may well be represented by Lanson:

> Son degout d'être ne parait pas un produit de mésaventures biographiques: il se présente comme une conception generale, supérieure à l'esprit qui se l'applique. Obsédé et assoiffé de la mort, Baudelaire, sans être chrétien, nous rapelle le Christianisme angoissé du XVe siècle. . . . Une originale mixture d'idéalisme ardente et de fétide sensualité se fait en cette poésie.[12]

This judgment, from no very enthusiastic admirer, picks out at once the fundamental difference between Swinburne and Baudelaire. The habit of dwelling on the perverse and the horrifying which they have in common is quite differently motivated in the two men. In Baudelaire it is not the result, or not merely the result, of *mésaventures biographiques*, it is the expression of a metaphysical disgust, the final horror of a man who believes in original sin, but not in the existence of God. Swinburne in comparison with him remains a naïvely rebellious asserter of romantic liberty, with specialised sexual tastes. Swinburne's idealised pagan world is Baudelaire's Cythère—

> Eldorado banal de tous les vieux garçons.
> Regardez! apres tout, c'est une pauvre terre.

Since Lanson's day Baudelaire's significance has been steadily growing: so that we find an English scholar of to-day, Miss Enid Starkie, defining his position in the European tradition as follows:

> For a variety of reasons, not all having a bearing on literature, Baudelaire seems to have been generally accepted as the European poet best able to make an appeal to modern man, and to express his essence, modern man the product of all the revolutions— political, social and industrial—which have ploughed up the world since the Revolution of 1789. . . . The problems which engrossed him were those which time has not changed, but to which it has only given a different colouring. What interested him was not the temporary manifestations of this contradictory and complex creature called man, but his eternal essence; the problem of his aspirations towards goodness and beauty combined with his proclivity towards sin and vice. The problem of sin—and particularly its illusory attraction—never ceased to

preoccupy him, and his aim was to discover its nature. . . .
Many are in revolt as he was, against the old hierarchy of moral
standards, like him they accept the inherent evil and sinful
nature of man—or of one side of him at least—but they do not
understand any more than he did the essence of sin, nor do they
know with what to replace the old disciplines and the old ideals,
much as they need some focus for their wandering aspirations.[13]

I quote this passage at length, for it says of Baudelaire pre-
cisely what we cannot say of any English writer of the time.
His perversities and disgusts are not the eccentricities of a
temperament, but powerful symbols of something that is
omnipresent in human life—what Baudelaire himself, however
untheologically, called original sin, the mitigation of which was
the only object of civilisation. So, at the end of the introduction
to *Les Fleurs du Mal*, the "hypocrite lecteur, mon semblable,
mon frère", cannot but be acknowledged by anyone who has
really discovered what Baudelaire was writing about. I doubt
if Swinburne, or any of the later writers, Wilde or Dowson,
who drew directly or indirectly from Baudelaire, ever began to
realise this. They dwelt rather on the difference between
themselves and their fellows: with the result that their eccen-
tricities remain eccentricities, their confessions remain at the
best private documents; at the worst, that most disgusting of
all kinds of literature, the intimate confession paraded before
the public in fancy dress. Baudelaire became the starting-point
for a whole new generation of writers; in France we have the
symbolists, one of the greatest and most far-reaching of modern
literary schools; in England we have only the nineties.

As a type of French-English literary relations at this time
we may take the case of Wilde's *Picture of Dorian Gray*. The
theme is typical enough—the degradation of a beautiful youth
by a cynical and immoral mentor. When Lord Henry Wotton,
the evil genius of the piece, wishes to further the process of
corrupting Dorian Gray, he lends him a certain yellow-backed
French novel.

It was a novel without a plot, and with only one character,
being, indeed, simply a psychological study of a certain young
Parisian, who spent his life trying to realise in the nineteenth
century all the passions and modes of thought that belonged to

every century except his own, and to sum up, as it were, in himself the various moods through which the world-spirit had ever passed, loving for their mere artificiality those renunciations that men have unwisely called virtue, as much as those natural rebellions that wise men still call sin. The style in which it was written was that curious jewelled style, vivid and obscure at once, full of argot and archaisms, of technical expressions and of elaborate paraphrases, that characterises the work of some of the finest artists of the French school of Symbolistes. There were in it metaphors as monstrous as orchids and as subtle in colour. The life of the senses as described in terms of mystical philosophy. One hardly knew at times whether one was reading the spiritual ecstasies of some medieval saint or the morbid confessions of a modern sinner. It was a poisonous book. The heavy odour of incense seemed to cling about its pages and to trouble the brain.[14]

Wilde never tells us its name, but it is easy enough to recognise Huysmans's *A Rebours*, which had appeared seven years earlier, in 1884. It probably remains anonymous because Wilde owed too much to it and was not over-anxious to advertise his sources. Gautier is the French writer who is most often mentioned in *Dorian Gray* (*Mademoiselle de Maupin* is obviously in the background), but the influence of Gautier in England was already more or less acknowledged: that of the later French writers who were lumped together in their own country as symbolists or decadents was still a rich and secret treasure-trove for English amateurs of the exotic, and it was very much to their interest that their fascinating eccentricities should appear as the result of their own private decadence, not as second-hand literary corruptions from abroad.

Wilde's paragraph quoted above is a fair description of *A Rebours*, and if it is highly coloured, it is not more so than the book itself. Des Esseintes, its hero, became a part of symbolist mythology. Mallarmé addressed some of his prose to this imaginary figure, and des Esseintes's library is a compendium of the tastes of the school. He was drawn in part from the actual Robert de Montesquiou, later to be immortalised as Proust's Charlus, but there is not much in common between the two portraits. Charlus is a portentous marionette; we watch its grotesque and tragic gestures, but we are hardly allowed to

see the forces by which it is moved; we only infer them from
its operations. Des Esseintes is an attempt at interior por-
traiture; his actions are irrelevant; indeed he hardly ever per-
forms any; the novel is a record of tastes and habits, of a
fantastic plan of life totally divorced from all the purposes of
ordinary existence. Des Esseintes shuts himself up in a house
in the suburbs of Paris which he turns into a sort of private
pantheon, the deities enshrined being his own esoteric caprices.
He has already exhausted most of the ordinary possibilities of
sensation; like the Byronic hero of earlier days, "he through
sin's long labyrinth has run", and his aim is now to withdraw
himself materially and spiritually as far as possible from the
life of his age. A good deal of the book is occupied with the
interior decoration and domestic arrangements of this strange
establishment. Then we have a chapter on des Esseintes's study
of the Latin writers of the decadence, one on his collection of
jewels, one on perfumes, one on modern ecclesiastical literature
and one on exotic plants; all these being objects from which
he has hoped to derive sufficient sensation to make it worth
while to continue his existence.

Dorian Gray duly becomes his disciple.

> Yes: there was to be, as Lord Henry had prophesied, a new
> Hedonism that was to re-create life, and to save it from that
> harsh, uncomely puritanism that is having, in our own day, its
> curious revival. It was to have its service of the intellect, cer-
> tainly; yet it was never to accept any theory or system that
> would involve the sacrifice of any mode of passionate experience.
> Its aim, indeed, was to be experience itself, and not the fruits
> of experience, sweet or bitter as they might be. Of the asceticism
> that deadens the senses, as of the vulgar profligacy that dulls
> them, it was to know nothing. But it was to teach man to con-
> centrate himself upon the moments of a life that is itself but a
> moment.[15]

A little Pater has got mixed up with the Huysmans here;
but when Dorian Gray takes up the study of jewels, he is simply
imitating, even to the names of the stones, one of the manias of
des Esseintes.

> He would often spend a whole day settling and resettling in
> their cases the various stones that he had collected, such as the

olive-green chrysoberyl that turns red by lamplight, the cymophane with its wire-like line of silver, the pistachio-coloured peridot, rose-pink and wine-yellow topazes, carbuncles of fiery scarlet with tremulous four-rayed stars, flame-red cinnamon stones, orange and violet spinels, and amethysts with their alternate layers of ruby and sapphire.[16]

Similarly with perfumes, ecclesiastical vestments, and all the other miscellaneous bric-à-brac with which these two precious heroes attempt to beguile the tedium of life. It is of course the putting into practice of part of the Paterian ideal, but without the element of *ascesis*, the real devotion to the best that the life of imagination has to give, that saves Pater from deliquescence. Other passages in *A Rebours* are closer to Pater than to Wilde. Des Esseintes has been brought up by the Jesuits, and is continually recollecting his clerical education. He cultivates an aesthetic admiration for the Church, not only for its ceremonies, but for its doctrines, for the writings of the Fathers and of modern theologians. And in all this, as in Pater, there is something more than superficial. If des Esseintes looks at Christianity from the outside, as a spectacle or an intellectual diversion, he has used his intelligence on it, and knows well enough what it involves.

> Il savait pourtant bien, en descendant en lui, qu'il n'aurait jamais l'esprit d'humilité et de pénitence vraiment chrétien; il savait, à n'en pouvoir hésiter, que ce moment dont parle Lacordaire, ce moment de la grâce, "ou le dernier trait de lumière pénètre dans l'âme et rattache à un centre commun les vérités qui y sont éparsés," ne viendrait jamais pour lui; il n'éprouvait pas ce besoin de mortification et de prière sans lequel, si l'on écoute la majeure partie des prêtres aucune conversion n'est possible; il ne ressentait aucun désir d'implorer un Dieu dont la miséricorde lui semblait des moins probables.[17]

Huysmans later became a fervent Catholic, and regarded *A Rebours* as an important stage in his progress. Dorian Gray copies des Esseintes's aesthetic dallying with Catholicism, but without giving the faintest sign of understanding what it is all about.

> It was rumoured of him once that he was about to join the Roman Catholic communion; and certainly the Roman ritual

had always a great attraction for him. The daily sacrifice, more awful really than all the sacrifices of the antique world, stirred him as much by its superb rejection of the evidence of the senses as by the primitive simplicity of its elements and the eternal pathos of the human tragedy that it sought to symbolise. . . . The fuming censers that the grave boys, in their lace and scarlet, tossed into the air like great gilt flowers, had their subtle fascination for him. As he passed out, he used to look with wonder at the black confessionals, and long to sit in the dim shadow of one of them and listen to men and women whispering through the worn grating the true story of their lives.[18]

The alleged poisonousness of *A Rebours* is largely verbal and retrospective. Des Esseintes, it is true, had in earlier life been through a course of systematic debauchery, but at the period dealt with in the book most of his avocations are singularly harmless. True, he picks up a poor boy in the streets and treats him to a regular night at a brothel once a week, with the object of turning him into a murderer and a rebel against society when he returns to his own squalid surroundings. This incursion of the wealthy exotic into the workaday life of the poor is echoed in Dorian Gray's affair with Sibyl Vane, the modest little actress. Again Wilde misses the point. The incident in Huysmans is a violent protest against bourgeois society: the best thing one can do for it is to turn men into murderers, that it may be smashed up the sooner. Wilde's is a commonplace mid-Victorian seduction story, given a "decadent" twist only at the end, when Sibyl Vane has killed herself, and Dorian Gray is persuaded by Lord Henry to regard the episode aesthetically, as an unusually complete and artistically satisfactory tragedy. Perhaps *A Rebours* is poisonous in the sense of being disgusting rather than immoral. Des Esseintes has some vividly realised and remarkably horrible dreams. His way of life undermines his health, and we are favoured with long accounts of the degeneration in his physical condition, culminating in a period in which he is unable to digest any food taken in the ordinary way, and is nourished, by a simple hydrostatic device, from below, an operation in which he takes a complacent and analytical interest. Wilde does not emulate Huysmans in this kind of thing; but the physical decay of des Esseintes is paralleled in the decay and corruption of Dorian Gray's portrait, the symbol of his soul, while his body remains unimpaired. And here we must grant that Wilde has found a far superior imaginative symbol.

The ultimate test of this kind of thing is, I suppose, the style. It was part of the aesthetic creed that style is more than matter, and of this kind of work at least it is true enough. If the quality of the writing is good enough to carry it off, it may succeed; if not, there is nothing to fall back upon, no "images which find a mirror in every mind, and sentiments to which every bosom returns an echo". In literature as in life, conscious eccentricity must be justified by some real distinction of mind if it is to be more than merely embarrassing. This is where Wilde, with his sham intensity and reach-me-down exquisiteness, fails to fulfil his professions. Some of the writing looks like common Victorian melodrama, like patches of bad Dickens; other parts are second-hand Pater, without any of Pater's distinction in handling these weary rhythms. Above all, the elaborate parade of the delights of the senses never convinces us that Wilde had any special delicacy of sense perception. One who sets up as a connoisseur of sights, sounds, odours and the like should at least satisfy us that he has experience and discrimination in these matters. Gautier defined himself as "un homme pour qui le monde visible existe", and his poetry bears it out. There is nothing in Wilde's writing to show that he had ever seen, smelt, tasted or listened with any special attention, had ever done anything but cull verbally impressive passages from his favourite literature. Huysmans's style is far more violently affected than Wilde's, and far more remote from the central French idiom than Wilde's from the English. Foreign judgments on these matters are generally unreliable, as Wilde's own reputation abroad can show us: but when Wilde describes Huysmans's writing as vivid and obscure at once, full of argot and archaisms, of technical expressions and elaborate paraphrases, he seems to put his finger on just that element of paradoxical vitality that his own style lacks. The extraordinary vocabulary and involved construction of Huysmans are the natural expression of an odd and contorted sense of life: Wilde's affectations are just the furniture of an *art-nouveau* drawing-room.

It is sometimes held that Wilde is saved by his wit. By all accounts it was delightful in private life: in literature there is nothing that reveals more constantly the unsureness of his taste. These slightly withered epigrammatic impertinences must have been invaluable over the dinner-table, where no doubt they had served several times before finding their way into print: but they have an air of incurable social smartness; and of all things social smartness is the most impossible to combine with the emotional and sensual intensity at which Wilde is aiming in *Dorian Gray* (This is why his only consummate success is in farce, in *The Importance of being Earnest*, where the smartness is part of the fun.) Apart from this intermittent crackle of epigram, *Dorian Gray* is an utterly humourless book. Huysmans, on the other hand, has found the proper condiment to season the otherwise rather monotonous richness of his invention. It is a grotesque humour, sometimes horrifying, sometimes purely comic, on the grand scale.

Half-way through the book one is excited by the prospect of an event. Des Esseintes has been reading Dickens, and stimulated by ths world of fantasy he determines to go to England.[19] It is raining hard as he drives through the streets of Paris, and already an imaginary London unrolls before his eyes, "un Londres pluvieux, colossal, immense, puant la fonte échauffée et la suie, fumant sans relâche dans la brume". He buys a Baedeker, reads about the London museums and falls to thinking about English paintings, "des tableaux de Millais, *La Veillée de Saint Agnès*, d'un vert argentée si lunaire, des tableaux de Watts, aux couleurs étranges, bariolés de gomme-gutte et d'indigo, des tableaux esquissés par un Gustave Moreau malade, brossés par un Michel-Ange anémié et retouchés par un Raphaël noyé dans le bleu". He goes to a bodega frequented by English tourists:

> La cave était pleine; accoudé sur un coin de table, des Esseintes attendait le verre de porto commandé à un gentleman, en train de déboucher d'explosifs sodas contenus dans des bouteilles ovales qui rappelaient, en les exagérant, ces capsules de gelatine

et de gluten employés par les pharmacies pour masquer le gout
de certains remèdes.

Tout autour de lui, des Anglais foisonnaient; des dégaines de
pâles clergymens, vêtus de noir de la tête aux pieds, avec
des chapeaux mous; . . . des mentons ras, des lunettes ronds, des
cheveux graisseux et plats; des trognes de tripier et des mufles
de dogues avec des cous apoplectiques, des oreilles comme
des tomates, des joues vineuses, des yeux injectés etidiots, des
colliers de barbe pareils à ceux de quelques grands singes. . . .

He goes to an English eating-house, where he perceives
robust Englishwomen, with teeth as large as paddles, attacking
"avec une réelle ardeur, un rumpsteak-pie". To enter into the
spirit of the thing he orders an oxtail soup, and regales himself
with this delicacy "tout à la fois onctueuse et veloutée, grasse
et ferme". He cannot of course understand the conversation of
those around him, but he concludes from their gestures that
they are unanimously discussing the bad weather. He feels
happy to be already, in a sense, a naturalised citizen of London.

Then he arouses himself with a start and consults his watch.
There is still half an hour before the train goes. He begins to
think of the only foreign country that has fascinated him—
Holland, and of the cruel disillusionment he suffered when he
actually went there. A wave of discouragement rolls over him;
he consults his watch again; still ten minutes to go; the door
of the tavern opens and people come in, bringing with them a
smell of wet dogs and oil. Des Esseintes suddenly feels in-
capable of moving. What is the use of bestirring oneself, since
one can travel so magnificently in one's chair? To go to
London will only be to court new disappointments. He looks
at his watch and decides that it is time to go home. He con-
trives to rise to his feet and order a cab. Then he returns, with
his trunks, valises, parcels, rugs, umbrellas and walking-
sticks, to his own house, feeling the physical and moral prostra-
tion of a man who has returned from a long and dangerous
voyage.

The picture of London might have been done in collaboration
by Dali and George Grosz. Huysmans began writing as a
realist, and fantasy is probably strongest on a realistic base.
It is, anyway, exactly what is needed to balance *A Rebours*,

otherwise too heavily loaded with chrysoprase, cymophane, benzoin, spikenard and scenes after Odilon Redon. It is no use making a dish of the richest and strangest meats if it has no salt in it. Huysmans's odd sardonic humour provides the right kind of salt. The English writers of the nineties never realised this; they dimly saw that their exotic delicacies required some supplement, but they were apt to decide that what was needed was some good plain boiled potatoes—a little solid morality to compensate for their flights into the perverse. Since they were none of them men of much original moral insight, the morality tends to be of the most commonplace type. At the end of *A Rebours* one can almost believe that Huysmans has been making a final moral experiment, that there is nothing left for him, as Barbey d'Aurevilly said, but the mouth of a pistol or the foot of the Cross. Wilde simply tells us that conscious cultivation of the sensations leads to ruin, in a manner as flat, as perfunctory, as remote from anything that he really believed, as any bourgeois journalist's attack on aestheticism.

Wilde is at his best when he is whole-heartedly frivolous: his serious work is nearly all pervaded by the same defect, which varies in intensity from a mere uncertainty of purpose to the emetic posturing of *De Profundis*. However, it is an ungrateful task to rub in the consequences of Wilde's "mésaventures biographiques", and criticism recoils from inquiring into the state of mind that led him to write "There is something so unique about Christ". The uncertainty that is always slipping into insincerity can be seen in a more analysable form in the essays and lectures, in the hopeless wavering between the Ruskinian and the later aesthetic ideal, without a sign of any real attempt to reconcile them. The best and most original of them is *The Soul of Man under Socialism*—an amusing and paradoxical attempt, not without ironical reference to the present day, to stand Socialism on its head and turn into it the sort of precious individualism that Wilde really wants. The most revealing are the lectures given in America. They were designed as an exposition of the new aesthetic doctrine, and they serve to show what a hotch-potch it had become. Fragments of Whistler rub shoulders with fragments of Ruskin and

Morris; these are interspersed with fragments of Pater, maxims of Gautier, and Wildian epigrams of the maddening kind that have the verbal form of wit without the intellectual content.

The lecture on Art and the Handicraftsman begins with a passage of Ruskin and water. (Even Ruskin's tricks of expression are copied.)

> No workman will beautifully decorate bad work, nor can you possibly get good handicraftsmen or workmen without having beautiful designs. You should be quite sure of that. If you have poor and worthless designs in any craft or trade you will get poor and worthless workmen only, but the minute you have noble and beautiful designs, then you get men of power and intellect and feeling to work for you. By having good designs you have workmen who work not merely with their hands but with their hearts and heads too; otherwise you will get merely the fool or the loafer to work for you.[20]

Yet in the lecture on the English Renaissance of Art we are told:

> The recognition of a separate realm for the artist, . . . forms not merely the essential element of any aesthetic charm but is the characteristic of all great imaginative work and of all great eras of artistic creation. . . . Art never harms itself by keeping aloof from the social problems of the day: rather, by so doing it more completely realises for us that which we desire.[21]

The gospel of Ruskin—that art is the expression of the life of the workman, faces the gospel of Japan—that the picture is a beautifully coloured surface and no more. Whistler in particular has been heavily raided for material on the position of the critic and the freedom of art from irrelevant ethical considerations; but not perhaps more heavily than Morris, for material about design and decoration. A good many of the borrowings from all these writers are direct verbal plagiarisms. The collection as a whole confirms the impression that Wildian aestheticism was little more than a series of attitudes and undigested notions, held together for the time by what must once have been a brilliant and attractive personality.

Wilde's literary influence, however, was nowhere very great, and was certainly not accepted by the younger men of the nineties. Yeats, with the psychological insight that he sometimes displays, says that he should have been a man of action rather than a writer; for indeed Wilde only really lived when in the public eye, when dominating a person, a group, or a dinner party; and he was willing to use whatever means came handiest to that end. Fidelity to a private vision is precisely what is lacking in his work. Yeats speaks of the "vague impressiveness that spoils his writing"; and in the introduction to his *Oxford Book* tells of the decisive rejection by his own group of the "rhetoric" of Wilde along with that of the earlier Victorians.

Yeats, Johnson, Dowson, Symons and the obscurer writers who formed the Rhymers' Club were trying to found a new school, with an austerer devotion to their own discipline than any that Wilde could understand. Yet from the thinnish trickle of original work and the fragmentary medley of personal reminiscence that go to make up our picture of the nineties, it is hard to extract any consistent impression; and from the *Yellow Book* and the *Savoy* it is hard to extract anything but a faint and unanalysable period flavour. It was an age of minor successes and minor failures, where fragments of delicate distinction emerge from a jumble of tasteless trivialities. Its ultimate importance in literary history is likely to be that it nourished the genius of Yeats. Yet as it did foster Yeats, as he felt an enduring piety for his companions of those days, and wrote of them in *Autobiographies* with more sympathy and more penetration than anyone else has done, something must have been stirring in the literary undergrowth, and we ought to find out what it was. Very little, of course, of actual achievement: Yeats calls his friends "the tragic generation", as Verlaine had called his "les poètes maudits", and their story is one of real but small talents, condemned for a variety of causes to obscurity and failure. Yet this group of the nineties is not a merely irrelevant episode in literary history; inconspicuous though their landmarks are, they are still landmarks; from them the road takes a new direction, and the ivory towers of to-day would not have quite the same *décor*, nor the Fabian committee-rooms quite the same absence of it, if they had never existed.

The Rhymers' Club was founded in 1890 or 1891, and its

meetings continued for three or four years. We learn of it from Yeats's *Autobiographies*, from Arthur Symons's introduction to Dowson's *Poems*. But both critical and biographical material is wanting. The principal members were Lionel Johnson, Dowson, Arthur Symons and Yeats himself, and among the minor figures were John Davidson, Victor Plarr, Richard le Gallienne and Selwyn Image. They met at an eating-house in Fleet Street, the Cheshire Cheese, in a conscious effort to reproduce the atmosphere of literary café society in Paris. The air of London was not congenial, and the attempt was not particularly successful, though Dowson and Symons, and, less assiduously, Yeats himself, were frequent visitors to France and students of the new French literature. In the background was the figure of Wilde, though he only attended the meetings of the club on the rare occasions when they met in private houses, having no taste for the sanded floor and the clay pipes of the Cheshire Cheese. Though the Rhymers met to read and discuss each other's poetry, and probably met at least as often as the P.R.B., we have not from them the ample supply of manifestos and declarations of faith that we have from the pre-Raphaelites. They had no conscientious historian like William Michael Rossetti, and since their principal theory was that all theories were vulgar, we can only attempt to describe an atmosphere, a vague community of sentiment, to be perceived only in hints and snatches.

Yeats tells us that he was made to feel provincial and insistent because of his determination in thrashing out his ideas. He was accused of talking like a man of letters and not a poet. It seems to us to-day that he was the only member of the group with sufficient intellectual and spiritual vigour to form a philosophy of poetry for himself. The evolution of this philosophy must be left to the next chapter; the others were strictly content with the pure impression, the isolated aesthetic emotion, and forbade all system-building. Let us nevertheless attempt a view of the unifying ideas that after all existed, and that make this group a not insignificant one, in spite of the smallness of its achievement.

In the first place, they professed to be traditionalists. The split between the progressive and the antiquarian elements that runs through all Victorian culture had by now become conscious. The only half-intentional reaction of the pre-Raphaelites against the scientific, forward-looking and democratic tendencies of their age was adopted by the Rhymers as a definite creed. Yeats's father, from being himself a pre-Raphaelite, had become a disciple of Huxley in philosophy and of the realists in painting; and, in a well-known passage of the *Autobiographies*, Yeats has described his resentment at this code, the feeling that it was depriving him of a spiritual heritage. Rossetti was the master of the Rhymers, especially the Rossetti who could not care whether the sun went round the earth or not, and turned away from all social and political questions to explore the byways of his own sensibility. The most disgraceful thing one could do was to write for the newspapers; even to write for the *Spectator* was a mistake, since one's friends read only the *Savoy*. Their ethics and pattern of life were derived from Pater; Lionel Johnson had been his disciple at Oxford, and all accepted his dictum that nothing which had strongly interested the human mind could ever wholly lose its validity. They were strongly drawn therefore to ancient beliefs and religious practices, to mystical cults, orthodox or otherwise, ranging from the strict neo-Catholicism of Lionel Johnson, through Dowson's emotional velleities towards the consolations of Catholicism, to the extremes of heretical occultism in Yeats. A familiar phrase of Johnson's was that all life should be a ritual; the Rhymers accordingly adopted a ceremonious manner, and, except for an occasional flowing necktie, a conventional correctness of dress. One remembers Yeats's use of the word "ceremony", and his irritation with his portrait by John, which made him look like an unshaven Bohemian.

In some cases this outward formality was the compensation for excessively untidy lives. Yeats first discovered Johnson to be a drunkard when he fell flat on the ground in the middle of delivering an austerely scholastic discourse justifying a certain point of conduct by the authority of the Fathers of the Church. But Johnson was an essential Catholic, and was perfectly clear about what he was doing. *Video meliora proboque, deteriora sequor.* Others combined an outward traditionalism, various kinds of leaning towards religion, with a considerable degree of social and moral antinomianism. Here no doubt the influence of Wilde and Beardsley counted for a good deal. Wilde's pose as leader of the younger aesthetes was never justified by his literary influence, but Wilde as a portent, the panache and personal charm with which he imposed himself, at his own valuation, on an unwilling society, exercised an enormous fascination on younger and obscurer men. Yeats has recorded how, after Wilde's trial in 1895, all literary London was stirred by the brilliance and audacity of his defence. "He has made of infamy a new Thermopylae." After that date, therefore, he began to assume something of the status of a martyr; the immediate cause of his persecution became irrelevant; the cause with which he became identified was a crusade for the freedom of the artist against the clapper-clawing of the vulgar. After the trial Beardsley came in for a share of the same adventitious homage. I do not suppose that anyone qualified to judge can ever have thought of him as a great artist, though he was a real one. But when, on account of a vague association with Wilde, he was summarily dismissed from the art-editorship of the *Savoy*, he too became a symbol of the persecution of the arts by society. He had nothing to do with Wilde's sexual aberration, but he had illustrated Wilde's work, some of his drawings were indecent, and many suggested a vaguely perverse sensuality. The presence of this pair of martyred heroes in the background therefore helped to make the reality or the affectation of vice a part of the aesthetic equipment. The reality was mostly confined to drinking and drabbing, neither of them particularly uncommon in any age: what was more or less new was making the suggestion of these things a conscious part of the literary stock-in-trade. Yeats moved among all this, remarkably unaffected by it, with a singular concentration on his own purpose; and the most generous commentary on it is his.

The critic might well reply that certain of my generation delighted in writing with an unscientific partiality for subjects long forbidden. Yet is it not most important to explore especially

207

what has been long forbidden, and to do this not only "with the highest moral purpose", like the followers of Ibsen, but gaily, out of sheer mischief, or sheer delight in that play of the mind. . . . I have felt in certain early works of my own which I have long abandoned, and here and there in the work of others of my generation, a slight, sentimental sensuality which is disagreeable, and does not exist in the work of Donne, let us say, because he, being permitted to say what he pleased, was never tempted to linger, or rather to pretend that we can linger, between spirit and sense.[22]

The English literary masters of the Rhymers were, as we have said, Rossetti and Pater. To these they added the French symbolists, with varying degrees of first-hand acquaintance with their work. Symons, a critic and a serious student of French literature, was no doubt clearly aware of the line of tradition in French poetry leading from the symbolists back through Baudelaire to Gautier. He wrote a useful book on *The Symbolist Movement in Literature*, and his best work was translation from Verlaine, Rimbaud and Mallarmé. Yeats, who was a bad linguist and read French only painfully, derived most of his knowledge of the French ideas from him. A version of the poetic doctrine of Mallarmé therefore became a part of Yeats's literary philosophy, and in life and personal conduct Villiers de l'Isle Adam's *Axel* became for a time his sacred book. Dowson translates from Verlaine and quotes from Rimbaud, and respectful references to Gautier, Baudelaire and the blessed name of Symbolism are tolerably frequent in the documents of the time. It is clear that the Rhymers felt that they were deriving new inspiration from France, but since they were so firmly opposed to the formulation of doctrines, it is hard to find out exactly what they supposed themselves to be getting. Let us make a guess at it.

It is not for me to offer an explanation of the ethos of symbolism, and even if I could do it, it would hardly be to the point; for to the writers of the nineties, symbolism was not a finished product, which they could read up in literary histories. It was something still in the making; its surviving heroes could still be met on visits to Paris, and knowledge of it was to be picked up as best one could in fragments from Mallarmé's

criticism, from Verlaine's poetry, from the reverent study of
Axel. The French influence meant in the first place the dis-
covery that Art for Art's sake had had its foundations, many
years ago, in Gautier's "L'art pour l'art"; that instead of being
a new aesthetic paradox it was already in France an established
doctrine, and had produced works far greater in scope than the
parallel movement in England. It meant too the discovery
that the protest against bourgeois society, the gradual closing
of the ranks of the artists against a steadily more hostile
world, was not a provincial or a merely English affair, but a
European movement: the beliefs of a small and obscure body
of English writers—beliefs in the superiority of poetic and
intuitive over scientific knowledge, in the pursuit of strange and
recondite forms of beauty—were given authority by the
practice of artists of assured achievement.

There was probably a considerable misunderstanding of
Baudelaire. His work was regarded as an authority for the
discussion of "forbidden" subjects, and the exploration of the
darker avenues of sensibility, but its real purpose and tendency
were almost certainly missed. The point of Baudelaire's pre-
occupation with "La sottise, l'erreur, le péché, la lésine" was
that if these things are clearly faced, if we do not stop short at
what is conventionally admitted, the result must be a vision of
metaphysical horror that henceforth changes the whole of
experience. Johnson, Dowson and Beardsley stop short at
fascinated contemplation of their "dark angels", but they make
no deductions from the activities of these mysterious beings,
and remain helpless to absorb and transmute the experience of
which they have caught glimpses. One begins to realise how
inadequate to Catholicism were the common literary concep-
tions of it at the end of the nineteenth century. Baudelaire the
unbeliever stripped his soul naked and achieved a new vision
of life that is far more Catholic than the uneasy alternation
between institutional religion and a private sensibility hope-
lessly at variance with it, such as we find in Verlaine and the
English nineties. It was, however, Verlaine who was to prove
their real master.

Verlaine was the greatest influence, too, in matters of form and diction. French symbolism was above all a technical revolution; but it requires a pretty thorough intimacy with French poetry to understand fully what was going on. Probably no one except Symons in the English nineties had studied French poetry to this extent, and what soaked through to England of the new *art poétique* was something very much less than the difficult and disturbing process by which Mallarmé and Rimbaud were transforming French verse. From Mallarmé was derived, mainly, it appears, through the influence of Symons, the notion of pure poetry, poetry stripped to its essentials, without doctrine, without detachable thought, without "impurities" of any kind. "Poetry, my dear Degas, is made not with ideas, but with words." This pronouncement constantly appears, under one disguise or another, in the nineties, along with an insistence on delicacy and beauty of form for their own sake. But in fact none of the English writers except Yeats even began to realise what an arduous discipline this meant: and Yeats, as we shall see, had to work through a long and laborious development before he grasped all the implications of a poetry freed from impurities. In the common poetical consciousness of the time, it meant little more than a rather finicking choice of subject and a rejection of the social and moral themes of the great Victorians. The esoteric doctrines of Baudelaire's sonnet *Correspondances* and Rimbaud's sonnet on the vowels, the attempt at a synaesthesia of different kinds of sense-impression, hardly seem to have crossed the Channel. Mallarmé's was a name to conjure with; but we may doubt how much of his exacting "poetical algebra" was generally understood. It was left for T. S. Eliot in a later generation to bring the full lesson of French symbolism to England. Verlaine's *Art Poétique*,[23] so much more dated, so much more a period piece, sums up the technical aspect of symbolism that was best understood in the nineties.

> De la musique avant toute chose,
> Et pour cela préfère l'Impair
> Plus vague et plus soluble dans l'air,
> Sans rien en lui qui pèse ou qui pose.

FIN-DE-SIÈCLE

Il faut aussi que tu n'ailles point
Choisir tes mots sans quelque méprise:
Rien de plus cher que la chanson grise
Ou l'Indécis au Précis se joint.

.   .   .   .

Prends l'éloquence et tords-lui le cou!
Tu feras bien, en train d'énergie,
De rendre un peu la Rime assagie,
Si l'on n'y veille, elle ira jusqu'ou?

In France, no doubt, this implies a far more precise pro-
gramme than it could in England—a revolt against the domi-
nance of the Alexandrine, against the strict rules of French
rhyme, against a certain kind of formal rhetorical effectiveness.
The Verlainian reforms were to bring French verse nearer to
the state in which English verse, except during the neo-classical
period, had always been, and most of what Verlaine meant
would have been more relevant to English poetry in the time
of Gray, or perhaps of Wordsworth. What the nineties drew
from it was a preference for slight musical effects, a deter-
mination to avoid the poetry of splendid abstractions, Miltonic-
Tennysonian blank verse and the grand style generally. Above
all they derive from Verlaine the idea that there is some ulti-
mate essence of poetry, something subtle and evanescent which
can be achieved, by mere isolation from all moral, logical and
rhetorical accidents, rather than by the elaborate mosaic-
making of Mallarmé.

De la musique encore et toujours!
Que ton vers soit la chose envolée
Qu'on sent qui fuit d'une âme en allée
Vers d'autres cieux à d'autres amours.

Que ton vers soit le bonne aventure
Éparse au vent crispé du matin
Qui va fluerant la menthe et le thym. . . .
Et tout le reste est littérature.

These seductive and mildly intoxicating ideas, so beautifully
exemplified in Verlaine's own best verse, were vaguely dis-
tributed among the Rhymers; but it would be difficult to show
that they produced much tangible result, except in the early

211

work of Yeats. This is not because he wished to write a different kind of poetry from his fellows, but because he is the only one who succeeded in doing what they all wished to do. The scattered minor poetry of the period should some time be thoroughly gone through, to find out what, if anything, it really added to the English tradition. But to do so would be outside the limits of this book. Dowson and Lionel Johnson may be taken as examples of the kinds of poetic success, and poetic failure, that are typical of the age. Both, if they had lived when there was an established poetical tradition, might have respectably continued it, each contributing his individual note. Johnson has something of the sensibility of a Gerard Manley Hopkins gone wrong, Dowson that of a less resilient Verlaine. But they were living in what should have been an age of poetical innovation. The great Victorian schools had done their work, and nothing had appeared strong enough to take their place. It is here that the impotence of the nineties becomes apparent. New sensibilities require new modes of expression, and these Johnson and Dowson are powerless to provide. Johnson writes like a man of taste who has read a great deal of poetry, but he has never a line or a phrase that sounds like the living voice, that sounds like anything except the poetical *lingua franca* which is available to almost any culti- vated man of some literary ability. And Dowson's languid rhythms and conventional vocabulary represent only the final etiolation of the pre-Raphaelite-Swinburnian diction, not with- out a pathetic charm, but utterly without the germ of new poetic life.

Johnson was one of those, like Hopkins, who arrived at the Catholic Church via an English public school and Oxford, a type so extremely unlike the Catholics of any other country or any other age. He was a scholar by temperament, and passed among his fellows for a deep student of the fathers and doctors of the Church. But he lived when neo-scholasticism was still new, and we may doubt whether his knowledge of Catholic philosophy was in fact very profound. He had the kind of love and knowledge of literature that makes a good critic, of the non-creative kind. His study of Hardy is still valuable, and his essays and critical papers, mostly short periodical causeries, are scholarly and agreeable. Sometimes the same note appears in his verse.[24]

> Now white Clarissa meets her fate,
> With virgin will inviolate:
> Now Lovelace wins me with a smile,
> Lovelace, adorable and vile.
> I taste in slow, alternate way,
> Letters of Lamb, letters of Gray:
> Nor lives there, beneath Oxford towers,
> More joy, than in my silent hours.

Respectable sentiments, but not of the kind that make poetry. There is a good deal of undistinguished devotional verse, some of it merely sectarian, and revealing the rather stuffy world of the clerically minded layman. The fundamental conflict in his verse is between a classical and a Christian ideal of human perfection, seen in such poems as *A Friend*, where he describes a serene Virgilian character who has won his love and admiration, for whom he yet prays at the end,

> God trouble him: that he may turn,
> Through sorrow to his only rest.

In *Men of Assisi* he contrasts and vaguely tries to reconcile the two sons of that town, Propertius and St. Francis; and the same picture of a spirit unhappily torn between the aesthetic and the religious ideal is seen in *To a Passionist*.

> Clad in a vestment wrought with passion-flowers;
> Celebrant of one Passion; called by name
> Passionist: is thy world, one world with ours?
> Thine a like heart? Thy very soul the same?
>
> Thou pleadest an eternal sorrow: we
> Praise the still changing beauty of this earth.
> Passionate good and evil thou dost see;
> Our eyes behold the dreams of death and birth.

It is the same dichotomy that runs through Hopkins's poetry: but the mere mention of Hopkins shows us where Johnson fails. The contrast may be ultimately in strength of nature: with more of Hopkins's terrifying iron control Johnson might have had a similar career to his: but for literature the point lies in Johnson's failure in expression, the inability to find language to match the intensity of his experience. Even in the poems which are obviously of immediate and terrible personal importance—*The Dark Angel*, addressed to his own shadow-self, and *The Destroyer of a Soul*, addressed to Wilde—the painfully literary and second-hand expression continues to obscure his utterance. And this means that, with more scholarship and more moral concentration than any of his fellows, he has yet very little that a later age will care to revive.

Johnson's story is one of obscure and painful conflict going on far below the surface and never finding an adequate outlet: Dowson's is a softer temperament. Yeats and Arthur Symons[25] have told his pathetic little story—the virginal and frustrated love, alternating with bouts of drinking and debauchery, the increasingly feeble health, and the sweetness of nature persisting through all the melancholy muddle. One of his poems, *Cynara*, has become a permanent anthology piece, the standing symbol of the split between an ideal love and that of the market-place, whose beginnings we see in early romanticism, whose end we do not see till Freud blew with his mouth and dissipated it finally from even the most minor verse, to find a last resting-place in the clinician's note-books. Dowson's Catholicism has none of the sternness of Johnson's; it is a vague relapse into unction and dreams of a white purity, between bouts of quite other emotion. His predominant sentiment is weariness, and the sense of exile from a consolation long desired and no longer hoped for; sometimes it achieves a faint wavering music which, however tenuous, is his own.

> In music I have no consolation,
> No roses are pale enough for me;
> The sound of the waters of separation
> Surpasseth roses and melody.
>
> By the sad waters of separation
> Dimly I hear from an ancient place
> The sigh of mine ancient adoration:
> Hardly can I remember your face.

FIN-DE-SIÈCLE

But again we have the fatal acceptance of the poetical common-place, the inability to find an individual language to express what was after all a very individual sensibility. His short tales, *Dilemmas: Stories and Studies in Sentiment*, though again tenuous, and with the narrowest range of feeling, are written in a prose which, in a quiet way, is far more distinguished than the more publicised pages of Wilde.

Now, I suppose, nobody actually reads these works at all, though some of them still have value in the first-edition market. There is no very strong reason why they should be read: yet they are not wholly insignificant. They represent a phase through which the poetic sensibility had to pass before it could emerge into new territory. But the taking of a new step in poetry is a more arduous process than the Rhymers supposed, or were capable of. Of their circle Yeats alone had the tenacity and spiritual energy to carry it through. And in considering him we shall have to consider the fusion of this French and English aestheticism with an Irish element that was permanently to change and enrich it.

Chapter VI

YEATS

I. THE REJECTION OF RHETORIC

For all its intense national feeling the Irish literary renaissance was not an insular movement. Besides a constant, even if antipathetic, relation with Catholic culture, it felt the influence of France, of India and even of England. Indeed, the return to the legendary Irish past, whatever it may have felt like to Irishmen, is likely to be regarded by the literary historian as a late continuation of the medieval and archaising tendency that had pervaded English literature for more than a century. Those who are addicted to such studies might find room for a thesis about the influence of the pre-Raphaelites on Irish culture. Yeats in the eighties, in his father's studio and among his painter friends, grew up in the pre-Raphaelite afternoon, and it is sufficiently evident that the gathering Celtic twilight owed something of its colour to the sombre glow from Rossetti's painting-room. Even as late as 1913 Yeats finds the old influence still capable of revival.

Two days ago I was at the Tate Galleries to see the early Millais's and before his "Ophelia" as before the "Mary Magdalene" and "Mary of Galilee" of Rossetti that hung near, I recovered an old emotion. I saw these pictures as I had seen pictures in my childhood. I forgot the art criticism of friends and saw wonderful, sad, happy people, moving through the scenery of my dreams. The painting of the hair, the way it was smoothed from its central parting, something in the oval of the peaceful faces, called up memories of sketches of my father's drawings on the margins of the first Shelley I had read, while the strong colours made me half remember studio conversations, words of Wilson, or of Potter perhaps, praise of the primary colours, heard, it may be, as I sat over my toys or a child's story-book. One picture looked familiar, and suddenly I remembered it had hung in our house for years. It was Potter's "Field Mouse". I had learned to think in the midst of the last phase of pre-Raphaelitism and now I had come to pre-Raphaelitism again and rediscovered my earliest thought.[1]

But Yeats is not a very pictorial poet; the precise enumeration of bean-rows did not detain him long; and pre-Raphaelitism for him was mainly a movement of ideas. He finds its natural continuation in the work of the *poètes maudits* of the nineties, Dowson and Lionel Johnson, and he attached himself to their school with the fervour he was wont to give to all mystic brotherhoods. Their concern with sin and salvation seems to have taken no root in his mind, but he absorbed their ideas on poetry, and all through the much annotated changes of his own conception of poetry the influence of the Rhymers' Club remained active. It is in Yeats's early essays that this late aesthetic doctrine finds its only adequate expression, for the other members of the band were too much preoccupied with absinthe and absolution to do much actual writing, while Yeats gives himself up to the full and luminous working out of his poetic doctrine. It is the richer for being quite untouched by conventional scholarship. Yeats surveys some of the classic grounds of European criticism as though they were quite unexplored; he is not concerned with what other men have said, but with the state of poetry in his own day and the development of his own vision. Besides the *Autobiographies*, *Ideas of Good and Evil* and *The Cutting of an Agate* are the major documents of this time: they are both the formulation of a party creed and an essential stage in the growth of a poet's mind.

As Yeats described it, the central doctrine of the school was the revolt against something called rhetoric: so called, it appears, largely because Verlaine had said "*Prends l'éloquence et tords-lui le cou*—Wring the neck of rhetoric". Yeats duly wrung it pretty hard, for the first twenty years of his poetical career, giving it an occasional twist in later life just to make sure: but he employs the word in some varied and highly individual senses, even for that Protean term. Sometimes it appears to mean "all that was prepense and artificial", and Yeats later came to feel that this conception forced upon his companions, and upon his own early work, "a facile charm, a too soft simplicity". More often, however, rhetoric seems to be vaguely extended to include propaganda of all kinds, everything to do with sociology and science, "impurities" in poetry generally. J. B. Yeats, the father, seems to have used the word in the same way.

> The whole land is crazy with rhetoric—the other night I happened to say to a lady near me, that a certain young lady was charming because in addition to good looks and graceful manners she had a serious mind. "You mean," she asked, "that she has a social conscience?" "No," I replied, "she is a serious student of the Irish language."[2]

To worry about society is to be contaminated with rhetoric: to study Irish is not. Had not Mallarmé said "Poetry is made, not with ideas, but with words"?

Imperial declamation in the manner of Henley (*a fortiori* of Kipling) is rhetoric: and this is not only dislike of the British political attitude, for later Yeats attacks the poetry of Young Ireland for the same reason: and his own verse was attacked by the Irish political poets, "Most of all for its lack of rhetoric, its refusal to preach a doctrine or to consider the seeming necessities of a cause". In middle life Yeats was to modify this view, and in his last years to write some almost jingo political verse: but even at this period the taboo on "causes" has nothing to do with a shrinking from conflict. It springs from the conviction that any political cause is temporary, that it is the business of poetry to deal with the permanent: and the conviction, though intermittently belied by flashes of satire or invective, remained with Yeats through his life. Unlike some of his own "dear shadows", he knew

> All the folly of a fight
> With a common wrong or right.

A man of affairs must deal with many trivial things, but the poet must be able to distinguish between them and the things of lasting importance. In modern metropolitan civilisation this is hard to do. "In London the first man you meet puts any high dream out of your head, for he will talk of something at once vapid or exciting, the moment's choice among those subjects of discourse that build up our social unity."[3]

Rhetoric, however, turns out to include moralising and science as well as propaganda. Rossetti, for the Yeats-Johnson group, marked the break with the earlier nineteenth-century tradition, "for he more than anyone was in reaction against the period of philanthropy and reform that created the pedantic composure of Wordsworth, the rhetoric of Swinburne, the passionless sentiment of Tennyson".[4] This feeling of course can be explained, with a considerable measure of truth, in sociological terms. Science and the social order were becoming too complex and too intractable for the old literary culture. The only large attempt at synthesis had been Tennyson's, and that was only doubtfully successful. Rossetti was half a foreigner, and his culture had no real roots in Victorian England. It was far easier and more natural for his poetry simply to turn away from it all. But this sort of explanation only works if you consider poetry as divorced from poets, as a stream of energy proceeding from the social organism. Rossetti was personally so indifferent to science and sociology, indeed to everything except erotic reverie and the technique of his two arts, that he hardly realised there was anything to turn away from. And he was spiritually indolent. Yeats's revolt against science and sociology had nothing to do with indolence or indifference, it was active and astringent. The narrowing of the bounds of poetry was not a lack of grasp, it was an *ascesis*. The intense spiritual excitement of his later years proved able to assimilate much craggy and indigestible matter; and his early attack on moralising in verse is not due to any debility in handling formidable ideas.

> I think that before the religious change that followed on the Renaissance men were greatly preoccupied with their sins, and that to-day they are troubled by other men's sins, and that this trouble has created a moral enthusiasm so full of illusion that art, knowing itself for sanctity's scapegrace brother, cannot be of the party. We have but held to our ancient church, where there is an altar and no pulpit, and founded, the guide-book tells us, upon the ruin of the temple of Jupiter Ammon, and

turned away from the too great vigour of those, who, living for
mutual improvement, have a pulpit and no altar.[5]

In spite of a strong period flavour, we should be wrong to
take Yeats's major beliefs at this time as the mere common-
places of aesthetic doctrine. The passage above has little in
common with the nineties' kicking over the traces of conven-
tional morality. It springs from a metaphysical belief in the
primacy of the altar over the pulpit: this is the period of
Yeats's experiments in theosophy and various mystical cults:
by them he reached the conviction that there is an actually
existent spiritual world beyond the range of normal moral
experience.

> He (Balzac) would have us understand that behind the momen-
> tary self, which acts and lives in the world, and is subject to the
> judgment of the world, there is that which cannot be called
> before any mortal Judgment seat, even though a great poet, or
> novelist, or philosopher may be sitting on it. Great literature
> has always been written in a like spirit, and is, indeed, the
> Forgiveness of Sin, and when we find it becoming the Accusation
> of Sin, as in George Eliot, literature has begun to change into
> something else. George Eliot had a fierceness hardly to be
> found but in a woman turned argumentative, but the habit of
> mind her fierceness gave its life to was characteristic of her
> century.[6]

Yeats regards the revolt against this moral fierceness as the
note of his time: but Blake is its forerunner, a version of Blake
very much adapted to Yeats's prepossessions.

> He announced the religion of art, of which no man dreamed
> in the world he knew; . . . In his time educated people believed
> that they amused themselves with books of imagination, but
> that they "made their souls" by listening to sermons and by
> doing or by not doing certain things. . . . In our time we are
> agreed that we "make our souls" out of some one of the great
> poets of ancient times, or out of Shelley, or Wordsworth, or
> Goethe or Balzac, or Flaubert, or Count Tolstoy, in the books
> he wrote before he became a prophet and fell into a lesser order,
> or out of Mr. Whistler's pictures, while we amuse ourselves,
> or at best make a poorer sort of soul, by listening to sermons or
> by doing or by not doing certain things.[7]

We may be permitted to wonder what kind of soul one could
make out of Mr. Whistler's pictures; the point here is that they

are emptied of all content but the purely aesthetic. How empty that could leave the spiritual vessel Yeats was not to see till somewhat later.

Science and miscellaneous knowledge were to disappear. Indeed, he tells us, he was always discovering some science or art that he might be rid of. The feeling of throwing away much useless lumber was delightful, and doubtless the jettison was accompanied by a few flourishes, *pour épater*. But for all Yeats's professed dislike of argument and self-justification, his vigorous mind had a passion for system: and he contrived to fit the new formula into a view of English historical development which exhibits him and his friends as returning to an older and sounder tradition. He writes of Spenser:

> He had lived in the last days of what we may call the Anglo-French nation, the old feudal nation that had been established when the Norman and the Angevin made French the language of court and market. In the time of Chaucer English poets still wrote much in French, and even English labourers lilted French songs over their work; and I cannot read any Elizabethan poem or romance without feeling the pressure of habits of emotion, and of an order of life, which were conscious, for all their Latin gaiety, of a quarrel to the death with that new Anglo-Saxon nation that was arising among Puritan sermons and Marprelate pamphlets. This nation had driven out the language of its conquerors, and now it was to overthrow their beautiful haughty imagination and their manners, full of abandon and wilfulness, and to set in their stead earnestness and logic and the timidity and reserve of a counting-house. . . . Bunyan's men would do right that they would come some day to the Delectable Mountains, and not at all that they might live happily in a world whose beauty was but an entanglement about their feet. Religion had denied the sacredness of an earth that commerce was about to corrupt and ravish, but when Spenser lived the earth had still its sheltering sacredness. His religion, where the paganism that is natural to proud and happy people had been strengthened by the platonism of the Renaissance, cherished the beauty of the soul and the beauty of the body with, as it seemed, an equal affection. He would have had men live well, not merely that they might win eternal happiness but that they might live splendidly among men and be celebrated in many songs. How could one live well if one had not the joy of the Creator and of the Giver of Gifts?[8]

THE LAST ROMANTICS

If a poet of the old nation were to come back to earth he would find some shadow of the life he knew, not in England, but among young men in Paris. In England it is young men who have been on a visit to Paris, like Yeats, who are returning to the old joy in the sacred earth. And the Irish had never lost it, had never had Puritanism and industrialism. Ruskin and Morris had hated the nineteenth-century degradation of life, but their work had come to nothing; England was still the slave of commerce and the machine.

> New from the influence, mainly the personal influence, of William Morris, I dreamed of enlarging Irish hate till we had come to hate with a passion of patriotism what Ruskin and Morris hated. . . . Ruskin and Morris had spent themselves in vain because they had no passion to harness to their thought, but here were unwasted passion and precedents in the popular imagination for every needed thought and action.[9]

From this point begins Yeats's enduring desire to find a foundation for his poetry in the life of his own people. Who, for a Protestant Anglo-Irishman, his own people are, must remain uncertain: this is ground where Angles fear to tread, and we are in any case concerned with his place in the English literary tradition. But it was precisely because the English literary tradition had moved so far from the common life, had lost its roots in the life of the people, that Yeats could not remain satisfied with it. Ireland with its relative simplicity of life and its stock of legends still active in the minds of the peasants could provide a better soil for the poet's passions to find maturity. The very early essay (1901) on "What is Popular Poetry?" provides a penetrating analysis of the situation and of the possibilities open to a poet of to-day. The question was, after casting out so much from poetry, what was to be put in? Here Yeats was met by conflicting ideals, none of them completely satisfying. The general answer was "symbolism", but when symbolism comes to be defined, it too seems to be approachable only by a series of negations—"a casting out of descriptions of nature for the sake of nature, of the moral law for the sake of the moral law, a casting out of all anecdotes, and of that brooding over scientific opinion that so often extinguished the central flame in Tennyson".[10] "The beryl stone was enchanted by our fathers that it might unfold the pictures in its heart, and not to mirror our own excited faces, or the boughs waving outside the window." But we still do not know, when all superfluities have been cast off, what the pictures in the heart of the beryl really are, what is the actual content of this central casket of poetry.

Yeats's first answer was that of uncritical aestheticism, pure reliance on the impressions of the delighted senses. But this phase did not last long. He early lost interest in describing outward things, and throughout his work he hardly used material objects except as symbols of something else. Towards the end of his life he expressed to Lady Gerald Wellesley his impatience with the English poetic habit of talking about flowers. For long, perhaps always, he loved the world of William Morris, with its naïve joy in physical things, its undisturbing passions, its tranquil faces. But it is not his world. To live in it is the way to be happy—he described Morris as the happiest of the poets—but Yeats, whether he knew it at the time or not, was bred to a harder school. He contrasts the poetry of Morris with that of Rossetti, in which desire can never be stilled, or satisfied by its simple bodily objects. "He listens to the cry of the flesh till it becomes proud, and passes beyond the world, where some immense desire that the intellect cannot understand mixes with the desire for a body's warmth and softness. His genius, like Shelley's, can hardly stir but to the rejection of nature, whose delight is profusion."[11] This idea of the rejection of nature haunted Yeats for the rest of his life.

> Once out of nature I shall never take
> My bodily form from any natural thing—

he wrote in the first "Byzantium". The poet's work is an analogy to the work of nature; for that very reason he should not spend himself in reminiscence of what nature has already done. The images drawn from the natural world in Yeats are used as symbols, as intellectual counters, but never as objects for gentle rumination in the manner of Wordsworth or Gray's letters.

Under my window-ledge the waters race,
Otters below, and moor-hens on the top,
Run for a mile undimmed in Heaven's face
Then darkening through dark Raftery's cellar drop,
Run underground, rise in a rocky place
In Coole demesne, and there to finish up
Spread to a lake and drop into a hole.
What's water but the generated soul?[12]

For Yeats the old man especially, the ashes of his younger self, nature offers no home.

That is no country for old men. The young
In one another's arms, birds in the trees,
—Those dying generations—at their song,
The salmon-falls, the mackerel-crowded seas,
Fish, flesh, or fowl, commend all summer long
Whatever is begotten, born and dies.[13]

But the intense spiritual passions of his later years were not yet come; in these early days he is much occupied with the contrast between two ways of love, the physical and the metaphysical, that he has typified in Morris and Rossetti, and that is the theme of his early play *The Shadowy Waters*.

FORGAEL. Now the secret's out;
For it is love that I am seeking for,
But love of a beautiful, unheard-of kind
That is not in the world.
AIBRIC. And yet the world
Has beautiful women to please every man.
FORGAEL. But he that gets their love after the fashion
Loves in brief longing and deceiving hope
And bodily tenderness, and finds that even
The bed of love, that in the imagination
Had seemed to be the giver of all peace,
Is no more that a wine-cup in the tasting,
And as soon finished.
AIBRIC. All that ever loved
Have loved that way—there is no other way.
FORGAEL. Yet never have two lovers kissed but they
Believed there was some other near at hand,
And almost wept because they could not find it.

And yet, however long it continues, this dialogue can lead only to the old impasse where we left Rossetti. It is indeed a conflict that persists throughout the poetry of Europe after the decay of the Roman self-sufficiency; almost reaching a solution for a moment in the thirteenth century—

>Guardami ben, ben son, ben son Beatrice;

but this was the momentary equilibrium of a system destined to fall apart again almost at once. The romantic solution has been even more unstable; and later psychology has provided an explanation but no way out.

>Man is in love, and loves what vanishes;
>What more is there to say?

Yeats could not remain at the level of uncritical romanticism, of Rossetti's mere confusion between the physical and the spiritual. And he never became content either to find the Holy Grail on Galahad's terms, or to forgo the search: so much of the scorched and angry verse of his last days remains a statement of blank conflict.

>A crazy man that found a cup,
>When all but dead of thirst,
>Hardly dared to wet his mouth
>Imagining, moon-accursed,
>That another mouthful
>And his beating heart would burst.
>October last I found it too,
>But found it dry as bone,
>And for that reason am I crazed
>And my sleep is gone.[14]

We can find here the personal myth that underlies much of Yeats's poetry at all periods: but in his early days he was almost obsessed by the idea that a personal myth was not enough. It is the vice of romantic poetry to become rarefied and thin because of the use of private symbols and the divorce from the general current of ideas. A major source of Yeats's strength is that he never remained content with this situation. Yet in the early essay *What is Popular Poetry?* he shows himself aware of all the difficulties. The question became epidemic again in the 1930's, but Yeats had said all that was relevant in 1901. He realises that the poetry that has actually become popular

in modern times—Longfellow, Mrs. Hemans, Macaulay's lays
—never came from the people at all, but was an impoverished
and vulgarised version of the written tradition, with the
"triviality of emotion, the poverty of ideas, the imperfect sense
of beauty" that we might expect from such an origin. The
religious and political ideas that actually move men to-day
have already been rejected, not simply because they are intract-
able material for poetry, but because for Yeats they explain
man's life in false and inadequate terms, and because they cut
men's minds off from the images and emotions that had once
carried their memories backwards thousands of years. For
Yeats private symbols could not be satisfying, and he feared
that they could never move the emotions powerfully, because
they had never existed in the heart of a people.

> I am certain there are many who are not moved as they would
> be by the solitary light burning in the tower of Prince Athanase,
> because it has not entered into men's prayers, nor lighted any
> through the sacred dark of religious contemplation.

Poetry, having been emptied of impurities and miscellaneous
rubbish, can only be filled again, not by images excogitated in
the study, but by a new mythology that could be valid in a
wider world.

II. THE SEARCH FOR A MYTHOLOGY

To trace in order Yeats's various attempts to find a satisfying
mythology would be almost to give a complete history of his
poetic development. The chronology of his work and the split
between his earlier and his later writing have perhaps been
over-emphasised, and his leading ideas are pretty constantly
active throughout his career. Underlying them all is the
realisation that poetry had lost its contact with religion: its
images no longer expressed man's deepest thoughts about his
own nature and own destiny. Industrial civilisation had
destroyed his relation with the natural world; and science and
Puritanism had vitiated his relations with the unseen. For
Yeats a mystical contemplation, not a moral code, was the
essential of religion; and by the time Tennyson and Browning

had finished with it poetry had little left to contemplate. Yeats at no time felt much inclination to faintly trust the larger hope. Nor did Christianity in its more uncompromising forms ever really occur to him as a solution of his difficulties. He contrasts the philosophy of Dante with that of Blake:

> This philosophy was the philosophy of soldiers, of men of the world, of priests busy with government, of all who, because of the absorption in active life, have been persuaded to judge and to punish. . . . Opposed to this was another philosophy, not made by men of the action, drudges of time and space, but by Christ when wrapped in the divine essence, and by artists and poets.[15]

Of course the Christ of this passage has nothing to do with historic Christianity, he is a figment constructed by Blake and Yeats between them. But for the most part, Yeats in his early days is not so much opposed to the Christian tradition as indifferent to it. The Erastian Irish Protestantism which was his native background could hardly offer much to the imagination; and for the same social and historical reasons he was irrevocably on the other side of the barrier from the Catholic Church. Once only in later life he records an attraction to it: but it comes through the agency of the hardly orthodox Hugel; and it is soon dismissed.

> I—though heart might find relief
> Did I become a Christian man and choose for my belief
> What seems most welcome in the tomb—play a predestined part.
> Homer is my example and his unchristened heart.[16]

He shows no disposition towards the aesthetic flirtations with the Church that Marius the Epicurean had made fashionable: and he is hardly more satisfied with Pater's final solution—the doctrine of the conclusion to the Renaissance. Much of Yeats's early prose, it is true, reminds us of this famous purple patch. "The poet, if he would not carry burdens that are not his, and obey the orders of senile lips, must sit apart in contemplative indolence, playing with fragile things." But Yeats is mentally far too vigorous for this religion of the "moments as they pass, and simply for those moments' sake". And having escaped the English university tradition, he is not disposed, like Arnold, to make a religion out of a Final Honour School of Literae Humaniores. He realises, as none of his contemporaries did, that the power of religious symbolism is not that it embodies the appeal of a graceful way of life, or supports a particular set of moral principles, but that it carries the mind back to the mystery that is at the heart of the universe, the mystery which the religious thought of the nineteenth century was bent on explaining away. For him, therefore, it is not possible to isolate a religious doctrine and express it in conceptual terms, apart from its own particular symbolism. "It is not possible," he writes, "to separate an emotion or a spiritual state from the image that calls it up and gives it expression." What can be announced in the pulpit is not that for which the altar was built, and symbolism is most often the only possible language for the expression of spiritual realities. This belief no doubt owes much to his own occult practices, and at times he shows an irritating preference for symbols which cannot be understood, as when he announces primly, "The arts are very conservative, and have a great respect for those wanderers who still stitch into their carpets among the Mongolian plains religious symbols so old that they have not even a meaning".

But out of this love of mystery, from which the element of mystification is not absent, Yeats constructs a valuable antithesis between symbolism and allegory. "I find that though I love symbolism, which is often the only fitting speech for some mystery of disembodied life, I am for the most part bored by allegory, which is made, as Blake says, by the 'daughters of memory', and coldly, with no wizard frenzy."[17] This is from the essay on Spenser, but the idea occurs first in an earlier one on Blake's illustrations to Dante. Symbolism is the only possible expression of some otherwise inexpressible spiritual essence, while allegory is an arbitrary translation of some principle that is already familiar, of something that has already been expressed in other terms. So that allegory is a bucket, from which you can get no more than has been put in, while symbolism is fed by an inexhaustible spring. Symbolism is what Blake calls "vision or imagination", and it represents what really exists, eternally and unchangeably. Yeats's essay on Shelley is devoted mainly to an elucidation of his symbols, which, he says, are more than metaphors or picturesque phrases, though they suffer from lack of definiteness, and from having never formed part of a living human tradition.

The power of the symbol is that it connects the individual imagination with bygone centuries of human emotion and experience, and beyond that with the great memory from which all human emotion and experience springs.

> Any one who has any experience of any mystical state of the soul knows how there float up in the mind profound symbols, whose meaning, if indeed they do not delude one into the dream that they are meaningless, one does not perhaps understand for years. Nor I think has any one who has known that experience with any constancy, failed to find some day in some old book or on some old monument, a strange or intricate image, that had floated up before him, and to grow perhaps dizzy with the sudden conviction that our little memories are but a part of some great memory, that renews the world and men's thoughts age after age, and that our thoughts are not, as we suppose, the deep but a little foam upon the deep.[18]

Later, when he came to write the preface to *The Words upon the Window-pane*, Yeats seems to know about Jung and the collective unconscious, and to be attracted to the idea: this, written in 1901, is a surprising anticipation. The form in which Yeats puts all this is variable; sometimes he uses more mystical, sometimes more historical terms. Later, too, he learnt to connect the remote state of consciousness to which symbolism can lead back with the *scienza poetica* of Vico, the primitive state from which all conceptual knowledge sprang. But even at this stage he derives the power of symbolism from its ability to cut through all modern experience and chatter about contemporary interests to the emotions and experiences that are eternally recurrent and are primitive in human life. If at one end his conception of symbolism is allied to trance and the communications of spiritualism, at the other end it is allied to the quite normal historical attempt (for instance, in Addison's papers on Chevy Chase) to base art on what is fundamental and unchanging in human nature. And this makes for Yeats the ideal transition (apart from patriotism and early associations) to Irish culture and legend as a basis for his myth.

In the essay on "The Celtic Element in Literature" he borrows from Renan and Arnold, and paraphrases their descriptions of the Celtic mind; its intense sensitiveness to nature, to her mystery rather than to her beauty; its melancholy that is inseparable from a realisation of nature's unaccountable and titanic force. But he goes on to say, what Arnold at his time perhaps could not have known, that this is the universal character of primitive humanity. To feel that nature is divine, to feel fascination and awe before her manifestations, is to do what primitive man has done all the world over; and it is utterly different from "the modern way, the way of people who are poetical, but are more interested in one another than in a nature which has faded to be but friendly and pleasant, the way of people who have forgotten the ancient religion." The old religion of the Irish with its magical view of nature, its unbounded sorrow at the universal victory of old age and decay, the ultimate rejection of nature by the lonely spirit of man, is only the old religion of all mankind: and it happens to have survived in the modern Irish longer than in others, a fact which is of far more than local importance.

> I will put this differently and say that literature dwindles to a mere chronicle of circumstance, or passionless phantasies, and passionless meditations, unless it is constantly flooded with the passions and beliefs of ancient times in Europe, the Sclavonic, the Finnish, the Scandinavian and the Celtic, the Celtic alone has been for centuries close to the main river of European literature. It has again and again brought "the vivifying spirit of excess" into the arts of Europe.[19]

The Celtic tradition therefore offers an escape from the modern impasse, a tap-root by which the arts can regain their sources of primitive energy.

Yeats is an extremely persuasive writer. One can believe almost anything he says while he is saying it. But here it might be worth while to pause and ask how far we can really accept all this, even how far it added strength to Yeats's own work. We find, as usual, that even Yeats's oddest ideas are not

mere abstract constructions; they have some foundation in
historic fact. The legends collected by Lady Gregory and
Yeats himself, the late survival of popular poetry in Gaelic,
the fact that Synge could base a superbly vigorous literary prose
on the actual speech of western Ireland, all point to the truth
that even if the primitive mind has not survived more un-
changed in Ireland than in other places, it was certainly in
Ireland that it had found the most accessible literary expression.
Among the "popular" elements in his verse, the folk-song
tradition, though how far this is specifically Irish I do not know,
served Yeats beautifully throughout his life. The "too soft
simplicity" he afterwards condemned is in the literary, the
un-Celtic poems; in

> Here will we moor our lonely ship
> And wander ever with woven hands,
> Murmuring softly lip to lip,
> Along the grass, along the sands,

not in the songs, such as "The Meditation of the old Fisher-
man":

> The herring are not in the tides as they were of old;
> My sorrow! for many a creak gave the creel in the cart
> That carried the take to Sligo town to be sold,
> When I was a boy with never a crack in my heart.

And popular song with its echoing refrain continued to haunt
Yeats most happily, and even among the complexities of his
later verse produced the lovely poem for Anne Gregory, and
the inspired insanities of Crazy Jane. But in reading the
strictly mythological poems one is driven to wonder how
much of this mass of purely Celtic tradition is really available
to the modern literary poet, how much of it even an Irishman
can use without becoming merely archaistic. Yeats's answer
has been often quoted: "I believed with my emotions, and the
belief of the country people made that easy." And it is true
that many of Yeats's most enduring attitudes are at least partly
derived from Celtic tradition—the exaltation of a doomed
heroism, the presence and power of terrible spiritual forces
from the Cuchulain cycle; the twilit romanticism, the presence

of a strange but prettier and less terrifying world of spirits from the later Ossianic legends. But it is hard to feel that the attempts to accommodate the legends themselves to modern narrative or dramatic verse are among his most successful achievements. Neither *The Wanderings of Oisin* nor the series of plays on the life of Cuchulain can compare with the best of the lyrical poetry of the corresponding periods. Perhaps this is just due to the accident that they are narrative and dramatic, and Yeats's narrative verse is less strong than the lyrical, and the dramatic less strong than the narrative. But from the point of view of English letters there is something faintly alien in the legends themselves, and the heart chills a little at Oisin and Cuchulain, Diarmuid and Grania, as it does not at Arthur, Lancelot and Guinevere. It is possible, too, that the ambition to revive ancient heroic legend was more of an abstract ambition in Yeats than a living impulse. Celtic legend is more useful to him when he uses it as Milton uses classical myth, to adorn and illustrate what sprang directly from his own immediate beliefs.

> And in Ausonian land
> Men called him Mulciber; and how he fell
> From Heav'n, they fabl'd, thrown by angry Jove
> Sheer o'er the Chrystal Battlements: from Morn
> To Noon he fell, from Noon to dewy Eve,
> A Summer's day; and with the setting Sun
> Dropt from the zenith like a falling Star
> On Lemnos, th' Aegean isle. Thus they relate,
> Erring;

Thus Milton accommodates delight in an antique myth to a seventeenth-century Protestant belief in devils. So Yeats, in the last section of "Nineteen Hundred and Nineteen", takes his violent mysterious horsemen from a surviving Celtic tradition, but uses them to typify a horrible turbulence that he felt to be actually inherent in history. This is more moving than the death of Cuchulain; and after all is it not the more symbolical way of using the old traditions? In this light, Irish myth takes its place with the images Yeats draws from the common European stock, with Oedipus at Colonus and Leda and the Swan: in fact he finds Helen a more powerful symbol than

Deirdre. What Ireland gave him in particular was not legends more noble or more primitive than others, but the feeling of historical continuity, of writing out of the heart of his own people and his own country. The don's ideal of a community of European culture can never wholly replace local loyalties, pre-literary associations from family and from childhood; though many of us may have to do without them, and so regard the deprivation as normal, Yeats's work is the stronger because he did not suffer it.

Actually, what he drew from the Ireland of his own day, from his family and his friends, furnished him with a more powerful and more moving mythology than Celtic legend. No doubt the mutual sympathy and respect between Yeats and his father had a good deal to do with this. It was a happy and a beautiful relationship, without afterthought or reserve, and may well have contributed to Yeats's strength. Much twentieth-century poetry has been written by people who appear to hate their fathers and expend their piety on purely intellectual ancestors: and this may be one of the reasons why Yeats's sense of tradition, having an organic and physical basis, has also more life. No poet in our day has written more about his family and his friends than Yeats, and no one has been more successful in enlarging them to heroic proportions. The only comparable modern attempt to make epic figures out of contemporaries is in *The Seven Pillars of Wisdom*. There is much magnanimity in the way that Yeats, who was not a companionable man, uses his very high sense of his own dignity to add to the dignity of his friends. This tendency is connected with a growing sobriety, a *romanitas* in Yeats's style, and a partial reconciliation with the rhetoric he had once condemned. The formal elegy on Major Robert Gregory and the less premeditated "Irish Airman" are often quoted; the pastoral on the same theme, "Shepherd and Goatherd", less often. But there is no poem that better illustrates Yeats's power of ennobling, with perfect simplicity, people he had known in the life of every day.

GOATHERD.   How does she bear her grief? There is not a
                        shepherd
                    But grows more gentle when he speaks her name

>   Remembering kindness done, and how can I,
>   That found when I had neither goat nor grazing
>   New welcome and old wisdom at her fire
>   Till winter blasts were gone, but speak of her
>   Even before his children and his wife.
>   SHEPHERD.   She goes about her house erect and calm
>   Between the pantry and the linen-chest,
>   Or else at meadow or at grazing overlooks
>   Her labouring men, as though her darling lived,
>   But for her grandson now; there is no change
>   But such as I have seen upon her face
>   Watching her shepherd sports at harvest-time
>   When her son's turn was over.

In these poems, in "All Souls' Night", "No Second Troy",
"On a Political Prisoner", the friends of his youth, George
Pollexfen, Lady Gregory and her son, Maud Gonne, Synge
and the rest, without ever losing their individual reality,
become symbols of something more than themselves.

>   And that enquiring man John Synge comes next,
>   That dying chose the living world for text
>   And never could have rested in the tomb
>   But that, long travelling, he had come
>   Towards nightfall upon certain set apart
>   In a most desolate stony place,
>   Towards nightfall upon a race
>   Passionate and simple like his heart.

In the same way, in the exquisite elegiac poem "In Memory of
Eva Gore-Booth and Con Markievicz" he sets a private
nostalgia in a whole landscape of wider references.

>   Many a time I think to seek
>   One or the other out and speak
>   Of that old Georgian mansion, mix
>   Pictures of the mind, recall
>   That table and the talk of youth,
>   Two girls in silk kimonos, both
>   Beautiful, one a gazelle.
>   Dear shadows, now you know it all,
>   All the folly of a fight
>   With a common wrong or right.
>   The innocent and the beautiful
>   Have no enemy but time.

It is curious to reflect on the material of which his heroic

234

idylls are constructed, that the Ireland of Yeats must at least
partly have overlapped (*horresco referens*) with that of Somerville and Ross; and that the lines

> When long ago I saw her ride
> Under Ben Bulben to the meet
> The beauty of her countryside
> With all youth's lonely wildness stirred,

might have appeared in the words of the Irish R.M. as "a
square-shouldered young lady with effective coils of dark hair
and a grey habit . . . riding a fidgety black mare with great
decision and a not disagreeable swagger".

In the magnificent "Easter 1916", he gives the lie to some
of his earlier convictions about political poetry, and finds the
most austere and splendid employment of his speaking voice;
here he attempts the exaltation not of individuals, but of a
people.

> I have met them at close of day
> Coming with vivid faces
> From counter or desk among grey
> Eighteenth-century houses.
> I have passed with a nod of the head
> Or polite meaningless words,
> Or have lingered a while and said
> Polite meaningless words,
> And thought before I had done
> Of a mocking tale or a gibe
> To please a companion
> Around the fire at the club,
> Being certain that they and I
> But lived where motley is worn:
> All changed, changed utterly:
> A terrible beauty is born.

He begins the evocation of figures from Irish history. In the
poems on the Lane pictures Parnell had appeared as a heroic
shade in the background. (Could any English poet have done
as much for Gladstone?)

> Go, unquiet wanderer,
> And gather the Glasnevin coverlet
> About your head till the dust stops your ear,

The time for you to taste of that salt breath
And listen at the corners has not come;
You had enough of sorrow before death—
Away, away! You are safer in the tomb.

Yeats now strengthens his sense of historical continuity by following the Irish Protestant tradition backwards and finding ancestors of the individualist and un-priest-ridden Ireland that he loved in Swift, Goldsmith, Berkeley and Burke. He celebrates them in "The Seven Sages" and "Blood and the Moon"; and they might have been not a little surprised to find themselves enshrined together in this pantheon. It is in these poems that Yeats finds the answer to his own early questionings about the right relation of poetry to the life of a people.

On account of this body of verse Yeats's career has sometimes been pictured as a progress from the Celtic twilight to a vigorous handling of actualities, from the wearing of a coat covered with mythological embroideries to the greater enterprise of walking naked. It is necessary to correct this view by returning to the point from which we started—Yeats's profound sense of the religious basis of poetry, and his feeling that poetry had lost touch with the spiritual world. Symbolism, he believed, could provide a means of reaching back to those primitive and fundamental modes of apprehension; and the old mythologies could be used by the modern poet to this end. This corresponds, in Yeats's peculiar kind of church, to the practice in other churches of the normal religious observances. But just as in other churches mystics have believed that there is another way, a direct apprehension that renders ritual and sacrifice irrelevant, so does Yeats. Beneath all his changes of theme and style there remains the constant conviction that the poet's experience is closely allied to the mystic's, that it may give direct access to a really existing spiritual world, and that this unseen world can make irruptions of various kinds into the world of every day. Writing in 1901 Yeats talks of the bloodlessness and etiolation of literature "unless it is constantly flooded with the passions and beliefs of ancient times". But he writes a footnote to this passage in 1924: "I should have added as an alternative that the supernatural may at any moment create new myths, but I was timid." Like most people whose beliefs are violently opposed to the whole contemporary climate of opinion, he tends to express them in veiled form, or in a deliberately provocative way which enables his audience to take them as amiable eccentricities. One recalls Max Beerbohm's cartoon of Yeats introducing Moore to the queen of the fairies. But this really will not do. In the first place Yeats really believed in magic, in the simple and literal sense; secondly, he was, it appears, at various times of his life the subject of some supernormal occurrences; and, most important, these experiences and beliefs gave rise to some of his greatest poetry.

Mild supernormal experiences have probably happened to most people, instances of telepathy, of unexplained foreknowledge, of precognitive dreams: because they do not fit into the standard world-view most people are content to dismiss them after a moment's gaping wonderment. Yeats on the other hand attached great importance to them; so much so that he was apt at times to invent supernatural romances around himself when there was nothing really happening;[20] and of course he spent a great deal of time and research in actually seeking such phenomena. In the eighties and nineties he was much in the theosophical circles of Madame Blavatsky and MacGregor Mathers, in both of which he became an initiate. They were concerned with magic in the traditional sense—spirit-compelling by means of rites and symbols. Later his interests changed, and he was attracted by a more recent spiritualism, and formed a friendship with the Hon. Everard Feilding, a prominent member of the Psychical Research Society. He sought, by automatic writing and other means, proofs of survival or immortality, information about the nature and constitution of the *vitam venturi saeculi*, and ultimately came to believe that he had exact information on the matter. Four days after his marriage in 1917 Mrs. Yeats spontaneously attempted automatic writing, and so began that extraordinary series of communications which was later systematised and published as *A Vision*. The story is told, with the most tenuous allegorical veil, in "The Gift of Haroun al-Raschid". In all these experiences the desire for system is to be observed. Yeats did not want mere strange experiences, he wanted exact and co-ordinated knowledge; partly because this would provide a set of symbols for his poetry that would have real and universal validity. Yeats says that the spiritual ministers who are omnipresent in Shelley's poetry give it "an air of rootless phantasy", because Shelley is ignorant of their more traditional forms, and is inclined to treat them as metaphors, only half-believing in their actuality. For Yeats the spiritual ministers were real, and supernaturally inspired metaphors were their gift. The unknown communicators of *A Vision*, speaking through Mrs. Yeats's automatic writing, said, "We have come to give you metaphors for poetry". Yeats hoped by this means to reach directly the supernatural reality from which the poet's images were derived; and he attributes the increased power and self-possession of *The Tower* and *The Winding Stair* to the experiences of *A Vision*.

That very ninetyish essay *The Autumn of the Body* hails the advent of a period

> when we are beginning to be interested in many things which positive science, the interpreter of exterior law, has always denied: communion of mind with mind in thought and without words, foreknowledge in dreams and in visions, and the coming among us of the dead, and of much else. We are, it may be, at a crowning crisis of the world, at the moment when man is about to ascend, with the wealth he has been so long gathering upon his shoulders, the stairway he has been descending from the first days.[21]

And in 1902 Yeats abruptly announced his belief in the practice and philosophy of magic and the evocation of spirits. If this philosophy were true, it could form the basis of a new myth-ology, one that could escape from all the falsehoods and banalities of contemporary opinion, and reach back to a more permanent reality. Yet the expression of this faith in Yeats's early poetry seems to demand the sort of acquiescence we give to an old wives' tale, rather than a settled belief. But it is quite possible that "Land of Heart's Desire" and "The Man who Dreamed of Fairyland" really mean what they say; that the slight prettiness of expression is due to Yeats's temporary

flirtation with the decadence, his dislike for rhetoric and argu-
ment. The word fairy, as E. M. Forster has remarked, is in
English consecrated to imbecility. But Yeats does not seem
to have felt this; for him the Sidhe, the Danaan, the fairies,
are all traditional avatars of the millions of spiritual beings
who actually walk the earth, and of whose presence he believed
himself to have direct evidence. Perhaps belief had come too
easily: "Only when we have seen and foreseen what we dread
shall we be rewarded by that dazzling wing-footed wanderer,"
he writes in *Per Amica Silentia Lunae*. And as the period of
that curious essay approaches, the period too of the beginnings
of *A Vision*, we begin to detect in Yeats the signs of a more
difficult faith in the supernatural. "I shall find the dark grow
luminous, the void fruitful, when I understand I have nothing,
that the ringers in the tower have appointed for the hymen of
the soul a passing bell."[22]

III. THE MASK AND THE GREAT WHEEL

The chief documents of this period, besides *A Vision*, to
which we will turn in a moment, are the prose essay *Per Amica
Silentia Lunae*, and the three poems "Ego Dominus Tuus",
"The Phases of the Moon", and "The Double Vision of
Michael Robartes". Yeats's mind was much occupied at this
time with what might be called the doctrine of the mask.
Many of his ideas seem to come to him initially as purely verbal
suggestions, and we can perhaps discern its origin in the much
earlier poem "Put off that Mask of Burning Gold", a dialogue
between a lover and his mistress, in which she tries to discover
whether it is his real self or his assumed mask that attracted
her. Perhaps too we can see traces of it in Yeats's concern
with the use of masks and the exclusion of individual character
in drama. However that may be, in *Per Amica* he develops the
theory that the poet in the act of creation is not seeking his
self, but a mask which is his anti-self, the antithesis of all that
he is in life.

> By the help of an image
> I call to my own opposite, summon all
> That I have handled least, least looked upon.[23]

He applies the idea to Keats, who out of poverty and ill-breeding made a world of luxurious beauty; to Dante—

> Being mocked by Guido for his lecherous life,
> Derided and deriding, driven out
> To climb that stair and eat that bitter bread,
> He found the unpersuadable justice, he found
> The most exalted lady loved by a man.[23]

And in *Per Amica* he speaks of a friend (evidently Lady Gregory) whose fault was harsh judgment of those who were not in sympathy with her, and who yet wrote comedies in which the worst people seem only naughty children. In the tragic poet there is conflict both with the world and with the self. "I am always persuaded that he [Dante] celebrated the most pure lady ever sung and the Divine Justice, not merely because death took that lady and Florence banished her singer, but because he had to struggle in his own heart with his unjust anger and his lust." Compensation, the psychologist would say; and as far as that goes, Yeats would agree; but he would not think that that explained very much. For he sees the mask also as the creative principle: out of the quarrel with the world we make rhetoric, out of the quarrel with the self we make poetry. All creative activity depends on the energy to assume a mask, to be deliberately reborn as something not oneself. Something of the theatrical element, of affectation even, is necessary to all active virtue. When the artist "found hanging upon some oak of Dodona an ancient mask", painted and regilt it to his liking, and at last put it on, he found that "another's breath came and went within his breath upon the carven lips and that his eyes were upon the instant fixed upon a visionary world". Both the man of occult learning and the practitioner of vulgar witchcraft are agreed that the other self is a daemon, that it may be a dead man speaking through the living; and Yeats added for himself that "the Daemon comes not as like to like but seeking its own opposite, for man and daemon feed the hunger in one another's hearts". "Ego Dominus Tuus", in which this doctrine is expressed, is the first of those poems of intense and passionate speculation which are the greatest triumph of Yeats's later style.

It is not evident at first how the doctrine of the mask leads on to Yeats's further religious and metaphysical speculations. But it does so; for the assumption of the mask is an *ascesis*, a denial of the personal life, and the poet's activity in assuming it is parallel with that of the saint and the hero, though not identical with theirs. The saint seeks the anti-self of the whole world, and renounces the world while it still has power to attract. But the hero finds his mask in defeat, and loves the world until it breaks him; and the poet finds his in disappointment and loves the world until it breaks faith with him. The saint assumes his mask for ever, and puts away the world and reduces his life to a round of customary duties. But the poet only assumes his mask while he is in the act of creation, and when it is all over Dante returns to his chambering; and as for Yeats himself, had he not written years before:

> All things can tempt me from this craft of verse,
> One time it was a woman's face, or worse.

At the end of the first section of *Per Amica* Yeats toys with the idea that the poet, growing old, might be able to keep his mask without new bitterness and new disappointment, settle down to a tranquil but not unfruitful old age. Then he remembers Wordsworth's fifty years' decay; and is willing after all to "climb to some waste room and find, forgotten there by youth, some bitter crust". In fact Yeats's quarrel with himself was to continue for twenty years longer. The conflict between an acceptance of the natural world and the denial of it involved in an assumption of the mask is the theme of his greatest verse —"The Tower" and the two Byzantium poems.

And now, after all attempts to edge round this daunting work, the problem of *A Vision*[24] must be faced: even for the most purely literary of critics, what a great poet regards as the central revelation of his life cannot be irrelevant to his poetry. The book presents us with not one but three incomprehensibles, its geometry, its astrology and its metaphysics. Regarded as coming from beyond this world, its doctrines are presumably not open to sublunary criticism, and I advance no theories about the origin of these or any other psychic communications.

Among much that I do not even begin to understand, this mysterious document contains, however, two things which have clearly had much to do with Yeats's poetry—a theory of psychological types, and a theory of history. The theory of psychological types springs from the mask theme of the quite naturally produced *Per Amica*; and an elaborate classification of men is built up on the basis of their combat with themselves and their combat with circumstance. There are twenty-eight types: they may be arranged in a circle and symbolised by the phases of the moon, but this is only an accident of notation. What is more interesting is that this symbolism expresses few ideas of which we have not already had hints in Yeats's earlier work, sometimes very long ago. Those phases in which man remains contentedly involved in nature and those in which he is engaged in the struggle with himself grow progressively more beautiful; until "at the full of the moon" the body is perfectly moulded by the soul, the result is perfect beauty: and this type is too perfect ever to lie in any earthly cradle; these are the beings whom countrymen meet with terror in the lonely hills, the Sidhe and the Danaan of Yeats's early poetry. The succeeding types are summarised as follows in "The Phases of the Moon":

> The soul remembering its loneliness
> Shudders in many cradles; all is changed,
> It would be the world's servant, and as it serves,
> Choosing whatever task's most difficult
> Among tasks not impossible, it takes
> Upon the body and upon the soul
> The coarseness of the drudge.
>
> .   .   .   .   .
>
> Reformer, merchant, statesman, learned man,
> Dutiful husband, honest wife by turn,
> Cradle upon cradle, and all in flight and all
> Deformed because there is no deformity
> But saves us from a dream.

Until, through the types of the Hunchback, the Saint, and the Fool, we return to the first phase, the dark of the moon, the stage of complete objectivity, where the dough is kneaded up again, to be formed again through the aeons after the old patterns.

Much of this restates, with a supernatural panache, what Yeats has implied before. The natural man, and he who struggles with his own soul, may be beautiful: the reformer, merchant, statesman, dutiful husband, are ugly and deformed. Have we not already heard, in the essay on Spenser, that beauty passed out of our culture with the coming of Puritan commercialism, and Puritan worry about other people's sins? Have we not heard that out of the quarrel with the world we make rhetoric; and was not rhetoric the tedious enemy of Yeats's early years? The difference is that what were formerly mere literary and social predilections have now assumed metaphysical status. The twenty-eight phases are the twenty-eight possible incarnations, to complete which is to complete a whole cycle of being. (Of course Yeats has always believed in reincarnation.) Man begins at phase one, the dark of the moon, complete objectivity: he seeks the opposite, finds it at the full moon, where body becomes only the complete expression of soul: then through the later phases he sinks back again to the undifferentiated mass. An analogous cycle is also traversed in an individual life, in a single judgment or act of thought: it is the rhythm of every completed movement of thought or life. Yeats called it the Great Wheel, and in the original form of *A Vision* described it as being traced on the desert sands by the feet of mysterious dancers. This symbol of the dance, seen as a kind of cyclical determinism, a predestined round which all men must tread, has left many traces on his poetry.

> All men are dancers and their tread
> Goes to the barbarous clangour of a gong.

So he writes in "Nineteen Hundred and Nineteen": in "The Double Vision of Michael Robartes" the image is different; it is of man being pounded, kneaded and formed by constrained mechanical creatures outside the temporal process. But in this difficult poem the dance symbolism occurs also—in the figure of the dancer, the girl who has brought her body to perfection by dancing, and has danced herself to death. She appears between two heraldic supporters, a Sphinx representing impassive

243

intellect, a Buddha in the attitude of benediction, representing universal love. The girl, by following the rhythm of the cosmic dance, has perfected her body so that it is only the expression of soul, has reached the phase of the full moon, of perfect beauty: and she is dead, for this state of existence is not a human state. The poet is obsessed by her supernatural image: yet he is divided and driven to madness,

> Being caught between the pull
> Of the dark moon and the full,

—the life of nature and the life of visionary contemplation.

The same figure appears in the next poem, "Michael Robartes and the Dancer", this time in a more human guise. The poem reads on the surface as dialogue between a man and a woman in which he tells her that the only job of a beautiful woman is to be beautiful, and that she must despise opinion and book-knowledge. It does, of course, say this, and so far connects with several other passages (in "A Prayer for my Daughter", "On a Political Prisoner", and elsewhere) on the same theme, with Yeats's own love experiences, and his hatred of rationalising and argumentativeness in women. But this is not all that the poem is about; Yeats describes it as an endeavour to explain his philosophy of life and death. It is not a piece of advice to young women, it is a statement about the human situation. The dancer is again the human entity—I must not say soul, for the point is that soul and body are not separable —whose function is to complete itself in beauty: and for Yeats physical beauty is the invariable accompaniment of spiritual completeness. All that is learnt in colleges, abstract thought, information, sociology and argument, is a dragon that must be killed ("Wring the neck of rhetoric"): when every thought is banished, except that which the perfected body can think too, then "the blest soul" is "not composite", body and soul are one, the moon is full. But, to complete the thought by refer- ence to *A Vision*, this blessed state is not permanent, man must return to the wheel; the succeeding incarnations, of reformers, learned men, "sophists, economists and calculators", are all phases of growing deformity and ugliness, till all at last sinks

in the undifferentiated life of nature, to start the round once
more. The dance symbolism appears again, at its greatest
pitch of intensity, in "Byzantium", in the dance at midnight
on the Emperor's pavement.

> Where blood-begotten spirits come
> And all complexities of fury leave
> Dying into a dance
> An agony of trance
> An agony of flame that cannot singe a sleeve.

To return to a more breathable air. This train of speculation
led Yeats to an interest in psychology and character that was
new to him. We see it reflected in his poems about his friends
and about historical persons. Yeats never tries, even in drama,
to "create character", in the conventional sense, and is said in
life to have been a bad judge of men. But he has what serves
him better, flashes of insight into certain mental states and
movements of the spirit, an insight that can be often acid and
ironical, as we see in the malicious passages of *Dramatis
Personae*. Among a varied assortment of strange riches, this
element is not absent in *A Vision*. Take the description of the
character of Phase Twenty-four, whose historical exemplars
are, somewhat oddly, Queen Victoria, Galsworthy and Lady
Gregory.

> There is great humility—"she died every day she lived"—
> and pride as great, pride in the code's acceptance, an impersonal
> pride, as though one were to sign "servant of servants". There
> is no philosophic capacity, no intellectual curiosity, but there is
> no dislike for either philosophy or science; they are a part of the
> world and that world is accepted. There may be great intolerance
> for all who break or resist the code, and great tolerance for all
> the evil of the world that is clearly beyond it whether above it
> or below. The code must rule, and because that code cannot be
> an intellectual choice, it is always a tradition bound up with
> family, or office, or trade, always a part of history.[25]

Suddenly the oddly chosen examples fit into place; one recog-
nises their kinship, and the state of the human soul, somewhere
between innocence and experience, to which they belong. It is
like reading the description of one of the psychological types
in Jung, and finding in it a picture of a real acquaintance.

More surprisingly, *A Vision* contains snatches of Yeats's peculiar humour. Humour came to him late—his early work has a hieratic solemnity—and when it came it was in the form of a sudden delighted recognition of incongruity in the midst of grave mysteries. My favourite is the victim of curiosity in the Eighteenth Phase (the one that includes Goethe and Matthew Arnold) who reflects "I was never in love with a serpent-charmer before".

But the twenty-eight phases are not mere fortuitous types of character, they are twenty-eight incarnations through which the soul of man must pass, and some of us are in one stage, some in another. As the same rhythm runs through all created things, human history passes through a similar cycle. Just as the psychological aspect of *A Vision* led Yeats to read biography in order to find examples of the phases, so its historical aspect led him to supplement the history he had read at school, hitherto left almost unamended, by reading a certain amount of ordinary historical writing, but more especially writers with a theory of the historical process, like Spengler and Toynbee; later Vico, whom he studied through Croce. These theories of a cyclical movement in history coalesced in his mind with the Magnus Annus of the Platonists, the Great Year in which a revolution of the whole stellar system is completed. Doubtless too, in his theosophical days he had heard of the *talpas*, the aeons of the Hindus, at the end of which the whole creation is dissolved into a formless unity, to be refashioned, when the whim takes him, by the imagination of the Uncreated. Yeats shares with the Hindu conception the unteleological feeling: there is no goal for humanity (for the individual human soul there may be), history moves in a circle and civilisations only emerge from the womb to sink into it again. An outline sketch of the process is given in "Dove or Swan", the fifth book of *A Vision*: Yeats's particular interest is in our own historical epoch, and the position in it of certain crucial events.

> I saw a staring virgin stand
> Where holy Dionysus died,
> And tear the heart out of his side,
> And lay the heart upon her hand

And bear that beating heart away;
And then did all the Muses sing
Of Magnus Annus at the spring,
As though God's death were but a play.

And indeed it is but a play, one which must be acted many times. The verse comes from *The Resurrection*,[26] in which Christ, risen from the dead, appears to his disciples in a room, at the same time as the frenzied worshippers of Dionysus, outside the house, are praying for the resurrection of their god. The same form recurs, but in a different material; they have their resurrection, but it is not Dionysus, it is another God who is reborn. The length of the Great Year has been variously calculated and there are smaller cycles within it: the whole Christian era is one such cycle, and it is now coming to an end. We are now passing through its last phases, the civilisation of policemen, schoolmasters, manufacturers, philanthropists, and fast approaching the phase of undifferentiated chaos. As before, the new era will be heralded by an incarnation, foreseen in *The Second Coming*.

Somewhere in sands of the desert
A shape with lion body and the head of a man,
A gaze blank and pitiless as the sun,
Is moving its slow thighs, while all about it
Reel shadows of the indignant desert birds.
The darkness drops again, but now I know
That twenty centuries of stony sleep
Were vexed to nightmare by a rocking cradle,
And what rough beast, its hour come round at last,
Slouches towards Bethlehem to be born?

If we still thought in that way, this terrific poem might gain for Yeats the reputation as a prophet that the fourth Eclogue did for Virgil. Let us throw our sop to literalism—Virgil was writing about a son of Asinius Pollio, or whatever it was, and Yeats about the Black-and-Tans: but Yeats himself believed that Virgil was "a wizard and a knowledgeable man", and that his symbol equally with Virgil's was "a vast image out of Spiritus Mundi", the Great Memory that is also the source of prophecy, since history repeats the same predestined cycles. To Yeats the incarnation of Christ was a violent and turbulent thing: it is "the uncontrollable mystery on the bestial floor", a desired and dreaded consummation which the Magi, unsatisfied by Calvary, are looking for again. It ushered in "a fabulous formless darkness" which dissolves all the constructions of previous civilisations.

> Odour of blood when Christ was slain
> Made all Platonic tolerance vain
> And vain all Doric discipline.

So the new incarnation that we await will be violent and turbulent, and will make vain all the disciplines which we have tried to think most lasting.

> We too had many pretty toys when young;
> A law indifferent to blame or praise,
> To bribe or threat; habits that made old wrong
> Melt down, as it were wax in the sun's rays;
> Public opinion ripening for so long
> We thought it would outlive all future days.
> O what fine thought we had because we thought
> That the worst rogues and rascals had died out.
>
> Now days are dragon-ridden, the nightmare
> Rides upon sleep: a drunken soldiery
> Can leave the mother, murdered at her door,
> To crawl in her own blood, and go scot-free;
> The night can sweat with terror as before
> We pieced out thoughts into philosophy,
> And planned to bring the world under a rule,
> Who are but weasels fighting in a hole.[27]

And so approaches the last phase, that marks the end of every historical era; "man awaits death and judgment with nothing to occupy the worldly faculties, and helpless before the world's disorder, drags out of the sub-conscious the conviction that the world is about to end".

Not only is the transition from one era to another naturally a period of turmoil; but the era which is approaching is in itself a turbulent one, a denial of Christian ideals.

At the birth of Christ religious life becomes primary, secular life antithetical—man gives to Caesar the things that are Caesar's. A primary dispensation looking beyond itself towards a transcendent power is dogmatic, levelling, unifying, feminine, humane, peace its means and end; an antithetical dispensation obeys imminent† power, is expressive, hierarchical, multiple, masculine, harsh, surgical. The approaching antithetical influx, and that particular antithetical dispensation for which the intellectual preparation has begun will reach its complete systematisation at that moment when, as I have already shown, the Great Year comes to its intellectual climax. Something of what I have said it must be, the myth declares, for it must reverse our era and resume past eras in itself; what else it must be, no man can say, for always at the critical moment the Thirteenth Cone, the sphere, the unique intervenes.[28]

The thirteenth cone, in Yeats's symbolism, is the domain of the incalculable; it is what, despite the common rhythm, prevents history from merely repeating itself. One cannot avoid the impression that Yeats looked forward to the coming ."masculine, harsh, surgical" dispensation with a certain sombre relish. The intellectual preparation he speaks of he found in the works of Gentile, and he notes that it underlies the political philosophy of Italy: his friendship with Ezra Pound may have helped him to admire this. The culture heroes of his later years tend more and more to violence and inhumanity, and he was for a moment taken in by a sort of shabby Irish fascism. He was lucky to die in 1939, before the thirteenth cone had shown what was at the bottom of its bag of tricks, if this is the bottom. What is remarkable is not that he found relief for a time in the smash-up sentiment: most people do at times. The remarkable thing is that he saw through all the contemporary claptrap, saw that however the struggle between civilisation and bestiality might be rigged, the result must be the triumph of bestiality.

> The best lack all conviction, while the worst
> Are full of passionate intensity.

Yeats had little experience of pity, perhaps fortunately for his verse, for in most hands it is a deliquescent emotion. In "Nineteen Hundred and Nineteen", the poem in which the decay of the liberal and humanitarian tradition is most searchingly analysed, he has no social consolation to offer; but the crux of the poem is that the solitary soul is not hopelessly involved in the chaos.

† *Sic.* But he must mean immanent.

He who can read the signs, nor sink unmanned
Into the half-deceit of some intoxicant
From shallow wits; who knows no work can stand,
Whether health, wealth or peace of mind were spent
On master-work of intellect or hand,
No honour leave its mighty monument,
Has but one comfort left: all triumph would
But break upon his ghostly solitude.

The interpretation of this "ghostly solitude" is the most difficult question offered by Yeats's later poetry. Phrases about the death-wish come easily into the mind: some of the imagery fits easily into the categories of Christian mysticism. But explanations along either of these lines are either inadequate or wrong: most of all in this part of Yeats's work it is important to remember that the poetry means what it says, that the idea cannot be separated from the symbol, though one may temporarily try to abstract it in an effort at exposition. Yeats's father said to him that his imaginations were always mundane, even if they were set in the other world; and it is true; his conception of the supra-terrestrial destiny of the soul is curiously concrete; it can be mapped and described; it can be embodied in apparitions and images; and this makes it very unlike the incommunicable experiences of orthodox mysticism.

The image which he uses most often to represent the solitary soul is the swan, one of the wild swans at Coole,

like the soul, it sails into the sight
And in the morning's gone, no man knows why.

The disappearance of the swan into the darkening appears sometimes as a mere image of annihilation.

The swan has leaped into the desolate heaven:
That image can bring wildness, bring a rage
To end all things.

But what distinguishes Yeats from other poets who might, in this phase, seem to resemble him is the endless energy and curiosity with which he explores this darkness, the darkness which has been so often seen as a cessation of energy and curiosity. There is no trace in Yeats of the Shelleyan tired child, longing for a dreamless sleep; and however nearly he may seem to approach it, he does not assert the mystical paradox that the darkness is light and the nothing everything. To the end of his life he is "caught between the pull of the dark moon and the full", the phenomenal world and whatever is beyond it. Neglecting the almost untraceable complications let us try to discern some of the main images on the web of belief that he stretched between these two poles.

In the first place Yeats had an assured belief in personal immortality, he believed that he had evidence of it that would satisfy any court of law. ("With a jury of metaphysicians?" Mr. Hone, his biographer, has pertinently asked.) He also feels passionately that the fact of personal immortality is of absolute and central importance. Valery's *Cimetière Marin* is expunged from his list of sacred books, because it rejoices that human life must pass. And F. H. Bradley is written off as "an arrogant, sapless man", because he neither believed nor wished to believe in the immortality of soul and body. Yeats also believed that he was in possession, partly as a result of his researches into magical tradition, partly as a result of actual supernatural communications, of detailed knowledge about the future destiny of the human soul. He expounds it darkly in *Per Amica*, more categorically in Book III of *A Vision*, called "The Soul in Judgment". His late plays, *The Words upon the Window-pane* and *Purgatory*, are both comments on the same theme. But it must be realised that the terms judgment and purgatory are used with only a very vague resemblance to their conventional meanings; mostly Yeats uses a terminology of his own, which I do not discuss here, though correspondences between it and the more ordinary dialects of philosophy and religion could be worked out. We might say that Yeats conceived both this life and the life to come as a continuous purgatory: but we should have to add immediately that it is a purgatory conceived in quite amoral terms, and having little analogy with the sacrament of penance. And it is a Purgatory almost without the expectation of Paradise. After reliving its earthly experiences the soul prepared for another incarnation, and the theme of escape from the wheel of becoming, central in Hinduism and Buddhism, plays a relatively small part in

Yeats's imagination. Individual responsibility, central to Buddhism and Christianity, is also greatly reduced. Yeats held always what he had announced in 1901 as two of the fundamental doctrines of magic—that the borders of our minds are ever shifting, that many minds can flow into one another; and that our memories are a part of one great memory, Anima Mundi, the memory of Nature herself. His belief asserts, too, far more fully and concretely than the Catholic angelology or prayer for the dead, a continual interaction between incarnate and discarnate spirits, so that the images which come in dreams or in artistic creation are actually produced by the action of the dead, or by irruptions, like Jung's archetypes, from the Anima Mundi.

The period between death and rebirth is elaborately systematised in Book III of *A Vision*. The main features are a reliving by the spirit, over and over again, of the events that have most moved it in life: this is at first compulsive; it is called the Dreaming Back, and can only be performed by the help of incarnate minds; it explains the apparitions haunting the places where they lived that fill the literature of all countries. This is followed by the Return, another repetition of the same events, but this time purposive: the experience is repeated in order that it may be understood, that all may be converted into knowledge. In another process the spirit follows out the consequences of its desires, fulfilling even its phantasies. (This sounds a dangerously attractive phase of the spiritual life.) When the spirit has thus exhausted all passionate events, it has liberated itself and the past life is dismissed. It is now no longer one of "the dead", but is a free spirit, and in further stages of purgation, less clearly conceived, it is purged of good and evil, and its intentions are purified of "complexity" and brought back, as it were, to certain spiritual norms. (Yeats connects this with his early conviction that the power of the lyric poet depends on his accepting one of a few traditional attitudes, lover, sage, hero, scorner of life.) The last stage is the Foreknowledge, a vision of the next incarnation, which the spirit must accept before it is reborn.

All this is of course only Yeats's personal systematisation of the world-wide and age-old tradition of the cycle of birth and rebirth. What is peculiar to Yeats is that the discarnate existence is filled with a repetition of what has already happened in the flesh, a continuation of its passions, and even its relations with other beings. So that the whole myth takes the form of an indefinite extension of the phenomenal world, as though it were that which Yeats wishes to make eternal. The Indian longing to escape from the wheel is hardly more than suggested, and, rather surprisingly, such symptoms of it as there are do not appear most clearly at the end of Yeats's life. It is at the close of *Per Amica*, in 1917, that he speaks of "the condition of fire", the state which seems to correspond most nearly with normal religious experience.

> At certain moments, always unforeseen, I become happy, . . . I look at the strangers near as if I had known them all my life, and it seems strange that I cannot speak to them: everything fills me with affection, I have no longer any fears or any needs; I do not even remember that this happy mood must come to an end. It seems as if the vehicle had suddenly grown pure and far extended and so luminous that the images from Anima Mundi, embodied there and drunk with that sweetness, would, like a country drunkard who has thrown a wisp into his own thatch, burn up time.[29]

The same state is described in "Vacillation".

> My fiftieth year had come and gone,
> I sat, a solitary man,
> In a crowded London shop,
> An open book and empty cup
> On the marble table-top.
> While on the shop and street I gazed
> My body of a sudden blazed;
> And twenty minutes more or less
> It seemed, so great my happiness,
> That I was blessed and could bless.

The language of *Per Amica* is obscure, but this experience seems to be connected with the full acceptance of the mask. The soul, having completed itself by assuming the mask, its own complement, is liberated, and momentarily at least is out of the wheel. At this time Yeats is disposed to interpret the liberation in something very like Christian terms.

> It may be an hour before the mood passes, but latterly I seem
> to understand that I enter upon it the moment I cease to hate.
> I think the common condition of our life is hatred—I know that
> this is so with me—irritation with public or private events or
> persons. . . . And plainly, when I have closed a book too
> stirred to go on reading, and in those brief intense visions of
> sleep, I have something about me that, though it makes me
> love, is more like innocence.[30]

And he wonders whether in a little time he will not give up his
"barbarous words", and grow old "to some kind of simple
piety like that of an old woman".

But this did not happen. The Byzantium symbol, which he
later uses for the Ultima Thule of the life of the spirit, is far
from simple and has little in common with what most people
call piety. Nor is there anything to suggest that the state it
represents is any more permanent than other phases of the
soul's journey. It cannot therefore be equated with Nirvana
or the beatific vision. To use the language of orthodoxy,
Yeats's experience is that of the ecstatic, not that of the true
mystic. Byzantium, the theme of what are perhaps Yeats's two
greatest and most complex poems, is a coalescence of ideas
derived from actual Byzantine art, and from the reading of
history undertaken to illustrate *A Vision*. Byzantine architec-
ture suggests to him that of the "Sacred City of the Apocalypse
of St. John": and he writes, whether prompted by vision or
history is not apparent, "I think if I could be given a month
of Antiquity and leave to spend it where I chose, I would spend
it in Byzantium a little before Justinian opened St. Sophia and
closed the Academy of Plato. I think I could find in some little
wine-shop some philosophical worker in mosaic who could
answer all my questions, . . . I think that in early Byzantium,
maybe never before or since in recorded history, religious,
aesthetic and practical life were one."[31] Therefore Byzantium
becomes the symbol of that state in which man, by a full
acceptance of the mask, attains a unity that is the antithesis of
the natural life.

> Before me floats an image, man or shade,
> Shade more than man, more image than a shade;
> For Hades' bobbin bound in mummy-cloth

May unwind the winding path;
A mouth that has no moisture and no breath
Breathless mouths may summon;
I hail the superhuman;
I call it death-in-life and life-in-death.

The key-word of this second Byzantium poem is "complexity".
The moonlit dome of the holy city disdains

all that man is,
All mere complexities,
The fury and the mire of human veins.

The miraculous bird seated on its golden bough scorns "all
complexities of mire or blood; and at the heart of the city is the
Emperor's pavement, where blood-begotten spirits come to
join in the dance which will rid them of "all complexities of
fury".

The state of soul which Byzantium represents exercises the
most powerful attraction and at the same time the most violent
resistance. "The Tower", "Blood and the Moon", the earlier
"Sailing to Byzantium", and other poems record this conflict.
This universal conflict between nature and what is beyond
nature coalesces in Yeats's mind with the physiological pro-
cesses of old age; to produce poetry in which Byzantium is
accepted, but unwillingly, as a *pis-aller*.

What shall I do with this absurdity—
O heart, O troubled heart—this caricature,
Decrepit age that has been tied to me
As to a dog's tail? . . .

It seems that I must bid the Muse go pack,
Choose Plato and Plotinus for a friend
Until imagination, ear and eye,
Can be content with argument and deal
In abstract things; or be derided by
A sort of battered kettle at the heel.[32]

Or we find bitter angry verse, explosions of sensuality; he said
all his last verse was prompted by rage or lust. The only
poem which accepts the prospect of death with equanimity is
not Yeats's own; it is the splendid and sombre adaptation from
Oedipus at Colonus which concludes "A Man Young and Old".

Even from that delight memory treasures so,
Death, despair, division of families, all entanglements of man-
kind grow,
As that old wandering beggar and these God-hated children
know.

In the long echoing street the laughing dancers throng,
The bride is carried to the bridegroom's chamber through
torchlight and tumultuous song;
I celebrate the silent kiss that ends short life or long.

The way of regarding love as something with historical conse-
quences is as un-Yeatsian as the "gay goodnight" of the last
stanza is un-Greek. The opposites between which his later
life were torn are best expressed by "Byzantium" on the one
hand, and on the other, the speech of self, in the "Dialogue
between Self and Soul".

I am content to live it all again
And yet again, if it be life to pitch
Into the frog-spawn of a blind man's ditch,
A blind man battering blind men;
Or into that most fecund ditch of all,
The folly that man does
Or must suffer, if he woos
A proud woman not kindred of his soul.

It is no use therefore to try to fit Yeats out with any last
words of serene assurance. If his late poems have been justly
compared to Beethoven's late quartets, it is for their complexity
and the intensity of their spiritual experience, and not for any
ultimate calm. For all the unearthly harmonies of Yeats's last
phase, we cannot liken it to the one that Dowden invented for
Shakespeare; and for Yeats there is no death-bed wisdom. How
should there be, his faith being as it was? How should there
be at the end of a process so little complete, so little sen-
contained as a single human incarnation?

IV. THE BELIEFS OF YEATS

So far I have only tried to explain some of Yeats's poetry in
terms of his beliefs: but what are we to say about the much
more difficult question of the beliefs themselves? One can

YEATS

observe a tendency, since Yeats's death, both in writing and conversation, to suppose that he somehow contrived to make great poetry out of ideas that were arbitrary, fantastic, or merely absurd. I do not think that this is true, or even possible: the beliefs underlying any great poetry must represent a permanently or recurrently important phase of the human spirit, and cannot be merely individual or fashionable fantasy. It is also sometimes held that the beliefs of a poet are only incitements to temporarily appropriate emotional attitudes, and that any further question about their validity is irrelevant. This does not appear to fit some kinds of poetical statement; "beauty is truth, truth beauty", for instance: but to apply it, say, to Dante's versification of scholastic philosophy—to the following lines, for instance:

> E quinci appar ch'ogni minor natura
> e corto recettacolo a quel bene
> che non ha fine, e se con se misura;

—is at best a patent travesty of the author's purpose—Keats's beliefs, if he had any, do seem to be merely auxiliaries to the texture and shape of the poems in which they occur. To talk of Dante's beliefs in this way is plainly absurd. Of course poetry can be read anyhow; but the poet's intentions should give some indication of the best method of approach. Dante writes poetry to express a faith, he does not excogitate a faith to provide a background for a poem, as, say, Keats does in *Hyperion*: and our appreciation of Dante cannot be wholly divorced from our attitude to medieval Christian philosophy. It is necessary therefore to find some means of defining one's attitude to a poet's ideas: and it is unlikely that many readers of poetry will be sufficiently metaphysicians to do so on strictly philosophical grounds. Perhaps the only generally available way is to try to see the poet's ideas in relation to others, to see where they coincide and where they clash with other ways of thought, and where they are simply irrelevant to them. This at least does something to connect poetry with other kinds of experience; and it gives a chance of setting technical criticism in a wider framework.

257

Yeats is essentially a poet to be treated in this way. He constantly asserts in his later days that he wrote poems "as texts for exposition", "to explain my philosophy of life and death", to express "convictions about this world and the next". Oisin and Cuchulain may legitimately be treated with "that willing suspension of disbelief that constitutes poetic faith", but the creative myths by which Yeats expresses his deepest convictions demand a different attitude. Let us avoid slick prejudgments about what is or is not evidence; and let us rid ourselves of the vulgar superstition that the pronouncements *de rerum natura* of a bishop, a physicist or a psychiatrist have necessarily more authority than those of a poet. If you believe that a "philosophy of life and death" can be a matter of organised knowledge, in which every additional piece of evidence is a permanent gain, like physical science, then most of the time Yeats is talking simple nonsense. If you believe that the only things which it is possible to talk sense about are those which are empirically verifiable, then he is talking nonsense in the Pickwickian sense of the logical positivists; but so, of course, is almost everybody else. If you believe that any attempt at such a philosophy must be a mythological approximation to a reality that is in any case inexpressible, Yeats's myth has as good a chance of being right as any other. This is the view I propose to take, and since on this view there is no final way of judging the truth or otherwise of a myth, one can only make a fragmentary attempt at showing its relation to other systems.

In practice we use as a criterion in these matters something like the *consensus gentium*, logically irrelevant though that may be: and the congruity of a particular world-view with our own private feeling about the nature of things. By these standards there is much in Yeats's system which is merely arbitrary. This, however, is hardly more than accidental: Yeats's four principles, twenty-eight phases and so forth are no more arbitrary than similar Catholic formulations—the three theological virtues and the seven gifts of the Holy Ghost: or Jung's two attitudes and four faculties. There seems no earthly reason why there should not be a fifth principle, a third attitude, an eighth deadly sin, or whatever it is. Nor is there any reason; but the authority of a great organisation or the prestige of science give some of these formulations a sort of classical status. This sort of psychological and metaphysical classification delighted Scholastics and Vedantists: to most people to-day it is unmeaning and repugnant. To a large extent Yeats is wilfully trailing his coat by using an unpopular mode of expression. Yet, as we have suggested already, he is only embodying in his own particular symbolism an ancient and widespread idea.

The belief in reincarnation has attracted two types of mind —one pessimist and quietist like Gautama, the other energetically in love with the whole of man's psycho-physical experience, like Blake. The one sees in human life "sabba dukkha, sabbha anatta, sabbha anikka", everywhere sorrow, everywhere impermanence, everywhere unreality; and it sees the wheel of becoming as a weary round from which it is the aim of the human soul to escape. The other, though it may sometimes pay temporary tribute to this Oriental attitude, is so deeply attached to the phenomenal world that it cannot bear to think of it except as eternally recurrent: if it believes in spirits, it gives them aerial bodies, if it has a remote and formal hope of being saved from the cycle of rebirth, it wants to postpone its salvation as long as possible. It is to this type that Yeats belongs. The irrevocable choice, the final judgment of Christian eschatology would have been infinitely repugnant to him, if he had ever seriously entertained it, which in fact he does not seem to have done. The belief in progress is equally repugnant, for it implies that the future will be different from the past, and Yeats is in love with experience, with the world as it has been. So he pictures man moving in a cycle of incarnations, which bring him back, after phases of various complexity, to his starting-point, the unselfconscious life of nature. History moves in a similar round, and when one cycle is completed it starts on the round again. The same rhythm is preserved, though the second cycle does not merely repeat the first, and its exact nature is always incalculable. Thus there is always the possibility of new experience, though it cannot differ fundamentally from the old.

Formally this may look like Hindu belief, but the emotional colouring is very different, and Yeats's belief actually springs from a very different central core of conviction. Hindu thought springs from a conviction that phenomenal experience is absolutely without value; Yeats's from a conviction that phenomenal experience is all we have, and that all value must be found within it. Christian and Indian religious beliefs have this in common with the belief in progress—that they all look for salvation in a state outside our present experience. Yeats does not believe that salvation is a goal to which we can attain by moral discipline or material development: it is something that we make, out of material already at our disposal.

> I mock Plotinus' thought
> And cry in Plato's teeth,
> Death and life were not
> Till man made up the whole,
> Made lock, stock and barrel
> Out of his bitter soul,
> Aye, sun and moon and star, all.
> And further add to that
> That, being dead, we rise,
> Dream and so create
> Translunar Paradise.[32]

His conception of the next life, as we have said, makes a good deal of it very like a recapitulation of this one. And in spite of his hatred for empirical science he was willing enough to use its methods on any subject that he cared about, for his belief in human survival is mainly based on empirical evidence, the evidence from psychical research. His concentration on "ancient wisdom" is not mere romantic antiquarianism: amid a good deal of fantasy in detail there remains the perfectly rational conviction that men in earlier ages had accumulated much knowledge and evidence of these matters which the modern world had tacitly agreed to neglect; and that the surviving beliefs and experiences of primitive people, and those who were outside the modern scientific tradition, were therefore of primary importance. Yeats's attitude to his evidence was an excessively uncritical one; but on the question of considering such evidence at all we can hardly do better than to remember the caveat of Professor Broad against confusing the Author of Nature with the editor of *Nature*, and of assuming that the one would not permit in his creation what the other would not accept as a contribution.

But of course the examination of psychic phenomena is only mildly unfashionable in our age; what is extremely unfashionable is to base a whole world-view upon it, as Yeats did. Yet Yeats is surely right to believe that if there is a possibility of survival it is of primary emotional importance to mankind; and that indifference to it is either affectation or stark insensibility. The almost universal belief in survival is no evidence of its truth, but it is evidence of its immense importance to the human mind.

I dwell on these unsympathetic and unpoetical themes because I believe that the general acceptance of Yeats's poetic greatness has been combined with a quite unjustifiable indifference to most of what he actually said. We may admit that his hostility to the prevailing modes of thought in his day may have had its root in prejudice and the conventions of a côterie; and the danger of this is of being left in a frowsty little backwater. Yeats's distinction is in his determination not to be so left, but to find another tradition more adequate to his experience. His opposition to the whole post-seventeenth-century climate of opinion nevertheless remains a formidable obstacle to the proper appreciation of his work; and the desire to find a connection between the thought of a poet whom we admire and other kinds of thought that we accept is a perfectly legitimate one. Let us therefore end on a more consolatory note. If we are to find any analogy in the contemporary world to Yeats's way of thinking it is in the analytical psychologists. They too have been driven to dreams and fantasies to explain man's total experience, and have found analogies between them and ancient and primitive beliefs. Of course the Freudian school has explored these irrational territories only in the interests of a scientific positivism; the connection we are looking for is between Yeats and Jung. Many of the parallels are sufficiently obvious. Yeats's Anima Mundi from which the images of the poet are derived is Jung's collective unconscious, from which come the archetypes of myth and legend. Yeats's mask is the unconscious, in Jung's sense, not in Freud's—not the wastepaper basket for discarded experiences and desires, but the vehicle of the buried faculties, those which are unused in the conscious life. The creative power which comes from the acceptance of the mask corresponds with the psychic rebirth which, in Jung's psychology, follows on the emergence of the submerged faculties. No doubt many similar elucidations could be worked out, by one who had the patience, the knowledge and the power of correlation; which probably means Jung himself. So great a mythologist as Yeats needs another mythologist to interpret him, and Jung's mythopoeic faculty is very much of the same kind. Like Yeats he is unsatisfied by the established religious formulas, yet is profoundly concerned with religion; like Yeats he uses sub-rational or supra-rational intuitions to complete the thin and abstract picture of the world given by logic and the senses. We find in both the same fertility and the same obscurity about the exact status of the myth. When Jung explains ecstatic and mystical experience in terms of the unconscious we feel the same uncertainty as we do when Yeats talks about "the condition of fire". Into what country are we being led? Are Byzantium and the collective unconscious psychological or metaphysical entities? All remains obscure, but involved with the obscurity is a sense of richness and adequacy, the antithesis of the cheap desire to explain away what cannot be immediately understood; and it is perhaps not an accident that the closest analogy to Yeats's thought is to be found in the work of the psychologist who has done most justice to the depth and variety of human experience.

CONVERSATION IN LIMBO

W. B. YEATS   H. G. WELLS

WELLS. But the bare truth is that such men are infantile defectives, who ought either to be referred back to a study of the elements of human ecology, or certified as incapable of managing public affairs.

YEATS. What spirit are you that roams through these fields, muttering fragments out of old mythologies?

W. Wells is my name, or was. Who are you?

Y. I have lived under many masks, spoken through many mouths, Aedh, Aleel, Forgael, Hanrahan, Swift, Berkeley, the old travel-wearied man of Colonus have lent me their voices. Out of Ireland have I come——

W. Ah, Yeats, of course. I never knew you, but I have seen your picture in the papers. Glad to meet you.

Y. Great hatred, little room. No, we never met; but the Great Wheel should school me in humility. Who am I that I dare fancy that I can better conduct myself or have more sense than a common man?

W. Pardon?

Y. I was quoting from my own works.

W. I'm afraid I do not know much of your later work. We scientists, you know, have had less time for poetry than we should. But I remember a little thing—years ago it must have been—*Innisfree*, was it called?

> There midnight's all a glimmer, and noon a purple glow
> And evening full of the linnet's wings.

To a serious student of human destiny such moments of relief are extremely delightful.

Y. That accursed poem! And my curse on the popular

education that has distributed it through the minds of all the bank-clerks in England.

W. Surely to touch and move minds, those of bank-clerks or any others, is precisely the aim we writers have always had before us?

Y. We writers! How generous of you to assume that you and I have had any purposes in common.

W. Not in the least. My relations with what you would call imaginative and aesthetic writers have always been most fruitful. Even Henry James, a mind as intricate and edentate as a pseudopodium, gave me some criticisms of my early work that were very valuable to me. Though it is true he never succeeded in seeing the novel from my point of view. If you and I had nothing in common, why should we be talking together now?

Y. We are talking now because it is part of our destiny to rehearse continually the actions, the ideas of our life on earth, till all has been converted into knowledge, until we can be rid of our experience by understanding it. Therefore I summon to myself my own opposite, all that I have least handled, least looked upon.

W. A few years ago I should have been very glad to help you. Years of research have enabled me to see some of the main trends of life, and I have perhaps had some success in presenting, instead of the masses of clotted and undigested fact that passes for academic history, an orderly view of human ecology.

Y. Ecology, pseudopodium, magic words.

W. But now it is finished. There has been a fundamental change in the conditions under which life is going on. Not simply human life, our whole world is at the end of its tether. As far as human life is concerned, the process is already at an end, or will be in a few years' or a few months' time. I am sorry, but I can do nothing for you. It has sometimes seemed to me a curious coincidence that the process of history should terminate at precisely the same time as my own earthly span, but so it is. The future has always been my special subject: henceforth there is no future.

EPILOGUE

Y. That is how the prospect of eternity looks to those who are accustomed to living in time. No, in your sense there is no future.

W. Not now. There used to be.

Y. Past and future, in your understanding of the words, have never really existed. Like others you have been forced to make your own philosophy, but whatever of philosophy has been made poetry is alone permanent. Your Whig myth is very recent, and it has never made poetry.

W. Oh, we are talking of mythology and poetry. I misunderstood you; I thought you were looking for the truth. I thought you wanted me to work out with you the strands of physical, biological, intellectual development, to trace their consequences——

Y. Some other time. Perhaps I have attended too little to the development of your myth. But you could tell me little of it now; your mind is hag-ridden with Jewish eschatology. Naturally; you are an Englishman; it is only the mind of Ireland that can reach out after the subtler intuitions of the Hindu.

W. Eschatology, last things; a theological conception. Though I have enlarged and deepened some of the cruder notions of traditional theology, I have never given much attention to the subject. Last things, indeed; but you are right—or rather I am: there is nothing else to talk about now.

Y. How did you find so much to talk about before?

W. I conceived the process differently. I did not foresee the final vast catastrophe; or I thought there was some way out or round or through the impasse.

Y. You conceived the process differently?

W. When I was a young man I seemed to myself to be living in the middle of a huge, crumbling confusion; aimless scurrying hither and thither; ill-defined desires and pointless sorrows. Yet I felt that something came out of it: I was able to say to myself, Through the confusion something drives, something clear and purposeful——

Y. Forgive me, as a poet I have an inveterately concrete mind. You say that something *drives* through the confusion—

something like a nail, is it, or something like an ass and cart?

W. How can I express the value of a thing at once so essential and so immaterial, something that is at once human achievement and the most inhuman of existing things? It emerges from life, generation by generation and age by age. From the simplest protozoon I saw it taking form ever more clearly until it reached that infinitely unsatisfactory, that wholly provisional creature, man. Among them I saw the rise of a class, clearer sighted than the rest, devoting their existence to a not unforeseeable future, the Samurai, the Open Conspirators of a new epoch in biological history. As technical efficiency increased, so a danger phase grew nearer: the danger that men's command of physical forces should outstrip their powers of social adaptation and control. Yet I saw them clambering painfully and uncertainly past the danger point. I saw that the devotion and persistence of countless forgotten workers gave form and clear purpose to what was at first mere floundering and clutching: until man struggles to such a level of assurance, understanding and safety as no living substance has ever attained before. As generation after generation passed I saw him becoming a new species, infinitely wiser and fuller than that weedy, tragic, pathetic, absurd and sometimes sheerly horrible being who christened himself in a mood of oafish arrogance Homo Sapiens.

Y. An interesting myth, but surely a very recent one.

W. It is only very recently that man has had the possibility of basing his world-view on real knowledge. It is because mine is recent that it is not a myth.

Y. Yet it has broken down. By your own account the something that drove through the confusion has driven so far only to tip its passengers into the foulest ditch.

W. Into the abyss of extinction.

Y. The abyss, if you prefer it.

W. But that does not invalidate what you call my myth. Suppose that I spend years in devising a piece of apparatus to perform an experiment of infinite scientific importance, an experiment that is morally certain of success. An hour before it is due to start, a drunken half-wit smashes the instruments and burns the formulae. Does that prove that my labour and my purpose were only an illusion?

Y. Since I died I have had time to learn a little logic. Your analogy is false. Your experiment was the expression of an individual purpose: it failed, but the purpose was really there. Your mythology would attribute the same purpose to the whole created world: that is an illusion.

W. Not to the world, to man. Man makes his own history.

Y. Yes, man makes his own history. Have I not said it myself?

> Death and life were not
> Till man made up the whole,
> Made lock, stock and barrel
> Out of his bitter soul.

But not according to his own will. He unwinds a skein that was wound before time began; when it is unwound he winds it up again. But your myth needs the old Overseer God to see that all this discordant coupling, breeding, killing, building and breaking is directed to a common end.

W. I deny it. The purpose that emerges from the confusion has nothing in common with that creaking old dummy of the priests and schoolmasters. It is true that the blind, muddled crowd of little people, endless, pointless variations of the same dull idea, never worked together for any common end. The purpose expressed itself through a class of enlightened ones, the Samurai, the Open Conspirators.

Y. Your kind of men, in fact; the noisy men, the men who write for the newspapers. Empty cigarette tins drifting down a gutter and thinking they direct its course. No poetry ever sprang from that wind-swollen vainglory.

W. When I was younger and less angry I sometimes thought it did.

> Be through my lips to unawakened earth
> The trumpet of a prophecy. O Wind,
> If winter comes, can spring be far behind?

Y. And if spring, can summer be far behind, and autumn, and the next winter? Shelley knew that the Great Year has its seasons, and it is only when he is versifying Godwin that he supports your myth. Let me quote him when he is writing as himself.

> Another Athens shall arise,
> And to remoter time
> Bequeath, like sunset to the skies,
> The splendour of its prime;
> And leave, if naught so bright may live,
> All earth can take, or heaven can give.
>
> Oh cease! must hate and death return?
> Cease! must men kill and die?
> Cease! drain not to its dregs the urn
> Of bitter prophecy.

But Shelley knows that there is no escaping that draught: there is only the insane necessity that what has been shall be again. Let me even quote myself.

> So the Platonic Year
> Whirls out new right and wrong,
> Whirls in the old instead;
> All men are dancers and their tread
> Goes to the barbarous clangour of a gong.

It is only when your philosophy of progress breaks down, when you change the end of the story, that it could be transmuted into poetry. When you see humanity take the last wrong turning you achieve a kind of limited nobility. For a moment you have a glimpse of the abstract joy, the half-read wisdom of daemonic images. Only a glimpse, for you see it through the dirty window that is the only light to men of your race and of your age. And what looks to you like the Gotterdämmerung is only the end of your shop-boy civilisation.

W. You are looking at a man with an inoperable cancer and talking as though he had a summer cold. While you are vapouring about the Platonic Year, one by one the lights are going out. The new tide of barbarism is already at half-flood, and the new barbarism is different from the old, for its powers of terror and destruction are so infinitely greater. The crumbling of the social structure that men have laboriously built up does not involve at once the decay of all the techniques that made it possible. In the end, of course they go, but some of the techniques of destruction are among the simplest and most persistent. Many of them are self-perpetuating. Some of them we have seen, soon we shall see others. We can expect again a crop of abortions and monstrosities; the viruses and pestilential germs will resume their experiments in variation; new blotches and infections will complete the deformation of what semblance of humanity remains. Mankind, which began in a cave, will end in the disease-soaked ruins of a slum. What else can happen, what other turn can destiny take?

Y. Suppose you are right; was there ever any reason in your mythology why this should not be so?

> So careful of the type? but no.
> From scarped cliff and quarried stone
> She cries "A thousand types are gone,
> I care for nothing, all must go."

Surely this was a fair statement of your premisses; and it was perfectly well known to the geologists of the 1830's. Yet out of this your fat-witted bourgeois complacency contrived to develop a kind of cosmic optimism. Your myth is a self-contradiction, and that is the only sense in which a myth can be a lie. You speak like a decadent megatherium, not like a man, not even like a man in your limited understanding of the word.

W. I speak like one of a class of men who, but for a crass accident, could have taken charge of human destiny.

Y. Godwin told humanity what to do, and thought that to tell them was enough.

W. But Godwin's justice was a pre-evolutionary fantasy, the static heaven of intellectualism, a home for little children above the bright blue sky. I and those who thought like me, for the first time in human history, knew life from its foundations. For the first time human thought had emerged from the jungle of superstition. My knowledge was built up step by step on a foundation of rock. I had placed man definitely in the great scheme of space and time. I had traced his lungs from a swimming bladder, step by step, with scalpel and probe,

K

through a dozen types or more: I had watched the gill-slits patched slowly to the purposes of the ear, I had followed all these things and many kindred things by dissection and in embryology, I had checked the whole theory of development again in a year's course of palaeontology, and I had taken the dimensions of the whole process, by the scale of the stars, in a course of astronomical physics. Turning then to social man——

Y. Old rags upon old sticks to scare a bird.

W. You spoke?

Y. Nothing. I said that I find it difficult to fix my mind upon such evidence.

W. Then to me your mind is not a mind at all. It is not, apparently, obfuscated with the dogmas of organised religion, yet you reject the only kind of thought that could be put in its place. On what kind of evidence do you rely?

Y. My spirit instructors have spoken to me sometimes in automatic writing, sometimes by the direct voice. They speak from beyond time, but even from there it is not possible to predict: for there is the Thirteenth Cone, the cone of the absolutely incalculable. It will be most easy to explain to you the mechanism of the Great Wheel by tracing its revolutions in our own historic period, and I will begin from that. Christ rose from the dead at a full moon in the first month of the year, the month that we have named from Mars, the ruler of the first of the twelve gyres. I do not know if my instructors were the first to make a new lunar circuit equal in importance with the solar out of that archetypal month. To this month, to touch for a moment on a less lucid symbolism, they give a separate zodiac when the moon falls at Capricorn. The two abstract zodiacs are so imposed the one upon the other——

W. Blimey!

Y. You spoke?

W. Nothing. I said that I find it difficult to fix my mind on such evidence.

Y. Anaximander, Plato, Plotinus, Vico——

W. Lyell, Darwin, Tyndall, Huxley——

Y. Spengler——

W. Haldane——

EPILOGUE

Y. Madame Blavatsky.——

W. Old Uncle Tom Cobley and all——

Y. We shall never get anywhere like this.

W. Yeats, we are both spirits by now. Your ghostly informers can claim no particular prestige, for they are only as you yourself, or even as I.

Y. And your experimental biology at the Royal College of Science in the Exhibition Road has no relevance here.

W. Let us give up trying to humbug one another. My applied science never gave me certain knowledge. It led me first up one blind alley, then up another. It even led me in middle age to the stuffed-nightshirt God of my childhood. But I needed it to support my self-conceit; and my pity. I was sorry for my shop-boy civilisation; sorry, if you like, for my old self; but also sorry for other people. So many of them looked like deformed children playing in a dark courtyard, when they could have been whole and in the sunshine.

Y. I have never been much troubled by pity.

W. It has been perhaps my most respectable impulse: sometimes pity for individuals, more often the pity we feel to see the kitchen-garden scratched up by dogs. But I am past it now. If Homo Sapiens is such a fool that he cannot realise even now what is before him, he is not worth pity. Those who see will not or cannot act: those who act are the blind and the greedy, the intriguers and the thugs.

Y. The best lack all conviction, while the worst are full of passionate intensity.

W. Who said that?

Y. I, years ago.

W. You were right: and the impotence and the passion between them have led to the last catastrophe.

Y. That I did not foresee.

W. You can hardly be blamed for that. You were not equipped to do so. Plotinus and Madame Blavatsky are hardly sufficient basis for scientific prediction of human affairs. I had less excuse: but it would have been very surprising if you could have discerned through the Celtic twilight this monstrous shadow looming out of the future.

271

Y.   Somewhere in sands of the desert
A shape with lion's body and the head of a man,
A gaze blank and pitiless as the sun,
Is moving its slow thighs, . . .
                    . . . but now I know
That twenty centuries of stony sleep
Were vexed to nightmare by a rocking cradle,
And what rough beast, its hour come round at last,
Slouches towards Bethlehem to be born?

W. You wrote that too?

Y. Yes. In 1921.

W. A gaze blank and pitiless as the sun. And in 1921 I was writing of the salvaging of civilisation and of men like gods! How were you of all people to know what was to come? How did you contrive to pull this astounding fragment of truth out of your rag-bag of obsolete theologies? How could you foresee Hiroshima?

Y. You must forgive me. I left the world in 1939, and since then I have paid very little attention to its affairs. Hiroshima is a Japanese name? But I know little of Japan, except for some study of the Noh plays. And Sato gave me a sword.

W. To hell with your intolerable affectations! I am talking of the bomb dropped on Hiroshima, the weapon with which man has armed himself for his own annihilation.

Y. A bomb dropped on Hiroshima? But there have been bombs before, of one kind or another, larger or smaller?

W. God defend us from the stark insensibility of the professional aesthete, the inheritor and transmitter of all the wilful obfuscations of the dark ages, with his head in the sand, his arse in the clouds, looking for fairies, while the fuse burns shorter, the spark approaches the powder, and he is too indolent or too addle-headed to lift a finger to put it out. For the moment your verses took me in: but of course you did not know what you were saying. I am talking about the total destruction of mankind, which is now for the first time possible: in the present mood of Homo Sapiens, therefore certain.

Y. You mean the total destruction of your kind of man.

W. I mean complete annihilation.

Y. Just before I died men expected a war which would

achieve just that. Yet, so far as I have observed, there are still men. Do you believe that the next time none would survive?

W. For a year or two, perhaps, a few blinded and scabrous parodies of the human form, crawling about the festering ruins of their cities. Then these feeble abortions too must perish.

Y. Of our quarrel with others we make rhetoric: but is it I who must remind you that rhetoric is not science? As a dispassionate observer of the something that drives through the confusion, as a calculator of probabilities, do you believe that *none* would survive?

W. No.

Y. None perhaps of your kind. None with whom you would feel at home: for you are the creature of your class and of your nation. But others beside myself have had the idea that as the Great Wheel revolves, the old classes and the old nations wear themselves out, that all must be beaten flat, that the worn and battered metal must go back to the melting-pot, to be tempered and hammered again into new forms, to be worn and battered in their turn. I will not speak to you of the Great Year of the Platonists, or of Vico's cycle of history, or of the heresy suppressed by the Bishop of Emessa which alleged that the Resurrection could happen more than once. . . . But Marx I suppose to have a place in your open conspiracy (or is he too an obsolete theologian?); those who have read him tell me that he foresaw something of the kind. If all goes back to the melting-pot to be moulded over again, that which first appears will not be anything that you can understand. The new forms are not such as can be studied in the Exhibition Road; they are instinctive, impersonal, "sapienza poetica". There are no abstract ideas; all is concrete, all natural forces are personified. Only the poet can understand that poetic wisdom from which all things have their birth, only the poet can civilise man by making himself the conscious and personal possessor of all that remains unrealised in that dim undifferentiated knowledge. For an age to come the world will know three kinds of men it has hardly seen for many generations—the Saint, the Hero, and the Fool. The Fool, for only a fool's lust for life and a fool's willingness to fling it away will allow the common man to

live through those days: the Hero and the Saint, for they alone
know that wisdom comes through beggary.

W. Your rhetoric at any rate is as good as mine.

Y. Though I have never shared your myth, all in my
generation have sometimes taken refuge in its shadow.

> We too had many pretty toys when young;
> A law indifferent to blame or praise,
> To bribe or threat; habits that made old wrong
> Melt down, as it were wax in the sun's rays.

Only the professional liars and the bestially ignorant, adminis-
trators and political men, can crawl under the shadow of that
rock now.

> Now days are dragon-ridden, the nightmare
> Rides upon sleep.

But spirits as we are, neither you nor I can tell what destina-
tion the nightmare rides. Her path is through the Thirteenth
Cone.

NOTES

As most of this literature is familiar and accessible, I omit exact references where they are not likely to be useful, and where the text indicates the source of quotations.

INTRODUCTION

1 *Modern Painters*, vol. III, part IV, chap. xvi, para. 13. All references to Ruskin's works are to the Library Edition, ed. Cooke and Wedderburn, 1903–9.

CHAPTER I. RUSKIN

1 "A Second Lecture on the Fine Arts." *Frazer's Magazine.* June 1839.
2 ibid.
3 *Stones of Venice*, vol. III, chap. iii, para. 53.
4 ibid., vol. II, chap. vi, para. 8.
5 *Modern Painters*, vol. I, part II, sec. 1, chap. vii, para. 21.
6 ibid., vol. III, part IV, chap. iv, para. 17.
7 ibid., vol. I, part II, sec. 3, chap. ii, para. 4.
8 *Seven Lamps*, chap. iii, para. 17.
9 *Stones of Venice*, vol. II, chap. v, para. 14.
10 *Modern Painters*, vol. IV, part v, chap. xv, para. 8.
11 ibid., vol. III, part IV, chap. xvi, para. 28.
12 ibid., vol. II, part III, sec. 1, chap. i, para. 2.
13 *Human Understanding*, ii.9.3.
14 *Modern Painters*, vol. I, part II, sec. 1, chap. ii, para. 2.
15 ibid., para. 4.
16 R. G. Collingwood, *Ruskin's Philosophy* (Kendal, 1919), p. 16.
17 Roger Fry, *Vision and Design* (Penguin edn.), p. 39.
18 *Modern Painters*, vol. II, part III, sec. 1, chap. i, para. 10.
19 ibid., chap. ii, para. 111.
20 ibid., chap. iii, para. 6.
21 *Stones of Venice*, vol. I, appendix 15.
22 ibid., vol. I, chap. xxvii.
23 ibid., paras. 21–3.
24 Roger Fry (ed.), *Reynolds' Discourses* (1905), p. 162.
25 R. H. Wilenski, *John Ruskin* (1933).
26 E. T. Cooke, *Life of Ruskin* (1911), vol. I, p. 271.
27 *Stones of Venice*, vol. II, chap. iv, paras. 17–20.
28 Wilenski, op. cit., p. 335.

[29] Cooke, op. cit., vol. I, p. 519.

[30] ibid., vol. II, p. 28.

[31] *Fors Clavigera*, 76.

[32] Cooke, op. cit., vol. II, p. 451.

[33] *Seven Lamps*, chap. v, para. 24.

[34] *Stones of Venice*, vol. II, chap. vi, paras. 10–17.

CHAPTER II. ROSSETTI AND THE P.R.B.

[1] W. Holman Hunt, *Pre-Raphaelitism and the Pre-Raphaelite Brotherhood* (1905), vol. I, p. 58.

[2] ibid., p. 59.

[3] W. M. Rossetti, *Dante Gabriel Rossetti: Family Letters and Memoir* (1895), vol. I, p. 109.

[4] Hunt, op. cit., vol. I, p. 91.

[5] W. M. Rossetti, *Pre-Raphaelite Diaries and Letters* (1900), p. 305.

[6] ibid., p. 267.

[7] Also reprinted in *Collected Works*, ed. W. M. Rossetti (1886).

[8] W. M. Rossetti. Preface to facsimile of *The Germ* (1901), p. 15.

[9] ibid., p. 10.

[10] Hunt, op. cit., vol. I, p. 92.

[11] ibid., p. 69.

[12] ibid., p. 94.

[13] ibid., p. 135.

[14] *The Germ*, No. 2, 1850, p. 72.

[15] ibid., p. 58.

[16] *The Times*, 7th May, 1851. Reprinted in vol. XII of Library edn. of Ruskin.

[17] *Pre-Raphaelite Diaries and Letters*, p. 318.

[18] "A Last Confession."

[19] "Sonnet on Leonardo's Virgin of the Rocks."

[20] "The Staff and Scrip."

[21] R. D. Waller, *The Rossetti Family* (1932), p. 204.

CHAPTER III. MORRIS

[1] *Lectures on Art and Industry*. Vol. XXII of *The Works of William Morris*, ed. May Morris (1910), p. 319. All references to Morris's works are in this edition.

[2] Quoted in Mr. Michael Trappes-Lomax's *Pugin* (1932). I am greatly indebted to this book, and also to Sir Kenneth Clarke's *Gothic Revival*, for the following material on earlier medieval revivalists,

NOTES

and for suggesting to me the parallel between Pugin's career and Morris's.

3 Trappes-Lomax, op. cit., p. 175. (Pugin, *Apology for the Present Revival of Christian Architecture* (1843), p. 6.)

4 ibid., p. 192. (Pugin, *Apology*, p. 39).

5 *Art and Industry. Works*, vol. XXII, p. 377.

6 Trappes-Lomax, op. cit., p. 179. (Pugin, *Apology*, p. 12.)

7 ibid., p. 154. (Pugin, *True Principles of Pointed or Christian Architecture* (1841), p. 1.)

8 *Art and Industry. Works*, vol. XXII, p. 169.

9 *Hopes and Fears for Art. Works*, vol. XXII, p. 40.

10 ibid, p. 77.

11 *Art and Industry. Works*, vol. XXII, p. 361.

12 ibid., p. 329.

13 *Hopes and Fears. Works*, vol. XXII, p. 361.

14 ibid., p. 134.

15 H. Read. "The Fate of Modern Painting." *Horizon*, November 1947, p. 249.

16 J. W. Mackail, *Life of William Morris* (1920), vol. I, p. 366.

17 *Signs of Change. Works*, vol. XXIII, p. 36.

18 ibid., p. 76.

19 Mackail, op. cit., vol. II, p. 116.

20 *Hopes and Fears. Works*, vol. XXII, p. 45.

21 The relevant chapters from *News from Nowhere* are x, xvi and xvii, which describe how the social change came about.

22 Mackail, op. cit., vol. II, p. 61.

CHAPTER IV. PATER

1 In *The Eighteen-Eighties*. Essays by Fellows of the Royal Society of Literature (1930).

2 *Appreciations*, p. 66. All references to the works of Pater are to the Library Edition, 1910.

3 *Plato and Platonism*, p. 195.

4 ibid., pp. 19 and 20.

5 ibid., p. 10.

6 ibid., p. 155.

7 ibid., p. 40.

8 *Renaissance*, p. 236.

9 ibid., p. 237.

10 *Plato*, p. 33.

11 A. C. Benson, *Pater*. English Men of Letters. 2nd edn. (1926.) p. 90.

12 ibid., p. 197.

13 *Appreciations*, p. 103.

[14] *Appreciations*, p. 68.
[15] *Marius the Epicurean*, vol. I, pp. 4 and 5.
[16] ibid., p. 8.
[17] ibid., p. 12.
[18] ibid., p. 145.
[19] ibid., vol. II, p. 11.
[20] ibid., p. 96.
[21] ibid., p. 103.
[22] ibid., pp. 106 and 108.
[23] ibid., p. 134.
[24] Benson, op. cit., p. 111.
[25] *Essays from the Guardian*, p. 67.
[26] St. Augustine, *Confessions*, X.
[27] *Renaissance*, p. 237.
[28] ibid., Preface, p. viii.
[29] ibid., p. x.
[30] ibid., p. i.
[31] *Plato*, p. 10.
[32] ibid., p. 125.
[33] ibid., p. 174.
[34] *Guardian*, p. 50.
[35] *Plato*, p. 269.
[36] *Appreciations*, p. 212.
[37] *Renaissance*, p. 135.
[38] ibid., p. 135.
[39] ibid., p. 176.
[40] *Miscellaneous Studies*, pp. 172–96. The following quotations not otherwise noted are all from this essay.
[41] *Imaginary Portraits*, p. 62.
[42] *Miscellaneous Studies*, p. 157.
[43] *Appreciations*, p. 261.

CHAPTER V. FIN-DE-SIÈCLE

[1] *Fors Clavigera*, 22nd July 1877.
[2] I am indebted to Mr. James Laver's *Whistler* (1930) for the biographical information that follows.
[3] Whistler, *The Gentle Art of Making Enemies* (1890). This reprints both the attacks on Whistler and his replies to them.
[4] ibid., p. 252.
[5] ibid., p. 128.
[6] ibid., pp. 135–59.
[7] ibid., pp. 133 and 136.
[8] ibid., p. 142.
[9] ibid., p. 144.

[10] ibid., p. 153.

[11] In *Emaux et Camées*.

[12] *Histoire de la Littérature Francaise* (1894), p. 1060.

[13] *Les Fleurs du Mal*, ed. Enid Starkie (1942). Introduction, pp. vii and viii.

[14] Wilde, *Plays, Prose Writings and Poems* (Everyman's), p. 173.

[15] ibid., p. 177.

[16] ibid., p. 181.

[17] *A Rebours*, chap. vii.

[18] Wilde, op. cit., p. 178.

[19] *A Rebours*, chap. xi.

[20] Wilde, *Essays and Lectures* (1909), p. 175.

[21] ibid., p. 128.

[22] *Autobiographies* (1926), p. 401.

[23] In *Jadis et Naguère*.

[24] *Poetical Works*, with introduction by Ezra Pound (1914). The poems mentioned below are all in this collection.

[25] *The Poems of Ernest Dowson*, with a memoir by Arthur Symons (1922). The definitive edition of Dowson is the *Poetical Works*, ed. Desmond Flower (1934): it contains forty newly discovered poems and much exact bibliographical information.

CHAPTER VI. YEATS

[1] *Essays* (1924), p. 429.

[2] Joseph Hone, *W. B. Yeats* (1942), p. 279. (Letter from J. B. Yeats to W. B. Yeats.)

[3] *Essays* (1924), p. 119.

[4] ibid, p. 436.

[5] ibid., p. 435.

[6] ibid., p. 125.

[7] ibid., p. 137.

[8] ibid., p. 453.

[9] ibid., p. 308.

[10] ibid., p. 200.

[11] ibid., p. 65.

[12] "Coole and Ballylee." All poems quoted, unless otherwise specified, are in *Collected Poems* (1937).

[13] "Sailing to Byzantium."

[14] "A Man Young and Old."

[15] *Essays* (1924), p. 364.

[16] "Vacillation."

[17] *Essays* (1924), p. 474.

[18] ibid., p. 96.

[19] ibid., p. 228.

NOTES

[20] For this, and the biographical information that follows, I am indebted to Mr. Hone's biography, cited above, to which all students of Yeats owe so much.

[21] *Essays* (1924), p. 235.

[22] ibid., p. 494.

[23] "Ego Dominus Tuus."

[24] *A Vision* (1925, second edition, revised, 1937).

[25] ibid. (1937), p. 170.

[26] In *Wheels and Butterflies*. But the poem quoted, with its companion piece, is reprinted in the *Collected Poems*.

[27] "Nineteen Hundred and Nineteen."

[28] *A Vision* (1937), p. 263.

[29] *Essays* (1924), p. 533.

[30] ibid., p. 535.

[31] *A Vision* (1937), p. 279.

[32] "The Tower."

INDEX

281

INDEX

Irish literary movement, 216

Johnson, Lionel, 204, 205, 206, 212–14

Jung, 229, 261, 262

Keats, 42, 116, 119, 121, 126, 257

Lanson, 193
Lewis, Wyndham, 114
Life and Death of Jason, 129, 130
Literary criticism, twentieth century, 113–16
Lovers of Gudrun, 128

Mademoiselle de Maupin, 189, 195
Mallarmé, xviii, 195, 208, 210
Marcus Aurelius, 150
Marius the Epicurean, 145–57, 168
Marx, 104, 106
Maurice, F. D., xi, 106, 135
Memlinck, 56, 58
Millais, 42–6, 66
    Lorenzo and Isabella, 62
    Christ in the House of His Parents, 63
    Ophelia, 65
    Autumn Leaves, 66
Modern Painters, xv, xvi, 6–18, 25, 29, 30
Morris, William, 39, 83–133, 222, 223
    compared with Pugin, 90–4
    aesthetic value of his designs, 97–8
    work of Morris and Co., 98, 101
    on popular art, 99–101
    News from Nowhere, 101, 107–12, 120
    entry into politics, 103–4
    mature political doctrine, 105–6
    position in Socialist movement, 113
    poetry of, 113–33
    Earthly Paradise, 122–5
    Defence of Guenevere, 127
    Norse poems, 128–9, 131, 132
    Life and Death of Jason, 129
    influence on Yeats, 222, 223

"Nature of Gothic, The," 32–9, 88–9
News from Nowhere, 101, 107–12, 120
Nineties, the, 153, 187–215
North and South, 136

Orchard, 60–2
Outcast, The, 136
Oxford and Cambridge Magazine, 83

Painting, abstract and representational, 184–5
Paley, 11, 32
Pater, xvi, xvii, 134–74, 196, 197, 227
    scepticism of, 137–41, 146, 147
    style, 138, 157, 172
    Renaissance, 138–44, 149, 156, 163–5
    Plato and Platonism, 138, 139, 157, 160
    Imaginary Portraits, 142, 145, 172
    Marius the Epicurean, 145–57, 168
    religious attitude, 145–6
    criticism and aesthetic theory, 157–166
    Guardian, Essays from, 160
    Appreciations, 161, 165
    The Child in the House, 166–7
    Denys l'Auxerrois, 168–9
    Apollo in Picardy, 168–9
Per Amica Silentia Lunae, 239–41, 251
Percy's *Reliques,* 117
Picasso, 23, 185
Picture of Dorian Grey, The, 194–200
Plato and Platonism, 138, 139, 157, 160
Praz, Mario, 192
Pre-Raphaelite Brotherhood, xv, 49, 55, 62, 65–6
    journal of, 49, 62
    attacked in the Press, 63
    decline of, 65–6
Pre-Raphaelitism, 40–67, 175, 216
    origin of the name, 57
    influence on Yeats, 216
Pugin, 85–8, 90–4
    and Ruskin, 86, 90
    compared with Morris, 90–4
    Contrasts, 91

Raphael, 6, 7, 56–7
Read, Herbert, 100
Reade, Winwood, 136
Reincarnation, 259
Renaissance, The, 138–44, 149, 156, 163–5
Reynolds, Sir Joshua, 1, 7, 9
"Rhetoric," 217–19

INDEX

Rhymers' Club, 204–15, 217
Rimbaud, xviii, 210
Robert Elsmere, 136, 154
Romantic Agony, The, 192
Romantic poetry, 113–22, 126, 132–3
Rossetti, D. G., xv, 43, 46–54, 67, 82, 175, 219, 223, 225
  Ecce Ancilla Domini, 41, 56, 63
  The Girlhood of the Virgin, 41, 62
  Dante's Dream, 40
  Found, 41
  Hand and Soul, 50–3
  poetry of, 67–82
  Early Italian Poets, 72–7
  The Blessed Damosel, 53, 54, 77–8
  The House of Life, 79–81
Rossetti, W. M., 43, 49, 54, 65
Rubens, 19, 92, 95
Ruskin, xiii, xv, xvii, 1–39, 86, 88–90, 175, 177, 222
  Modern Painters, xv, xvi, 6–18, 25, 29, 30
  sensibility to visual appearances, 5–10
  philosophical basis of his aesthetics, 13
  on Theoretic and Aesthetic faculties, 15–17
  The Stones of Venice, 19–22, 25, 26, 32–9, 86, 88–9
  The Seven Lamps of Architecture, 20, 22, 25, 26, 32
  Protestantism of, 20–1, 25, 88
  "unconversion," 27
  natural religion of, 29–32
  Munera Pulveris, 32
  Political Economy of Art, 32, 89
  Unto This Last, 89
  influence on P.R.B., 41, 42, 44, 56, 60
  defends P.R.B., 64
  and Pugin, 86, 90
  and the Gothic revival, 88–9
  libel suit with Whistler, 177
  influence on Yeats, 222

Salvator Rosa, 6
Scott, 118
Seven Lamps of Architecture, 20, 22, 25, 26, 32
Siddal, Elizabeth, 41, 75, 81

Sigurd the Volsung, 131
Shelley, 116, 118
Social Democratic Federation, 104
Socialism,
  Utopian and economic, 103
  in the 'eighties, 104–5
Spengler, 246
Spenser, 221
Starkie, Enid, 193
Stephens, F. G., 49, 56, 60
St. Francis, 28
Stones of Venice, 19–22, 25, 26, 32–9, 86, 88–9
Swinburne, xviii, 180–1, 189–90, 192
  and Gautier, 189–90
  and Baudelaire, 192
Symbolism, xviii, 208–11
Symons, Arthur, xviii, 204, 205, 208

Taylor, Warrington, 128
Ten o'Clock Lecture, 182–6
Tennyson, xi, xii, 135, 219
Thackeray, 2
Theoretic faculty, 15–17
Tower, The, 238, 255
Toynbee, Arnold, 246
Trappes-Lomax, Michael, 276
Turner, 6, 41, 65

Van Eyck, 55, 56, 58
Verlaine, xviii, 209–11
Veronese, 19
Vico, 229, 246
Villiers de l'Isle Adam, xix, 209
Vision, A, 238, 241–52
Vita Nuova, 68, 75–7, 79

Waller, R. D., 73, 78, 79
Walpole, Horace, 84, 85
Wanderings of Oisin, 232
Wells, H. G., 263–74
Whistler, 175–87, 220
  relation to Ruskin and P.R.B., 176–178, 187
  early career, 178–9
  aesthetic doctrine, 179–81
  Ten o'Clock Lecture, 182–6
  relation to aesthetic movement, 186
Wilde, Oscar, 191, 194–200, 202–4, 207

283

INDEX

THE LAST ROMANTICS

The arts and their relation to religion and the social order were major pre-occupations of the leaders of thought in late Victorian times. Professor Hough here examines some æsthetic theories of Ruskin, Rosetti, Morris, Pater and finally Yeats.

'A thoughtful critic with no axe to grind—exceptional also in his freedom from vulgarity, obscurity and pretentiousness. The section on Yeats is arresting; and the rest of the book must impress every student of the Victorian Age.'

Raymond Mortimer in the *Sunday Times*

UNIVERSITY PAPERBACKS

U.P. 27